DATE DUE

DEMCO, INC. 38-2931

JESUS AND JUSTICE

JESUS AND JUSTICE

Evangelicals,
Race, and
American
Politics

Peter
Goodwin
Heltzel

Foreword by
Mark A. Noll

Yale University Press
New Haven & London

Published with assistance from the Kingsley Trust Association
Publication Fund established by the Scroll and Key Society of
Yale College.

Set in Postscript Galliard Oldstyle by The Composing Room
of Michigan, Inc. Printed in the United States of America by
Sheridan Books, Ann Arbor, Michigan.

Library of Congress Cataloging-in-Publication Data
Heltzel, Peter.
Jesus and justice : Evangelicals, race, and American politics / Peter
Goodwin Heltzel ; foreword by Mark A. Noll.
p.   cm.
Includes bibliographical references and index.
ISBN 978-0-300-12433-0 (cloth : alk. paper)
1. Christianity and politics—United States.   2. Evangelicalism—
United States.   3. United States—Church history.   I. Title.
BR516.H45 2009
261.7—dc22   2009006564

A catalogue record for this book is available from the British
Library.

This paper meets the requirements of ANSI/NISO Z39.48-1992
(Permanence of Paper). It contains 30 percent postconsumer waste
(PCW) and is certified by the Forest Stewardship Council (FSC).

10 9 8 7 6 5 4 3 2 1

To Sarah, *mio tenero amor*

CONTENTS

FOREWORD

Since the 2004 presidential election, when "values voting" was considered a key to the victory of George W. Bush, a spate of books has appeared on the relationship between religion and politics. Most concentrate on evangelical voters; many are marked by partiality or panic. The general result has frequently been to heighten cultural conflict without improving political understanding or deepening religious insight.

Peter Heltzel's *Jesus and Justice* is a different kind of book. It offers a singular interpretation of the recent history of the evangelical Christian Right by way of theological analysis. At its heart is patient, but also prophetic, attention to race as a critical factor in evangelical history, contemporary evangelical politics, and theological assessment of America's evangelical communities. The result is an insightful grasp of evangelical movements, an intriguing expansion of the category "evangelical," and a powerful statement of evangelical theology.

Heltzel's contribution to historical understanding comes from several convincing arguments. First is his contention that Martin Luther King Jr., along with much of the civil rights movement as a whole, represented a kind of evangelicalism that can be traced back to the same stock from which the New Christian Right sprang. Second is his claim that the theology of Carl F. H. Henry, longtime editor of *Christianity Today* magazine and intellectual leader of postwar "neo-evangelicalism," contained resources for a much more progressive social stance than developed by "Christian conservatives." The theological payoff from this fresh reading of history is Heltzel's persuasive case that the perspectives of King and Henry can and should be amalgamated to form a more progressive political stance, yet one that is still strongly in line with the historic affirmations of the Protestant evangelical tradition.

Heltzel does not try to hide his own progressive bias, but this standpoint does not prevent him from sympathetic treatment of a wide range of evangelical political efforts. He is, thus, as fair in his treatment of James Dobson's conservative Focus on the Family as he is of the liberal Sojourners movement of Jim Wallis. The historical importance of Heltzel's argument is to show how the strong and obvious differences among groups like Sojourners and Focus on the Family represent branches from a common evangelical tree. The broader significance of this historical interpretation becomes clear when Heltzel shifts roles to speak as a theologian. With that voice he makes a vigorous appeal—that the merger of strands he describes in the book might lead to an active evangelical theology that maintains the best of Carl Henry's emphasis on the Kingdom of God experienced in personal terms and Martin Luther King Jr.'s beloved community expressed in social transformation. No one, to my knowledge, has joined history and theology in quite this way before.

Readers from across the spectrum of political and theological convictions will find much to ponder in these pages. Incisive social analysis, innovative history, and forceful theology are a rare combination in contemporary America. The book before you is a striking exception. Take it, read it, ponder its implications. If in fact it is true, as Heltzel claims, that much of what is considered "white evangelicalism" and much of what he describes as "black evangelicalism" can in fact be merged into a political position that is both theologically conservative and socially progressive, a new day of hope may be about to dawn.

Mark A. Noll
   Francis A. McAnaney Professor of History
   University of Notre Dame

ACKNOWLEDGMENTS

This book began and ended as an ongoing, open-hearted conversation with my colleague Eleanor Moody-Shepherd. In many ways this book is an attempt to understand the difference between her upbringing as a black woman in Alabama and mine as a white man raised in Mississippi. Every year we co-teach a course called "Going Home: Southern Religion and the Civil Rights Movement," walking the freedom trails together from Montgomery, Alabama, up through the Mississippi Delta to Memphis, Tennessee. During these trips we have gotten to know each other's families, eaten barbeque together, sung together, and grown in our understanding of the Christian faith and race relations in the Deep South. I could not have made this journey without her faithful and festive friendship.

I made many new friends along this journey. Many people and institutions deserve thanks for helping bring this book to publication. Recognition and gratitude must go first and foremost to the Association of Theological Schools for their generous support of my research through their Theological Scholars program. I would also like to thank Chris Rogers, my editor at Yale University Press, for his perceptive eye and steady encouragement throughout the writing of this book, and Eliza Childs, my copyeditor, who with gentle encouragement helped me more clearly articulate my argument with style. I also thank Laura Davulis and Margaret Otzel for the kindness and patience with which they guided the manuscript through completion.

I would like to thank my research assistants on this project for their scholarly acumen and boundless enthusiasm: Ian Doescher, Rafael Reyes III, and Amy Reynolds. Several of my students at New York Theological Seminary also helped with research, including Alvin Bunis, Luis-Alfredo Cartagena, Nina Delho, and Gail Badger Morgan. I am also grateful to Geraldine Howard, Ron McKoy, Anthony Rivera, and Bowie Snodgrass for proofreading the manuscript, and to Blake Edwards for preparing the index.

President Dale T. Irvin and New York Theological Seminary have provided overwhelming support for this book at every stage. I have enjoyed many conversations about this project with colleagues, including Humberto Alfaro, Diane Ashley, Paul Bradley, Leslie Dawn Callahan, Katie DiSalvo, Shirvahna Gobin, Jin Hee Han, Obery M. Hendricks, Jr., Max Herman, Edward L. Hunt, Dale T. Irvin, Michelle Lim Jones, Lois Gehr Livezey, Lowell W. Livezey, C. Vernon Mason, Eleanor Moody-Shepherd, Peter J. Paris, Laura Pires-Hester, Rebecca M. Radillo, Jerry Reisig, Lester Edwin J. Ruiz, Keith Russell, Jeffrey C. Slade, David Vidal, and George "Bill" Webber. I offer a hearty thanks to my colleague and friend Lowell W. Livezey for letting me use an empty Ecologies of Learning office during 2007. Lowell passed away during the writing of this book, but he always believed in the importance of my work, and his passion for prophetic black Christianity in northern urban centers lives on in my scholarship.

My chief intellectual debts in this book are to Randall Balmer, Bruce Ellis Benson, Malinda Berry, Edward J. Blum, Rita Nakashima Brock, J. Kameron Carter, James Cone, John Jefferson Davis, Donald W. Dayton, Gary Dorrien, Eddie S. Glaude Jr., David P. Gushee, Barry Hankins, Job Henning, Dale T. Irvin, Catherine Keller, Charles Marsh, Eleanor Moody-Shepherd, Christopher Morse, Robert C. Neville, Mark A. Noll, Ted Ownby, Kurt Richardson, Robin Rogers, Lester Edwin J. Ruiz, Phillip Luke Sinitiere, Mark Toulouse, Corey D. B. Walker, Wesley J. Wildman, David F. Wells, and Christian T. Collins Winn, all of whom combine an insightful mind with a lion's heart. A stouthearted thanks to Bruce Herman, who has been a true intellectual companion, reading and commenting on most of my papers and chapters since seminary.

I am grateful to the following individuals who read or discussed topics in the book with me: Wallace Best, Peter Beyer, Chris Boesel, Derrick

Boykin, Steve Brooks, Don Browning, Michael Buddy, David Bundy, Virginia Burrus, Jennifer Butler, Henry Carrigan, Pia Chaudhari, Rodney Clapp, Eric Convey, Michael Cromartie, Creston Davis, Richard Fern, William A. Gamson, W. Clark Gilpin, Michael Hamilton, Lisa Sharon Harper, Lilly Henning, David Hempton, Jeffrey Hensley, George Hunsinger, Robert P. Jones, Serene Jones, Thomas S. Kidd, Tim Kumfer, Peter Kuzmic, Kwok Pui Lan, Timothy Larsen, Michael Lienesch, D. Michael Lindsay, Martin E. Marty, Caleb J. D. Maskell, Carey Newman, John Nunley, Christine Pae, Chad Pecknell, Richard Pieard, Mark Richardson, Lynn Robinson, Garth Rosell, Jonathan Sassi, Joel Scandret, Osagyefo Uhuru Sekou, Jim Skillen, Christian Smith, Douglass M. Strong, Douglass Sweeney, Mark Lewis Taylor, J. Terry Todd, Daniel J. Treier, Kevin Vanhoozer, David L. Weddle, W. Brad Wilcox, Newell Williams, Ashley Woodiwiss, Robert Wuthnow, Robert Yarborough, Amos Yong, and Glenn Zuber. I am deeply grateful to my friend Stephen Spencer, who has helped illuminate my understanding of the theology of Carl F. H. Henry while we mined the Henry archives together as I worked on this project. I would also like to thank Peter Beyer for his help in letting the last chapter sing.

I would like to thank several scholars who helped deepen my understanding of Martin Luther King Jr., especially Malinda Berry, J. Kameron Carter, James Cone, Gary Dorrien, Vincent Harding, C. Vernon Mason, Peter J. Paris, Tony Pinn, Arnold Isidore Thomas, Corey D. B. Walker, and most of all my good friend Rufus Burrow.

I would like to thank the archivists and librarians at the Alderman Library and Special Collections at the University of Virginia; the Burke Library at Columbia University/Union Theological Seminary; the Firestone Library at Princeton University; the Widener Library at Harvard University; the Billy Graham Center Archives, the National Association of Evangelicals Archives, and the Sojourners Archives at Wheaton College (IL); the Carl F. H. Henry Archives at Trinity Evangelical Divinity School; the King Center in Atlanta, Georgia; and the Harold John Ockenga Papers at Gordon Conwell Theological Seminary.

Throughout my research, I made several pilgrimages to the Institute for the Study of American Evangelicalism at Wheaton College. I would like to thank Edith Blumhoeffer and Larry Eskridge, of the institute, for their help. Hearty conversations with Larry about the southern character of evangelicalism have inspired my ongoing conversation about southern evangelicalism with Randall Balmer, Edward J. Blum, J. Kameron Carter, Valerie C. Cooper, Amy Laura Hall, Barry Hankins, Mark A. Noll, Ted Ownby, Philip Sinitiere, and Lauren Winner.

I would like to thank Charles B. Strozier and the Fundamentalism Seminar at John Jay College for Criminal Justice in New York City for the invitation to present chapter 5, "Focus on the Family: Nurturing and Defending the Family," in April 2007. I am grateful for the comments and suggestions offered by the participants in the seminar as well as at the festive dinner afterwards. I would like to thank Mark Douglas of Columbia Theological Seminary and Joel Hanisek of the United Nations Office of the P.C. (U.S.A.) for the opportunity to present chapter 9, "Evangelical Politics in a Shade of Blue Green," in January 2008 for a D.Min. seminar on "The Church in a World of Displaced Persons."

I am grateful to Laura Smidt and the Office of the Chaplains for arranging a lunch conversation with faculty from Calvin College and Calvin Theological Seminary in fall 2006 and to Joel Carpenter for the opportunity to participate in the seminar "Global Liturgical Identities" during summer 2007. During visits to Calvin College I was able to discuss the project with John Bolt, James Bratt, Joel Carpenter, Robert Hosak, Randall Jelks, Stephen Moonsma, Jim M. Penning, James K. A. Smith, Corwin Schmidt, and Nicholas Wolterstorff.

I am grateful to James Davison Hunter, Slavica Janesik, and Josh Yates at the Institute for Advanced Studies in Culture, University of Virginia, for their warm hospitality during January 2007. I would also like to thank Jacob Goodson and Charles Marsh of the Center for Lived Theology for making available the Civil Rights Papers and the John Perkins archives for my research.

Unless otherwise noted, all quotations are drawn from interviews I conducted for this book. The following are the individuals that I interviewed or spoke with concerning the project. From Focus on the Family, I would like to thank Paul Batura, James Dobson, Carrie Gordon Earll, Robert Flanegin, Melissa Fryrear, Mike Haley, Paul L. Hetrick, Leon Lowman, H. B. London Jr., Yvette Maher, Bill Maier, Tom Minnery, Glen Stanton, and Bob Waliszewski. From the Family Research Council, I would like to thank Kenyn M. Cureton, Thomas E. McClusky, and Peter Spring. From the National Association of Evangelicals, I would like to thank Leith Anderson, Donald Argue, Richard Cizik, Heather H. Gonzales, Carolyn Haggard, Ted Haggard, Kevin Mannoia, and Bob Wenz. From Sojourners, I would like to thank Aaron Graham, Kevin Lum, Duane Shank, Sondra Shepley, Adam Taylor, and Jim Wallis. From Christian Community Development Association, I would like to thank Shane Claiborne, Louis Carlos, Lowell Noble, John Perkins, Vera Mae Perkins, Dolphus Weary, and Barbara Williams Skinner. In addition, I would like to thank Gary Bauer, American Values; Deborah Fikes, president, D. H. Fikes International, Inc.; Harry Jackson, founder and chairman of the High Impact Leadership Coalition; Benjamin Marsh, Dalit Freedom Network; Brian McClaren, Emergent Village; David Miller, CBS News.com; Jesse Miranda, AMEN; Gabriel A. Salguero, Hispanic Leadership Program, Princeton Theological Seminary; Senator Rick Santorum (R-Pennsylvania); Ron Sider, Evangelicals for Social Action; Samuel Rodriguez Jr., National Hispanic Christian Leadership Conference; Tim Tseng, Institute for Asian American Christianity; Jerald H. Walz, Institute on Religion and Democracy; and Rick Warren, Saddleback Church.

I am also grateful for the support of my family: Sam and Ann Heltzel, Bruce and Meg Herman, Ben and Laura Herman, Rachel and Darryl Rankin, Margie Heltzel, and Robert Heltzel, and Eric Convey. Finally, I thank my wife Sarah for her passionate love and endless song that eternally inspire me.

INTRODUCTION

The American political establishment's fascination with evangelicals is entering its fourth decade. Beginning with Jimmy Carter's 1976 candidacy for the presidency and continuing through Barack Obama's 2008 election, evangelicals have stood, conspicuous and vehement, on the political stage, and the world has watched with wonder.

From the spin-based efforts of the Sunday morning pundits to the emotional and personal responses of journalists and writers, there has been no shortage of tools used or perspectives drawn from in the attempt to quantify this phenomenon. Historians have considered the past. Sociologists have looked at demographics. Political scientists have analyzed tactics.

Yet all this scrutiny lacks one essential element. To understand politically active evangelicals in all their diversity—from Pentecostals in storefront churches to members of established black churches to white suburbanites who attend megachurches—one must explore their theologies of Jesus Christ.

Who is Jesus?

Ask evangelicals this question, and you will get a revealing glimpse into their thoughts—and not just about theology but also about the social order and even partisan politics. Clearly theology and politics overlap in the evangelical mind, and both can be seen as an outgrowth of who Jesus was when he walked on the earth—what he exemplified, what he preached, what he did—and as he remains today within the evangelical worldview, both as ideology and as living God.

Theology matters to evangelicals; it is an active, physical, daily ritual. They read about it, talk about it, preach about it, and watch television shows about it. In the evangelical worldview it is, quite literally, a matter of life and death. This book is similarly obsessed with theology, because it is the shared theology commissioned by Jesus of enacting the Gospel in the world that so directly drives evangelical politics and provides insight into that tantalizing question: who is this intriguing group of Protestant Christians who have emerged to wield so much political power?

Since forays by evangelicals into politics are guided by their understandings of the Bible and Jesus, I study their use of biblical narratives, and stories of Jesus in particular, in the political enterprise. In chapter 1, I explore the theological beliefs that evangelicals hold in common as well as the different ways these beliefs are deployed in the political sphere. American politics and religion are embedded in the deeper conflict in race relations, traced throughout America's history of slavery, oppression, and unrest. The ways evangelical social movements approach race become an important barometer of their commitment to holistic social justice, vividly illustrating the divergent and emergent streams of evangelical public theology. While conservative evangelicals have often practiced a warrior politics in the post–cold war milieu, viewing evangelicalism from the standpoint of black Christianity in the Americas reveals a prophetic evangelical politics that is growing into a broader post–civil rights coalition for peace and justice.

In chapter 2, I begin to offer a new genealogy of American evangelicalism in an attempt to cast light on American evangelicalism's complicated relation to American politics. The question of race, that is, the divide between black and white in America, is central to understanding this relationship. It is vital to narrate the religious drama that is America from the vantage point of American evangelicalism's quest, from its earliest revivals for justice, to be intentional in engaging the pressing public concerns of the nation. American evangelicalism is not ancillary to the drama that is America but is a story that must be understood as living at the heart of the American story. Embedded within the religious saga of American evangelicalism is the deeper saga—no less religious and evangelical in character—of race.

Antebellum revivalism provides a common heritage for the growth of the black and white evangelical traditions. While blacks and whites worshiped together at revival meetings, there was a deep division in the antebellum evangelical church around the issue of slavery. The populist preaching and partisan politics of the antebellum period help to illuminate the fault lines of contemporary evangelical politics today.

The political activity of contemporary evangelicals can be traced directly to two towering twentieth-century figures: Martin Luther King Jr. (1929–68), the courageous leader of the civil rights movement, and Carl F. H. Henry (1913–2003), the visionary public theologian of the evangelical movement. Heirs to the spirit of antebellum revivalism, King and Henry were charismatic communicators and subtle public theologians, leading movements in the 1950s and 1960s that set new directions in postwar politics in the United States.

Martin Luther King Jr. transformed American religion and politics. Imbued with a deep theology of the cross, he deployed a robust prophetic theological imagination through leading a Word of God movement for love and justice (chapter 3). By helping lead the civil rights movement, King demonstrated that Christians in the United States could be mobilized in support of a righteous cause. Through nonviolent direct action, Christians partnered with other activists in various communities to overthrow centuries of racial segregation and oppression. King is the icon of this largely church-based movement for racial and economic justice, a movement that continues to fuel the fires of a growing evangelical justice movement.

As a theology professor at Fuller Seminary and as the editor of *Christianity Today,* Carl F. H. Henry distinguished himself as the most rigorous evangelical public theologian of his generation (chapter 4). While Billy Graham was the front man for the evangelical movement, Henry was the brains behind the operation. In emphasizing Jesus as Lord over all, Henry enabled an enclave of separatist fundamentalists to mature into a robust, socially engaged movement of evangelicals. All the while, Henry lamented fundamentalism's abandonment of America's great social reform movements. He fired an initial salvo for justice in his manifesto *The Uneasy Conscience of Modern Fundamentalism,* confessing the irony of fundamentalism's social isolationism, given the nineteenth-century evangelical struggle to end slavery and to empower women in the ministry. By the early twentieth century, however, many fundamentalists had become apolitical, focusing exclusively on matters of personal piety. Henry called upon midcentury evangelicals to wake up to a broader justice agenda, but his conscience remained uneasy over several social issues, including race. He and other white evangelicals anguished over the problem of racism but ultimately did not develop a theological vision, social analysis, and collective motivation to form a substantive and sustained response.

As we consider the ways that King and Henry relate their understandings of Jesus to public life, many parallels become apparent. King and Henry arose from two different alienation experiences—black suffering and white fundamentalist separation, respectively—but both exhibit evangelical responses to their circumstances. Both proclaimed that Christian belief should lead to action, with Henry calling for personal transformation with a gesture toward social engagement, and King for personal as well as systemic transformation. Both sought to awaken their community to a broader justice agenda via a distinct political vision: King's beloved community and Henry's vision of the Kingdom of God.

Although there are affinities between their two theological visions, there are fundamental differences in the ways that they understand Jesus and justice. King emphasizes Jesus's suffering and death, while Henry emphasizes Jesus's resurrection and triumph. King emphasizes Jesus's mission to set people free from the oppressions of systemic sin, while Henry emphasizes Jesus saving people from personal sin. The difference in the way they treated racism demonstrated the differences in their understandings of Jesus. King developed a theological account of racism and a collective strategy to dismantle it in societal institutions, whereas Henry identified race as a problem but limited his response to interpersonal reconciliation. Racism was the watershed issue that divided these two primary streams of evangelical politics in the United States, streams of public theology that have come to dominate contemporary American politics.

This deep influence can be traced through various evangelical social movements that emerged in their wake, and I will examine four of the most prominent: Focus on the Family, the National Association of Evangelicals, Christian Community Development Association, and Sojourners.

From the theological roots of Carl Henry grow the branches of Focus on the Family (chapter 5), a vast global network of ministries that includes eleven magazines, a radio show heard by more than seven million people weekly, and a column that appears in more than five hundred newspapers. Focus on the Family (FOF) was founded by child psychologist James C. Dobson (1936–) in 1977 and shaped by narratives of Jesus as Lord applied to the American family. Dobson quickly began to assert his theological principles to the political sphere, establishing the Family Research Council (FRC) in Washington in 1983. Because the Republican Party was unresponsive to his agenda, he formed Focus on the Family Action in 2004 and helped launch and lead the "I Vote Values" campaign to reelect George W. Bush as president and lend support to other pro-family candidates. Focus on the Family, FOF Action, Family Research Council, and FRC Action have created a powerful evangelical coalition for the pro-life, pro-family movement, and their emphasis has been squarely on those issues.

On a related branch, also grown from the Henry root, stands the National Association of Evangelicals (chapter 6). Founded in 1942, the National Association of Evangelicals (NAE) is a fellowship of evangelical churches and organizations joined to pursue a common unity and justice agenda. Historically the NAE had pursued a narrow social agenda, including service projects in the United States and abroad focused on helping individuals, but recently it has broadened its purview, engaging the more collective issues of poverty, human rights, and the environment. The understanding of Jesus as transformer of souls and society became increasingly instrumental in this theopolitical transformation, an emphasis brought about largely by Richard Cizik (1951–), who has lived and breathed NAE politics within the organization's Office of Governmental Affairs since 1980. In the NAE's *For the Health of the Nation* statement, Richard Cizik's vision of Jesus Christ as Lord over all creation has emerged as an important theological narrative, guiding the evangelical creation care movement as well as a vast array of social justice efforts.

Martin Luther King Jr. has been an enduring inspiration to both black and white evangelical communities. Two branches that grow from the theological roots of Martin Luther King Jr. are the Christian Community Development Association (CCDA) (chapter 7) and Sojourners (chapter 8). Thinking about evangelicalism through its history in antebellum revivalism, including its prophetic embodiment in the black church's struggle for freedom, opens up a new horizon for thinking about evangelical social movements. The ministry of John M. Perkins (1930–) embodies a prophetic black evangelicalism that is a synthesis of Biblicism, the black church tradition, and communitarian politics. Black, white, Hispanic, Asian, and Native American evangelicals have played an important role in the development of his Christian Community Development Association, started in 1989, and are currently taking it in new directions—for example, the work of the new urban monastics like Shane Claiborne, a CCDA board member.

Since the late 1960s, Jim Wallis (1948–), the leader of Sojourners, has provided a progressive witness for justice within the broader evangelical world. Sojourners has emerged as a progressive evangelical voice that is providing a vital prophetic evangelical alternative to the Religious Right and the secular left. Like the other evangelical social movements under examination, Sojourners generates its political vision and identity from retellings of the stories of Jesus. The portrait of Jesus held by Sojourners is as a peacemaker who is in solidarity with the poor and who subverts the forces of empire. Sojourners has increased its ministry with and to the poor through the founding in 1996 of Call to Renewal, an ecumenical, multiethnic social movement that has recently been transformed into the Mobilization to End Poverty.

Following this discussion of Sojourners, I will conclude by assessing how these four movements have succeeded and failed in building cultures of peace, justice, and love. In my examination, the maturation of evangelical public theology is cast in a shade of blue green (chapter 9). Blue symbolizes the tragedy of black suffering in the Americas, and green symbolizes an emerging holism within evangelical public engagement, particularly focused on the issues of poverty and the environment.

Dramatized by a debate between James Dobson and Richard Cizik on global warming, the greening of evangelicalism is receiving new public visibility in the United States today. Not only has it been the wedge issue dividing a prophetic evangelicalism from the Religious Right, it has also signified a deeper structural change within evangelicalism. Evangelical megachurch ministers like Rick Warren and Joel Hunter are moving from an agenda focused on traditional Religious Right foci—abortion, gay marriage, and pornography—to a broader agenda that includes poverty, AIDS, and creation care.

These and other emerging coalitions in the tradition of King point to a political evangelicalism with a broader moral agenda, encompassing many social issues. Likewise, the NAE's *For the Health of the Nation* document demonstrates that evangelicals in the tradition of Henry espouse a worldview that includes both personal salvation and social justice. Although evangelicals will continue to organize around issues that animate the pro-family movement, they will not be limited to those issues alone. Nor can they afford to be; the complexity of the problem of race in the United States grows increasingly important in the Obama era, as the current immigration debate illustrates, and the need to care for creation grows more urgent every day. As a new generation of evangelical activists embraces King's vision for racial equality and reconciliation, and as evangelicals in the Henry tradition seek to live into his call to justice and reform, a growing intercultural evangelical coalition is embodying a prophetic politics of hope.

PART

I

EVANGELICAL HISTORY

It is time that the evangelical movement sees itself for what it is: a lion on the loose that no one today seriously fears.
Carl F. H. Henry, 1976

1

THE LION IS ROARING

Democratic presidential candidate Barack Obama won the Iowa caucus on Thursday, January 3, 2008. In his column the next morning, David Brooks spoke for millions when he wrote: "You'd have to have a heart of stone not to feel moved by this. An African-American man wins a closely fought campaign in a pivotal state. He beats two strong opponents, including the mighty Clinton machine. He does it in a system that favors rural voters. He does it by getting young voters to come out to the caucuses. . . . This is a huge moment. It's one of those times when a movement that seemed ethereal and idealistic became a reality and took on political substance."[1] Like Jesse Jackson winning the Michigan caucus by a landslide 55 percent in the 1988 presidential primary, Obama's victory was a watershed moment in American politics: an African American was a serious candidate for president of the United States.

At the same moment, Southern Baptist preacher Mike Huckabee won the Iowa caucus for the Republican Party. A socially conservative former governor of Arkansas, Huckabee delivered speeches that sounded like sermons. He frequently mentioned his faith in Jesus Christ and its relevance for American public life, a message that went over well with many Iowan evangelicals. Huckabee's vision captured the hearts and minds of the Religious Right, and his passionate populist message also appealed to a growing number of evangelicals who were increasingly concerned about racial, economic, and environmental justice.

Obama and Huckabee, and their victories in the Iowa caucuses, symbolize the two primary streams of American evangelical politics: the prophetic black Christianity of Martin Luther King Jr. and the socially engaged evangelicalism of Carl F. H. Henry. With Obama's invocations of Frederick Douglass and Martin Luther King Jr., and Huckabee's summoning of Billy Sunday and Billy Graham, these two political candidates self-consciously worked out of these two religious traditions. With common roots in an antebellum revivalist past, black and white evangelicalism were coming together again, but a deep, persistent, and intractable problem remained: racism.

The convergence of the black and white evangelical traditions in the third millennium is still plagued by the problem of white supremacy, the moral contradiction on which America was built. From slavery to segregation, America's tragic past demands a robust evangelical theological accounting. In the eighteenth and early nineteenth centuries, chattel slavery divided blacks and whites in the southern interior, but today black and white evangelical Christians are coming together in a post–civil rights moment. Prophetic black Christianity that had been tucked away within a white evangelical modernity gradually emerged to redirect evangelicalism to its deepest prophetic roots.

We are witnessing a major paradigm shift in evangelical political life: the birth of a new prophetic evangelical politics. Within the evangelical world, prophetic evangelical politics are biblically based and theologically conservative, marked by a broad focus on racial justice, internationalism, environmentalism, and decreased identification with partisan politics.[2] Drastically different from the warrior politics that defined the Religious Right and the Republican Party in past decades, the prophetic politics of a growing group of evangelicals is serious about proclaiming and embodying peace and justice. Among prophetic evangelicals, we see the emergence of a strong aversion to violent, warrior discourse; disillusionment with party politics of all stripes; and a broadening of social concerns beyond issues such as abortion. Although prophetic evangelicals generally oppose abortion and support the traditional family, they are engaging a broad array of social justice issues, such as racial justice, poverty, sex trafficking, AIDS, and the environment. They not only vote in elections but also daily seek to work collectively for the common good locally, nationally, and internationally. Prophetic evangelicals have come of age.

Carl F. H. Henry likened the evangelical movement to "a lion on the loose" in 1976, the year *Newsweek* dubbed the "Year of the Evangelical."[3] At the beginning of the 1970s, evangelicals were largely invisible in American public life; by 1976 they were taking their first tentative steps away from the fringe of American society. Today they have taken center stage. The lion is roaring and people everywhere, both within and beyond the United States, are scared and quaking. Yet many people don't understand that evangelicalism is moving from a warrior politics to a prophetic politics or that Carl Henry's and Billy Graham's late internalization of the egalitarian ideal of the civil rights movement is the reason why.

The election of George W. Bush as president in 2000 and 2004 was the symbol par excellence of a new evangelical political establishment, but also symbolized the twilight of evangelical warrior politics. As Esther Kaplan writes, "Bush's religiosity [was] so widely embraced on the Christian Right that when Pat Robertson resigned as president of the Christian Coalition at the end of 2001, American Values president Gary Bauer told the *Washington Post*, 'I think Robertson stepped down because the position has already been filled. [Bush] is that leader right now.'"[4]

Evangelicals delivered key swing votes in the 2000 and 2004 presidential elections, becoming the foundation of Karl Rove's strategy to maintain "permanent" Republican hegemony through the evangelical voting base. One Pew survey showed that 87 percent of "traditionalist" evangelicals (10.7 percent of the adult population) voted for President Bush in the 2004 election.[5] Those overwhelming statistics verify that although not all evangelicals categorically embraced Bush, his presidency has nevertheless symbolized a form of conservative warrior politics.

When asked who his favorite philosopher was, George W. Bush responded, "Jesus Christ," although Bush's form of strong-arm, cowboy politics did not reflect the prophetic values of Jesus Christ.[6] A self-identified evangelical, George W. Bush has moved through a series of conversions in his life. His first conversion to faith came under the influence of Arthur Blessitt in Midland, Texas, and his second came by way of the best-known world evangelist of the late twentieth century, Rev. Billy Graham. Within a year of his encounter with Graham, Bush had traded in bondage to alcoholism for a newfound strength in his Christian faith. Renouncing exclusive pursuit of personal self-fulfillment, he turned to a life of public service. Years later, the horrific events of September 11, 2001, triggered in President Bush what he described as a moment of religious-like calling. As he tried to come to terms with this terrorist attack, a new "presidential mission" was visited, like a religious conversion, upon him: to protect American citizens from terrorists. With the confidence of a nineteenth-century postmillennialist, President Bush assured U.S. citizens that safer days lay ahead as America continued to implement its providential destiny in the international sphere.

It has often been observed how evangelical faith has significantly shaped the staff and practices of the Bush White House. Inclined toward prayer and Bible reading, the president surrounded himself with Christians both inside and outside his two administrations, including former Attorney General John Ashcroft and his speechwriter and friend Wheaton College graduate Michael Gerson. Furthermore, this climate was maintained at the highest to the lowest levels; in 2004, seven of almost one hundred interns in the White House came from Patrick Henry College, a small evangelical liberal arts college founded in 2000 in Purcellville, Virginia.[7]

Beyond their presence in central leadership and intern positions within the George W. Bush administration, evangelicals also have exerted considerable influence through lobbying efforts and business networks. The explosion of evangelical political action committees (PACs) throughout the 1980s and 1990s was noted by Kevin Philips: "In recent years, as evangelicals have gained importance, corporations have begun to take note, hiring more Washington lobbyists with biblical worldviews or Christian Right connections."[8]

The networking extends beyond PACs: evangelical businessmen gather as part of a "Fellowship," arranging throughout the year to have heads of state meet with the president at the National Prayer Breakfast.[9] Furthermore, the visionary Hispanic evangelical leader Luis Cortés Jr., president of Nueva Esperanza and Esperanza USA, founded and hosts the National Hispanic Prayer Breakfast and Conference, providing an opportunity for the Hispanic community to interact with the president. Clearly, evangelicals—ranging from powerful politicians to influential businesspeople, from college presidents to internationally renowned artists—have been on the rise in American public life.[10] This potent network, referred to by sociologist D. Michael Lindsay as the new "evangelical elite,"[11] evinces the current influence evangelicals have in American political society; their voices *are* being heard.

But whose voices are they, and who exactly are the evangelicals? The label itself remains highly contested among historians of American religion. It takes on many meanings, and many theological traditions make claim to it. The terminological debate surrounding the word "evangelical" has become so knotty that Donald W. Dayton argues for an outright moratorium on the term.[12] As much as one might sympathize with Dayton's frustration, there is no getting around the fact that the term "evangelical" is not going to go away. Its use is constantly reinforced by talk show hosts, political strategists, academics—indeed, by members of countless disciplines— and perhaps most indelibly, by regular churchgoers themselves. Drawing a common thread through such disparate multitudes is a delicate study and one that requires a step back and a look at historical roots.

Meaning "gospel" or "good news," the term "evangelical" originates in the magisterial Reformation that began in Germany with Martin Luther's nailing the Ninety-five Theses to the door of the Wittenberg Cathedral in 1517. In Germany, *evangelisch* continues to be used in this Reformation tradition to signify both Protestants in general and Lutherans in particular. The primary tenets of the European Reformation continue to shape the theologies and ethos of both black and white evangelicals in the United States; however, the revivalist background of American evangelicalism has played an even greater role in the emergence of postwar twentieth-century evangelical politics. To better understand evangelicalism in America today, we need to place it in its historical context, paying special attention to revivalism and race.

British historian David Bebbington provides an excellent starting point, citing four distinctive features of evangelical faith and practice: (1) an experience of conversion to Jesus Christ, (2) a view that the Bible is the ultimate religious authority, (3) an activism expressed through evangelism and social witness, and (4) an emphasis on Jesus's death on the cross and bodily resurrection from the dead.[13] Bebbington's definition has become a standard in the field of American religious history. To these four points I would add a fifth: transdenominational populism.

Evangelicalism has long been characterized by "shifting movements, temporary alliances, and the lengthened shadows of individuals."[14] Na-

than Hatch has argued forcefully for evangelicalism's democratic character, which I describe as populism.[15] The concept of transdenomina-
tionalism is borrowed from John Stackhouse, who rightly argues that
evangelicals are found throughout traditional denominational structures
as well as outside of them, within nondenominational and parachurch
structures.[16]

Evangelicalism has been able to adapt, grow, and engage the world in
many ways precisely because of its fluid character. Considering evangelicalism in terms of transdenominational populism provides a way to expand
analyses of evangelical churches and denominations and apply them to
broader evangelical social movements that seek to effect political change.
Viewing American evangelicalism as a populist movement provides a theoretical landscape for thinking about its various submovements, and it al-
lows us to draw on the particular historical and theological heritages that
different evangelical submovements represent. This is a crucial step in our
efforts to historicize the term "evangelical."

Within the wide parameters of Bebbington's definition of evangelicals
(biblical authority, conversion, cross, activism), all four of the Christian social movements discussed in this book would be considered evangelical,
yet each is formed by a different theological and cultural heritage. One of
the limitations of Bebbington's definition that is indicative of most of the
genre of "defining evangelicalism" literature is its focus on Christian theological identity without deeply engaging social location and cultural history. For example, according to Bebbington's definition, many Roman
Catholics and many African Americans would be considered evangelicals,
yet this quick designation can mask important theological and cultural differences. Definitions like Bebbington's do provide various degrees of theological boundaries for those who identify themselves as evangelicals, but
they do not properly address the movement's historic and cultural complexity.

One of Bebbington's students, evangelical theologian Timothy Larsen,
takes up the challenge of historicizing the definition of evangelicalism.
Larsen engages the historical context when he argues that an evangelical is
an "orthodox Protestant who stands in the tradition of the global Christian networks arising from the eighteenth century revival movements associated with John Wesley and George Whitefield" while at the same time

stressing key Bebbingtonian theological characteristics: biblical authority; reconciliation with God through Jesus's work on the cross; and the work of the Holy Spirit in conversion, fellowship, and evangelism.[17] Larsen thus builds on Bebbington by addressing the historic and global dimensions of evangelicalism. Furthermore, through mentioning the work of the Holy Spirit, Larsen introduces the pneumatological motif that has become so important in twentieth-century evangelicalism, influenced by the explosive rise of Pentecostalism.[18]

This historical grounding of evangelicalism in eighteenth-century revivalism helps us to answer the question: are African American Protestants like Martin Luther King Jr., Jesse Jackson Sr., John Perkins, and Barack Obama evangelicals? Many African Americans experienced conversions during the eighteenth-century revival meetings of Wesleyan preachers like George Whitefield and also John Wesley himself, but these occurrences alone were not sufficient to create a new space for African Americans to work out of a broadly evangelical theological orientation. That evolution began to emerge during the nineteenth century through increased participation by black and white evangelicals in a collective struggle for the abolition of slavery.[19] In this situation, a purely Bebbingtonian, ahistorical definition of evangelical theology becomes limited. It is chiefly through an inextricable welding of theology onto a historical and political context that African Americans began to emerge within the evangelical tradition on a broader scale, transforming it from the outside in.

The complexity and controversy of black-white interaction in the antebellum period reverberates today. Mark A. Noll draws similar conclusions: "The decades before the Civil War constitute, thus, not only the most intensely partisan period in American history but also the period in which theology was most directly applied to public issues. The only era that comes close is our own."[20] Noll goes on to identify two parallels between the antebellum period and the contemporary period (1956–present): both periods exhibit a deep cultural divide that expresses itself along political lines, and both exhibit contentious public debate. In contrast to religious leaders in colonial New England, evangelical populist preachers of the antebellum period often chose to incite religious controversy, a tactic for which there is obviously no shortage today.

The arguments of Larsen and Noll demonstrate that the term "evangelical" must be historically grounded. Their common focus on the revivalist roots of evangelicalism in the United States provides an important lens to help us view both the origins and the present character of this movement. By retracing the threads of evangelicalism back to antebellum revivalism, we are given a better understanding not only of white evangelicalism but also of black Christianity in the United States. But this understanding can truly begin to set in only when we venture beyond abstraction and attempt to evoke material conditions as they existed then.

Antebellum revivals were sites of both solidarity and oppression among blacks and whites in the United States. Human slavery was a scourge on America and an ethical crisis for Christianity. Race created a deep problem within white evangelicalism, and the experience of white evangelical slave owners beating, raping, and lynching blacks in the American South presents an ongoing theological problem for histories of evangelicalism and evangelical theology. J. Kameron Carter argues that the black experience of suffering in America "dislocates" the white evangelicals' understanding of Christianity in order to "relocate" it in the experience of black Christianity.[21] Carter frames his analysis of suffering around the "politics of death," observing that African Americans suffered in a literal, physical sense—beatings, killings—but further defining this suffering as a social and cultural death.[22]

Carter points to Harriet Jacobs, the author of the earliest known female slave narrative, as an example of both the depth of black suffering and the breadth of the black theological imagination.[23] In her narrative, Jacobs recounts her struggle with her white owner, Dr. Norcom, who attempts to rape her. She climbs into "an airless, mice-infested, nine-feet long, seven-feet wide, and three-feet high attic-like garret, which was part of the roof of her grandmother's house" in order to evade Dr. Norcom's attacks.[24] She lives hidden from view, in this claustrophobic space for seven years, in the hope that her children would eventually be sold away toward the North and move a step closer to freedom.

To reconcile the cruel reality of her life to the hope inherent in her Christian faith, Jacobs prayerfully reflects on the life and death of Jesus Christ. The crucifixion of Jesus Christ becomes an entry into an entombed God-forsakeness that Jesus experiences on Holy Saturday. This "in-between" state provides a theological space of freedom where Jacobs can identify with the suffering of Christ and where she can express her own theological voice. Christ was alienated from the land of the living and his Father in heaven, and Jacobs was alienated from human connection and her children on earth.

Jacobs's conception of Jesus is very different from that of many white evangelical preachers and theologians. The Jesus that Jacobs is looking at is not the triumphal Lord of the Resurrection but the Jesus who shares our suffering in those vacuous in-between spaces of life. As both a historical and theological subject, Harriet Jacobs exposes the problems of white evangelicalism, complicating its dominant theology of Jesus, and points also to the promise of new theological perspectives abundant in black Christianity.

Many historical accounts classify evangelicalism as an almost entirely white phenomenon, but that tells the story only from the surface. Once slaves became Christians, they forever transformed the American evangelical experience. Carter points to Jacobs's life and theology as a starting point for reclaiming the term "evangelicalism" in a way that expresses the intricacies of the black Christian experience. Following Carter, we seek to develop the contours of a new genealogy of evangelicalism—one that unearths what has often been overlooked or obscured by its deep white evangelical root system. As Carter argues, there is a "theologically profound counter-tradition that is tucked within the tradition of American evangelicalism. This is the tradition of black Christianity, which in fact retrieves crucial aspects of the broader catholic Christian traditions that were in some sense lost to modernity. Black Christianity provokes a continued interrogation of persons black, white, and all shades in between who, at present, want the name 'evangelical.'"[25] Carter's question—"What would it mean to receive the Jewish Savior, to enter into the body politic of the wounded, not triumphalist, flesh disclosed there, and so be saved?"—makes an important theological connection between the "Jewish" flesh of Jesus Christ and the black flesh of enslaved Africans in the Americas. Carter is concerned with the ways in which Jews and blacks have been racialized throughout Christian history, an injustice, he argues, in which the church has been compliant and at times intentionally instrumental. He thus challenges the evangelical church to meet Jesus the Jew, for it is in the Jewish flesh of Jesus that white evangelicals can find the woundedness of

Jesus's human flesh—the same woundedness looked to by Africans in the Americas, whose physical flesh has suffered for more than three centuries.

In the incarnation of Jesus Christ all space and time is condensed in a single human, Jewish life. Through Jesus the Jew, all people, including the Gentiles, are grafted into the divine family. As early Christianity moved from being a Jewish sect, the "Jews" were racialized according to a theological logic of European Christendom. As a result the Jews were seen as outsiders and faced persecution and oppression throughout the centuries. In the early modern period, European Christendom once again racialized an Other, but this time it was the "black." The black was racialized in the period of European colonization on Christian theological grounds. Thus, in order for white evangelical Christianity in the Americas to confront its racist past, it is vital to uncover the theological logic that created "blacks."[26] From Immanuel Kant to Thomas Jefferson, the white architects of a Euro-American modernity must be interrogated concerning the problem of race. Renarrating church history from the standpoint of those with dark skin has a theological basis in the dark skin of Jesus the Jew. Thus, there is an important theological connection between Jesus Christ and race in the complex history of trans-Atlantic Christianity that must be explored genealogically in order to understand evangelical contemporary public theologies in the Americas.

2

REVIVAL, RACE, AND REFORM:
THE ROOTS OF MODERN EVANGELICAL
POLITICS

On Saturday, August 9, 1801, thousands of settlers assembled at Cane Ridge, Kentucky, for a revival that would transform the face of American religion. Black and white, rich and poor, northern and southern, people from all over the country poured onto the Cane Ridge to revive their souls. With apocalyptic thunderclaps, this revival produced spiritual shock waves, a signal of the social crisis that was about to spread throughout the land. As blacks and whites worshiped together, it became clear there would eventually have to be a holy reckoning concerning the enslavement of Africans in the southern interior. In the process of deep cultural interaction, an independent black Christian voice—a distinctive social and political vision—was born. At Cane Ridge in Kentucky the nation witnessed the emergence of a robust, prophetic evangelicalism and the birth of the Bible Belt.[1]

The Cane Ridge revival became a symbol of a new egalitarianism on the American frontier, as the countertradition of prophetic black Christianity emerged from under the white evangelical culture in the Second Great Awakening. This symbol is poignant today, and an understanding of prophetic black voices in the context of American revivalism provides a new horizon for understanding the evangelical political past and present. Thus it is vital that the story of evangelicalism in North America be renarrated from the perspective of those on the underside of a white evangelical modernity, including women and people of color: African Americans, Asian Americans, Latino/a Americans, and Native Americans. This is a monumental historical task. In this book I focus on a part of that project: the interaction between black and white evangelicals.

David W. Wills has argued that American religious history has been dominated by two central themes: pluralism and Puritanism.[2] He also suggests a third theme: the encounter of black and white. Wills argues that colonial southern religion cannot be understood as a religion of white southerners alone but is better understood as a dynamic interaction between black and white cultures. The black-white encounter model of southern evangelicalism provides a better explanation of the phenomenon than a "diluted Puritanism or a benign pluralism."[3]

In the wake of Billy Graham's successful mass crusades, southern evangelicalism became one of the most dominant forces in twentieth-century postwar politics. Since the encounter between blacks and whites has been so central to the southern evangelical experience, it provides an important window into the "southernization" of American politics. From President Jimmy Carter to President George W. Bush, born-again southern evangelical political leaders have become a fixture in American public life.

Most white historians of evangelicalism have developed the "Puritanism theme," focusing on the northern evangelical experience. This historical perspective often misses the centrality of a countertradition in the American evangelical experience—black Christianity. White male evangelicals have been prominent in narratives of evangelical politics, from Jimmy Carter and George W. Bush to James Dobson and Jim Wallis, but there is also a stream of black Christianity that is bubbling up in our early twenty-first-century milieu, a heritage that arises from Harriet Tubman and Sojourner Truth to Fanny Lou Hammer and Martin Luther King Jr. What would our narration of evangelical history look like if we considered evangelicalism as an antislavery, antisegregation, antiracism, reconciliation movement seeking to bear witness for Christ through being a parable of the Kingdom God?

The story of black Christianity is an important starting point for the creation of a new genealogy of evangelicalism in the United States. This story has been largely excluded in white accounts of evangelical history, which have focused primarily on the thought and activities of white men; however, these early accounts are currently being challenged and transformed by a growing body of literature in the field of history.

Early accounts of black evangelicalism were written primarily by African Americans whose work was often marginalized within mainstream scholarship.[4] Recently, though, black and white historians of evangelicalism have begun to move the topic of the black Christian experience in America from the margins to the mainstream in the field of history.[5] These works are complemented by a growing body of historical monographs on race, religion, and politics in the United States, especially in post–Civil War America.[6] We are witnessing a transformation in the field of religious history, and it is now time for evangelical theology to catch up.

The genealogy offered in this book is unique in its attempt to identify where white evangelicals and black Christians shape each other throughout American history. From the beginning, black and white Christians have lived in conversation, conflict, and collaboration with each other. Evangelical social movements cannot be fully understood without a sustained analysis of this deep cultural interaction. Furthermore, the theological subjectivity and subversive political agency of black Christians is an integral part of renarrating America's evangelical past and constructing a prophetic evangelical future.

Conceptually, I consider the black-white interaction in American history as a call-and-response dialogue analogous to the structure of traditional black spirituals and gospel music. While some black slaves heard Christ's call through the preaching of white evangelicals, they also transformed the motif into their own language, music, and culture when they responded. The black Christian musical tradition has had an influence on white evangelical culture that has never been fully recognized. From slave songs to black spirituals, the African singing tradition helped shape many of the revivalist hymns of white evangelicalism. As whites and blacks were free to express themselves bodily and emotionally in the context of eighteenth- and nineteenth-century revival meetings, a process of mutual mimicry emerged that became a metaphor for the present multicultural diversity within evangelicalism.

The story of the black church is central to the white evangelical story because both are organic, independent, and interdependent movements within American religious history. Thinking historically about the relation between black and white evangelicalism in the formation of different streams of American political culture requires revisions in the way we think of the theological ideas, political practices, and legacies of evangelicalism. The objective of this intercultural approach to religious history and Christian theology is therefore not merely to define evangelicalism but to explore it genealogically.[7] As evangelicalism stands at this historical crossroads, the need to examine its genealogy leads right back to the social and spiritual shock waves of Cane Ridge and to evangelicalism's revivalist roots.

The history of "awakenings"—revivalist movements with religious services marked by passionate prayer and preaching to mobilize people to commit or recommit themselves to religious faith—is foundational in this genealogy centering on the interaction between blacks and whites.[8] In his masterful *The Great Awakening*, Thomas S. Kidd argues that revivals provided the site for massive conversions of African Americans, who in turn reshaped white evangelical piety, producing prophetic evangelicalism, both black and white.[9]

From its earliest days in colonial America, evangelicalism's deepest roots lie within religious awakenings and revivalism, and within the conversionist and pietistic strands of the American evangelical experience. Early American revivals played an important role in transatlantic religious expansion and development, as well as in breeding new forms of evangelicalism in the Americas.[10] This evolution was characterized by both black and white voices. America's greatest white evangelical theologian, Jonathan Edwards, preached passionately to African Americans, accepting nine as members of his Northampton church.[11] As increasing numbers of African Americans converted to evangelical Christianity, the church gradually, in fleeting moments, began to embody the Gospel's egalitarian ideal that would undergird the evangelical abolition movement.

John Wesley and George Whitefield arrived in the South during the late 1730s. Wesley met his first black slave on August 1, 1736, and quickly began to share his faith with African Americans.[12] After Whitefield came ashore in the Carolinas in 1738, many African Americans found solace in evangelical faith. "The evangelical rejection of earthly status and authority, coupled with an emphasis upon an intense personal conversion experience, proved attractive to thousands of black slaves," writes Milton C. Sernett.[13] As a result of these conversions, a strong African American evangelical presence emerged in the lower South and the mid-Atlantic states.

The conversion of African Americans was arguably the greatest contribution of the evangelical revivals to the future of American Christianity. "Early American white evangelicals' commitment to evangelization set in motion perhaps the most remarkable change in American religious history: the nearly wholesale conversion of African Americans to some form of evangelical Christianity. That great transformation began in force in the mid-1780s, and by the early nineteenth century African Americans were converting at almost unparalleled rates," writes Thomas S. Kidd.[14] The conversion of black slaves, and attempts to evangelize them by whites, represented the first egalitarian contact between whites and blacks that moved relations between the two races beyond the level of master and slave. Evangelical revivals were the first instance of southern slave-holding whites looking at blacks as more than some sort of economic tool or resource on the level of livestock. The challenge for white evangelicals would be whether or not they could fully perform the egalitarian logic of the Gospel by dismantling the slave system on which the southern economy was built.

With the fires of revivalism spreading around the country and crossing racial lines, evangelicalism became the most robust form of Protestant religion during the eighteenth century. Although moderates were content to focus on the spiritual conversions of individuals, white prophetic evangelicals added an emphasis on the Gospel's social implications. Within the culture of revivalism a stream of radical abolitionist Christianity emerged that impacted both black and white evangelicalism. In the eighteenth century, white prophetic evangelicals like Hugh Bryan and John Hopkins began to see that the logic of conversion meant that slavery must be condemned. A Whitefield convert in 1740, Hugh Bryan was a prophetic visionary. Prefiguring Benjy in William Faulkner's *The Sound and the Fury,* Bryan was a brilliant southern "idiot character" who understood the injustice and idiocy of the current situation and saw apocalyptic fragments of a new future. In 1742 he dreamed that Charleston, South Carolina, would be burned to the ground for the sin of slavery, a prophecy fulfilled almost one hundred years later with Nat Turner's rebellion in 1831.[15] Bryan had a series of prophesies impressed on him of a coming time when slaves would rise up, and he imagined he would play a strategic leadership role in this rebellion. He stood between the poles of vibrant personal piety and political radicalism.

At the same time there was a rising of antislavery consciousness in some white radical evangelicals in the southern interior, a number of black northern preachers carried the spiritual fire and evangelistic rhetoric of the First Great Awakening into the Mid-Atlantic and lower South. These black prophetic evangelicals preached a message of Jesus and justice that galvanized people to join the struggle against injustice. In 1784, Richard Allen left eastern New Jersey and traveled into the Pennsylvanian interior. In his journal, Allen described a church visited by visible supernatural signs. He wrote of preaching "on a Sabbath day to a large congregation of different persuasions, and my dear Lord was with me, and I believe there were many souls cut to the heart, and were added to the ministry. I stayed in Radnor several weeks. Many souls were awakened and cried aloud to the Lord to have mercy upon them. . . . It was a time of visitation from above, many were the slain of the Lord."[16] Allen appropriated the Edwardsian rhetoric of awakening and added to it a new evangelical discourse that included being "slain of the Lord." Allen represents one example of black Christianity drawing on and creatively modifying motifs from within the white European revivalist tradition.

Whereas colonial America bore a broadly Calvinist vision of public life, the revivalism and radical reform of the nineteenth century increasingly embodied a Wesleyan and Baptist piety.[17] The Calvinist tradition emphasized the sovereignty of God in electing certain individuals to eternal salvation, but in contrast, John Wesley and Francis Asbury began to preach persuasively through the frontier that one could choose to have faith in God. This emphasis on free will also implied that one could choose to work for the common good, including actively joining social struggles— for example, working for the abolition of slavery.

John Wesley emphasized the doctrine of entire sanctification, maintaining that upon coming to faith, one gradually becomes purified through the vital and cleansing powers of the Holy Spirit. Wesleyan doctrines of sanctification were often applied both to personal piety and to societal transformation. With the free-will orientation of Armenian forms of Methodism and a postmillennial eschatology, nineteenth-century evangelicals were often engaged in ministries of social transformation, including the struggle to abolish slavery and the struggle for the equality of women.[18]

During the mid-nineteenth century, Protestantism was largely evangelical, and as such it was passionately committed to a personal faith with a variety of strategies for social transformation. Evangelical Christianity was "the largest, most formidable subculture in American society" during this period.[19] Growing out of the religious awakenings of the eighteenth and nineteenth centuries, evangelicalism was being energized and transformed by both pietist and Reformed theological streams. In addition to the cross-fertilization between Reformed and Wesleyan pieties in the nineteenth century, a similar relationship developed between black and white evangelicals, who were together shaped by the revivals of the First and Second Awakenings.

Revivalism created a new religious landscape for black and white Americans to engage one another on more equal footing, as thousands converted, regardless of race or ethnicity. Revivals offered a message of hope and solidarity among African Americans whose bodies and spirits were bound by the shackles of slavery. Yet although many African Americans came to faith through the revivals of the eighteenth and nineteenth centuries, they were often initiated into an individualistic form of faith that did not address the social inequalities of the day. Still, a slave response to the underlying Christian call of deliverance from bondage rang out, deliberate but hidden, heard in the double meanings of slave songs like "Swing Low" and "Steal Away."

Revivals were sites for increased spiritual interaction between blacks and whites, functioning as a new space for racial integration where all were equal at the altar of God. Within the revivalist ethos there were fleeting moments of spiritual unity between black and white. Mechal Sobel writes, "Virtually all eighteenth-century Baptist and Methodist churches were mixed churches, in which blacks sometimes preached to whites and in which whites and blacks witnessed together, shouted together, and shared ecstatic experiences at 'dry' and wet christenings, meetings and burials."[20] It was through the shout that African Americans mediated an ecstatic spiritual medium as a communal cry for social justice unveiling the Afrocentric form of prophetic evangelical politics.[21] Revivals provided African Americans with both a message of equality before God and a physical space where they were free to express themselves through singing, shaking, running, dancing, chanting, and shouting.

Outside the rigid hierarchy of the plantation, revivalism created a new space for African Americans to sing and dance and express themselves in the rituals and cultural forms of their African past. Influenced by the rhythms of West African religions, black evangelicals joined with white evangelicals in passionate music-making and hymn singing. David Hempton observes that in the Methodist tradition, black evangelicals formed their own "empire of the spirit" in which they embodied Christian community in a manner that was distinctively African and socially engaged.[22] Music was a liturgical bridge between West African religious customs and American revivalist Methodism.[23]

Black evangelicals found their own voice through preaching and exhortation. Revivals provided unique opportunities for many African American men to preach to both blacks and whites. For example, Harry Hosier, nicknamed "Black Harry," preached on the circuit with Francis Asbury in the 1780s. Audiences along the revivalists' journeys consistently preferred Hosier's passionate preaching to Asbury's staid sermons.[24] In a culture that usually silenced and despised African Americans, preaching provided a vocational platform of honor and dignity for the few black men who entered the pulpit. Revivalism provided a place where African Americans could creatively express their African past through their vibrant evangelical faith.

The spiritual fervor of antebellum revivals was deployed by some white evangelicals to resist slavery and by others to defend it. At their best, revivals provided positive social consequences. Black and white Christians joined together in worship. Some white slave owners felt compelled to free their slaves and others to treat their slaves more humanely.[25] But the spiritual fervor of the antebellum revivals was not always channeled so cleanly toward racial equality, and a revival could become a forum for more subtle, "spiritually" sanctioned forms of white oppression. A number of evangelical slave owners continued to employ injunctions of scripture—"slave obey your master"—within the revival setting in order to shore up the white male power base of the southern interior.

Regardless of the messages preached at the revivals, blacks and whites nearly always returned to their assigned roles in the antebellum social hierarchy once the revival concluded. The two races were able to unite and worship together during the services, but they remained divided by the institution of slavery. During the early nineteenth century a heated debate emerged among evangelicals of both the North and the South around the issue of slavery. The transatlantic slave trade had built the agrarian economies of the South, and southern whites were dependent on African slave labor for their very livelihood. But as the slaves became Christians, the theological questions were too obvious to ignore, and both blacks and whites began to examine the ethics of this peculiar institution.

Passionate debates erupted concerning scripture and slavery. While European Christianity placed the responsibility of interpretation on church authorities, American evangelicals argued for the private interpretation of the Bible, further intensifying the dialogue. The proslavery evangelicals gathered an arsenal of scriptural verses to deploy in defense of slavery (e.g., Gen. 9:25–27; Deut. 20:10–11; 1 Cor. 7:21; Rom. 13:1, 7; Col. 3:22, 4:1; 1 Tim. 6:1, 2). Although the antislavery evangelicals could not amass as many scriptural references that explicitly rejected slavery, they argued that the whole of redemptive history presented in the Bible disclosed the dignity and value of all human individuals, regardless of their race and ethnicity. Populist preachers emerged in both camps. These preacher-activists traveled around the country spreading their views, often in the context of revivals.

A cadre of proslavery evangelicals, men like Robert Louis Dabney, James Henley Thornwell, and Thornton Stringfellow, deployed biblical apologies for slavery through their preaching and teaching in the southern interior. White Baptist minister Thornton Stringfellow was a fierce biblical defender of the institution of slavery, arguing that "Jesus Christ recognized this institution as one that was lawful among men, and regulated its relative duties."[26] The fault line of the slavery debate, fundamentally an exegetical debate, produced severe and lasting division in the U.S. church and society.

Southern evangelicals who owned slaves or benefited from a slave-based economy dug in their heels to protect the southern way of life. Slavery benefited the white southern establishment not only economically but in every dimension of life. In the antebellum period, whites enjoyed the privilege of stores, banks, hospitals, and restaurants set up to serve them, while black slaves were relegated to the resources of the slave quarters on the plantation.

To secure their position in the social hierarchy, white men developed a mythology that was a synthesis of continental aristocracy and evangelical religion.[27] The aristocratic mythos that animated southern life had its roots in the slave culture of Roman civilization. As Orlando Patterson writes, "In the U.S. South there developed the last and most perfectly articulated slave culture since the fall of the Roman Empire. The religion that had begun in and was fashioned by the Roman slave order was to play the identical role eighteen hundred years later in the slave system that was to be Rome's closest cultural counterpart in the modern world."[28] The proslavery southerners thus articulated a European aristocratic mythology that framed the collective imagination of the white South within a temporal narration of history, creating a social space that provided psychic distance from the horror of the daily practice of slavery.

Christian theology became very fluid and adaptable to this southern mythology, which was used to justify a set of systems and mores that primarily benefited white males. Highly prized in southern culture was a distinctive concept of honor, which for many southerners often trumped the theological virtues of faith, hope, and love. As John Hope Franklin writes: "The honor of the Southerner caused him to defend with his life the slightest suggestion of irregularity in his honesty or integrity; and he was fiercely sensitive to any imputation that might cast a shadow on the character of the women in his family. To him nothing was more important than honor. Indeed, he placed it above wealth, art, learning, and the other 'delicacies' of an urban civilization and regarded its protection as a continuing preoccupation."[29] The defense of slavery became the defense of white male honor, which in turn was dependent on the degradation of black slaves. White male honor entailed protecting the purity of white women, who were confined to the sanctified space of the home. The fight to defend slavery was a fight for the very way of life of white southern men. If the practice of slavery were overturned, the white men of the South had the most to lose.

In the mythology of the white southern honor culture, the subjugation of slaves became the basis of the slave owner's social status. Eugene Genovese writes, "The slaveholders, not the South, held the power to accede or resist. To these men slaves were a source of power, pride, and prestige, a duty and a responsibility, a privilege and a trust; slavery was the foundation of a special civilization imprinted with their own character."[30] Furthermore, the institution of slavery benefited white men not only economically and culturally but also sexually. Robert J. C. Young argues in *Colonial Desire* that racism and sex are inextricably linked in the colonial imagination.[31] The racialization of the "black" in the Americas also entailed a sexualization.[32] For white southern men, the black slave women were simultaneously objects of desire and repulsion, while black men where viewed as sexual predators who were a threat to white female purity. The politics of race was animated by the politics of sex, seldom spoken about but often performed.

An underlying duality also existed within the aesthetics of the time, reinforcing social attitudes and racism. Whiteness was considered blessed and beautiful, a reflection of godliness, and blackness was seen as cursed, ugly, and sinful.[33] The dark and despised flesh of the black African was viewed as a living embodiment of Noah's curse on the Canaanite lineage of Ham. Within the white supremacist Christian imagination, a distinctly southern mythological appropriation of the ancient Near Eastern theology of covenantal blessings and curses took root, where whites were blessed and blacks were cursed.

This racist evangelical theology was further reinforced by the racialized science of the time, exemplified by a growing number of books in craniology published in the 1830s and 1840s. Samuel George Morton's *Crania Americana* (1839) and *Crania Aegyptiaca* (1844) argued that whites were superior to blacks because of skull size and capacity.[34] Morton's claim that racial difference was inherent and unchangeable was interpreted by proslavery evangelicals as evidence for the inferiority of Africans. Evangelical preachers theologized through this moment by developing polygenetic accounts of creation that differentiated the ancestral lines of blacks and whites. Thus, the southern mythology was grounded not only in continental aristocracy and evangelical theology but also in nineteenth-century pseudoscience. Myth, theology, and science converged in a proslavery evangelical social imaginary, producing a cultural logic of white over black as a de facto social principle in the antebellum South.

Driven by the binary of white (good) over black (evil), the Manichean theology of racist southern evangelicalism became institutionalized within the social hierarchy.[35] The hierarchy placed white males on the top and black females on the bottom, with white females and black males between them. Within this social hierarchy, white females and black males were in the greatest spatial proximity—a site of sexual danger.

Miscegenation was the unpardonable sin in the antebellum South. Within the aristocratic mythology of the southern interior, the chastity of the white woman was held in highest esteem. Southern white men would go to extremes, sometimes including chastity belts, to prevent their white wives and daughters from having sex with black male slaves. The belief in the "purity" of the white race provided the rationale for avoiding inter-racial sex and was also the source of an irrational fear of black sexuality and of mulatto offspring. Robert L. Dabney, a Southern Presbyterian theolo-gian of the time, exemplified this fear and ignorance when he wrote, "The offspring of an amalgamation must be a hybrid race, stamped with all the feebleness of the hybrid, and incapable of the career of civilization and glory as an independent race."[36]

Sexual sins had always cast a long shadow in the American Puritan imag-ination, most famously illustrated in Nathaniel Hawthorne's *The Scarlet Letter* (1850). As punishment for adultery, the heroine of this novel, Hes-ter Prynne, is branded with a scarlet A and condemned to a life as an out-cast. But for a woman in the antebellum South who had sexual relations with a "black man," the stigma was even worse—not only had she com-mitted adultery, but she had had sex with someone whose race was viewed as inferior and any child she might bear would suffer from the weakness of being a "mixed breed." Thus strict lines of social demarcation were drawn between whites and blacks to prevent miscegenation at all cost. Yet human desire for the cultural Other was insatiable.

Although white southern men staunchly defended the purity of white females, they often crossed the color line themselves to satisfy their own sexual desire.[37] White southern plantation owners often thought their "ownership" of slaves entailed being able to use black female bodies for their own sexual fulfillment. The logic of lordship as deployed by the mas-ter entailed absolute control over the bodies of his slaves, and the logic of submission embodied in the slave entailed a life-essence of seeking to obey and please the master.

The sexual encounter between white masters and black slaves unveils the fundamental contradiction of the antebellum slave economy: although slaves were narrated in the antebellum mythology as dependent on their independent masters, in reality the masters were dependent on their slaves. Given the black and white moral polarity of southern antebellum culture, the honorable, godly white male master was magnetically drawn to the black, shameful, sinful flesh of his female slaves. The eroticization of the wild and dirty black woman stood in dark contrast with the mannerly and pure white woman in the sexual imagination.[38] Colonial desire was exacerbated by the economic demand for more slaves.

White men having sexual relations with black women unveils the psychic destruction that was unleashed on black women's identity and black men's masculinity. As a result of white male sexual liaisons with black women, black women sometimes rose above black men in the social hierarchy. When this happened, white men were on the top of the hierarchy, black men on the bottom, and white and black women met in between.

Forced to embody purity in a sanctified home, white southern women resented the perceived "free" sensuality of black women and, in some instances, sought sexual encounters with black men. The white male desire for total domination through sexual control of a sanctified home and enslaved farm drove this sexual economy. Untangling this web of desire reveals vicious brutality driven by the logic of objectification and death-bound subjectification.

The white male defense of white female purity coupled with the nurturing of a sadistic desire for black flesh exposed the psychosocial dimension of the moral contradiction of slavery. White male slave owners and black female slaves were on the opposite ends of the social hierarchy of the antebellum South. When white male slave owners objectified and sexually violated black female flesh through rape, they participated in a ritual of vicious evil that unveiled the dark underside of chattel slavery. As Young explains, "The controlling power relation between slave-owner and slave was eroticized . . . [and] public corroboration of this white desire for 'black flesh,' [was] carried out through either rape or coercive exploitation. . . . At the same time, the white male's ambivalent axis of desire and repugnance was enacted through a remarkable ideological dissimulation by which, despite the way in which black women were constituted as sexual objects and experienced the evidence of their own desirability through their own victimization, they were also taught to see themselves as sexually unattractive."[39] In the context of the sexual encounter between the white male slave owner and the black female slave, we witness the exploitations of black females who were not only used as disposable economic flesh in public fields but also as disposable, despised sexual flesh in secret places.

The sexual exploitation of black women in the context of slavery was a vicious evil; it destroyed black women in mind, body, and soul. Fortunately, a few female slaves were able to resist the advances of their white owners, one inspirational example being Harriet Jacobs, who actively resisted the sexual advances of her owner.[40] During her time of hiding in an attic-like garret, Jacobs came to terms with her oppression *theologically.* Reflecting on Christian existence from the margins of the white antebellum economy, Jacobs found strength in Jesus's life and death, and particularly in that period between life and death. Like Jesus, she was living in an in-between state. In this sense, she found a Christological rationale for resistance and sustenance during her struggle against earthly evil. Thus, Harriet Jacobs becomes one of the first prophetic evangelicals who actively resisted slavery and racism at its most vicious point—the white male's attempt to rape a black female.

Harriet Jacobs is followed by a long line of black women who resisted slavery, segregation, and racism, including Sojourner Truth, Harriet Tubman, Ida B. Wells, and Fanny Lou Hammer. White males had settled within the power and privilege of the system of slavery. This vicious system and the racism behind it would eventually be transformed through the collective power and strength of those on the lowest underside of a white evangelical modernity—black women. Charles Finney's and Jonathan Blanchard's abolition efforts can not be fully understood unless they are read together with the abolitionist struggles of Sojourner Truth and Harriet Tubman.

The national debate about slavery intensified early in the nineteenth century as reports of the British repeal of slavery reached the United States. The fight against slavery in Britain was led by a passionate, eloquent, visionary leader named William Wilberforce, a Christian British member of Parliament.[41] Through the influence and resolve of Wilberforce, Parliament ended the West Indian slave trade in 1807. Slavery itself was formally abolished in all British territories in 1833, just as the debate was beginning to heat up in the American South.[42]

Out of the interracial communion that characterized the best compo-
nents of American revivalism, a growing group of white and black abolitionists emerged. The revolutionary egalitarianism of the evangelical revivals inspired prophetic evangelicals, both black and white, to join in
dismantling the institution of slavery. From Hugh Bryan's prophecy of
Charleston, South Carolina, being burned in judgment to Nat Turner's
rebellion in Southampton County, Virginia, in 1831, the radical egalitarian
vision of evangelicalism led to revolutionary, subversive political activities.[43] The success of the abolition movement in Britain provided growing
inspiration for the abolition struggle in the United States among both
black and white evangelicals.

White evangelical abolitionists in the early nineteenth century included
Jonathan Blanchard, the founder of Wheaton College in Illinois; Charles
G. Finney, the father of modern revivalism; and Asa Mahan, the first presi-
dent of Oberlin College in Ohio. During the period 1840 to 1860, the
"new measures" revivalism of evangelists like Jacob Knapp, Theodore
Dwight Weld, and Finney often led to radical abolition efforts in the
North. Preachers in Finney's Oberlin stream of theology sought a higher
life of entire sanctification that also had a strong social dimension.

Charles G. Finney was a religious virtuoso.[44] A fiery preacher, thoughtful scholar, creative entrepreneur, and president of Oberlin College, he became the symbol of mid-nineteenth-century revivalism. His egalitarian
message of all people having the freedom to choose Jesus Christ was well
received, given the rugged individualism and voluntarism of the period.
Through his "new measures" techniques, Finney's revival meetings were
set up to create the social conditions for religious revival.[45] He went on to
develop a coherent Wesleyan theological account of revivalism in his
twenty-two lectures on revival.[46]

Central to Finney's theology of revival was the integral role that reform
played in it. According to the logic of Finney's understanding, spiritual renewal expressed itself in concrete political struggles. Finney concretized
his public theology through preaching against the war with Mexico and
the practice of slavery. When people came forward during the altar calls of
his revivals, he would often recruit them to join the abolition movement.
His commitment to the abolition movement was so strong that he denied

slaveholders access to Communion. Opposing the practice of slavery was integral to being a prophetic evangelical in Finney's brand of nineteenth-century evangelicalism.

Phoebe Palmer, a popular woman evangelist who focused on the experience of "perfect" love, joined the Oberlin preachers in promoting a more socially engaged Wesleyanism. Jonathan Blanchard joined the Wesleyan abolition struggle from his base near Chicago. From Finney to Blanchard, nineteenth-century evangelicals viewed revival as both a spiritual and social happening. It was not enough to revive the souls of individuals, but rather to revive communities to transform society according to biblical norms of love and justice.

Yet the abolition struggle led by white evangelicals in the North was not without problems, as can be illustrated in the tortured life of Theodore Dwight Weld, whose passionate preaching was a fascinating synthesis of revivalism and reform. Weld had a complex relationship to the Oberlin School; although he shared abolitionist convictions with Finney, he did not subscribe to the desire to place individual conversion over abolitionism. Weld became increasingly frustrated with the pockets of vanity, corruption, and dogmatism within the evangelical movement before the Civil War. As he became more aware of certain blind spots of the tradition, including its individualism and racism, Weld eventually abandoned evangelicalism altogether.

The conflict between Finney and Weld reflected a deeper fissure that lay at the heart of Finney's reformist evangelicalism. Finney's revivals were a smashing success in upstate New York in the mid-1820s, but he experienced tougher audiences in New York City and other urban centers, revealing new challenges to his form of revivalist evangelicalism. James D. Bratt acknowledges the importance that Finney played in consolidating revivalist evangelicalism in the antebellum period, and he argues that 1835 marked a number of important religious departures from evangelicalism's revivalist logic.

Bratt sees an important transition in American Protestantism taking place between 1835 and 1845. During this period the Oberlin School of abolitionism struggled. Finney had stubborn health problems; Weld was often shouted down in slavery debates and was beginning to lose faith; the Tapan brothers, who funded the abolition effort, went bankrupt. With the influx of European and Catholic immigrants, new religious developments emerged outside of the evangelical mainstream, including a small but influential group of critics of revivalism.[47] The collective weight of these internal tensions and external forces unveiled weakness in the northern evangelical abolitionist struggle, a weakness due in part to a northern vision of whiteness, in which good-hearted whites were encouraged to help oppressed blacks without a deeper questioning of white power and privilege. Thus, there was an inability to develop a counterinsurgency strong enough to dismantle institutionalized white power and privilege. A deeper river was needed to successfully push through the abolition struggle: prophetic black Christianity.

The robust strength of black evangelicalism filled in the gaps left by the budding but not altogether effective abolitionism of white evangelicals. White northern evangelicals played a vital role in building the momentum of abolitionism as a political movement, but black evangelical abolitionists struggled against slavery as those who, in the words of Howard Thurman, had their backs up against the wall. Revival and reform shape a seamless garment of life for those who were directly affected by injustice, like black slaves in the antebellum era. Those who came out of the Egypt of slavery like Sojourner Truth were able to help lead others into the promised land of freedom.

Black abolitionist voices in the antebellum era, the voices of those such as Frederick Douglass, Harriet Tubman, and Sojourner Truth, led the struggle against slavery from the prophetic underside of a white evangelical modernity drawing from the great wealth of black prophetic religion. Through personal witness, powerful rhetoric, and stinging revelations, black abolitionists were a mighty force in the effort to end slavery. These black abolitionist voices provided a human face to the issue of slavery, proving to whites everywhere that black people were indeed human, were indeed children of God, and ought to be treated as such.

Born a slave to James and Elizabeth Baumfree in 1797 in Ulster County, New York, Sojourner Truth was originally named Isabella Baumfree. Serving several slave masters throughout her youth, she witnessed the severe cruelty of the system of chattel slavery. Truth interpreted her suffering and the suffering of blacks through the Christo-drama presented in scripture. Every time she saw her mother grieve the loss of her children who were ripped from their family, it would "crucify her heart afresh."[48] When Sojourner and the other children were discouraged by their dire estate, their mother, "Mau-Mau," would tell them in Low Dutch, the only language she knew, about a God "in the sky" who listened to their cries and prayers. Mau-Mau encouraged Sojourner, "when you are beaten, or cruelly treated, or fall into any trouble, you must ask help of him, and he will always hear and help you."[49]

Sojourner Truth prayed fervently for her release and her prayers were answered. A Quaker couple, Isaac and Maria Van Wagener, purchased and emancipated her. Her being set free was a type of conversion. From that point on she felt God's presence throughout the world and knew that Jesus loved her. Truth then began attending a Methodist church in Kingston, New York.

As she grew in the Christian faith, Truth felt a call to preach. On June 1, 1843, Isabella Baumfree changed her name to Sojourner Truth—Sojourner because she was embarking on a prophetic journey and Truth because she was going to speak the truth about the evil of chattel slavery. She traveled around the country lecturing against slavery in the 1840s and 1850s. A statuesque and sonorous speaker, Truth's prophetic message rang out across a nation, North and South, which was dominated by white supremacy. Truth wrote, "Such an abominable state of things is silently tolerated, to say the least, by slaveholders—deny it who may. And what is that religion that sanctions, even by its silence, all that is embraced in the '*Peculiar Institution*'? If there can be any thing more diametrically opposed to the religion of Jesus, than the working of this soul-killing system—which is as truly sanctioned by the religion of America as are her ministers and churches—we wish to be shown where it can be found."[50] Truth laid out her position in the clearest terms, revealing slavery as "diametrically opposed to the religion of Jesus," and dedicated her life to putting an end to this "soul-killing system."

Like Sojourner Truth, Harriet Tubman was a black prophetess on the move. As a "conductor" on the Underground Railroad, she made at least thirteen trips into the southern interior to rescue slaves. When asked how she survived multiple trips into the South, Tubman responded, "I just asked Jesus to take care of me, and He never let me get *frost-bitten* one bit."[51] This deep personal faith and communion with Jesus Christ in the

context of survival in the freedom struggle unveils the depth of the suffering and the resilience of faith in the black abolitionist tradition. Jesus is not
just a Lord and an atoning sacrifice, but Jesus is a true and real friend, an
ever-present help in a time of need; Jesus will see you through. Helping
free over two hundred slaves, Tubman was called "Moses" by many of her
contemporaries. As an emancipator of slaves, she demonstrates the extent
to which the black Christian experience inhabits the Exodus narrative as a
religious reality. As Frederick Douglass was speaking out against slavery in
public assemblies by day, Harriet Tubman was smuggling slaves to freedom through the Underground Railroad by night. Douglass writes of
Tubman, "The midnight sky and the silent stars have been the witnesses of
your devotion to freedom and of your heroism. Excepting John Brown—
of sacred memory—I know of no one who has willingly encountered more
perils and hardships to serve our enslaved people than you have."[52]

One difference between white and black activists is rooted in their application of the Exodus symbol to the American nation. White evangelicals
generally viewed America as a New Canaan, where chosen people (whites)
enacted a Christian civilization, whereas black activists like Frederick Douglass interpreted America as Egypt and white Americans as pharaohs. The
vocation of the black abolitionist was to prophetically confront the white
establishments of both North and South to "let my people go!" Jesus
Christ was understood as an earthly prophet, and like Moses in the Old
Testament, it was Jesus who would lead the black people out of their
bondage of slavery into a promised land of freedom and peace. Jesus's saving work on the cross lived on in the struggle for love and justice in the
world among all of God's people. Sojourner Truth and Harriet Tubman
helped black southern slaves, in exile, find a way out of their captivity.
Black liberation was fundamentally a theological enterprise. Their understanding of Jesus was of one who understood their suffering and empowered them to work for a more just and peaceful world.

After the passing of the Fugitive Slave Act in 1850, Frederick Douglass
and Sojourner Truth joined forces, traveling to address abolitionists in
Boston. Douglass launched a passionate critique of America and the inability of the American church to overcome its sins and the social death of
slavery. For Douglass, the physical and social death that the slave system
caused for African Americans entailed a form of the "death of God."

Douglass's speech posed an important theological question: how could anyone in good conscience call themselves a Christian when they lived in a culture based on a moral contradiction?

When Douglass finished his diatribe, Sojourner Truth turned to him and asked a simple question, "Frederick, is God dead?"[53] Like Douglass, Truth saw that there must be a divorce between evangelicalism and the spirit of the empire; however, unlike Douglass she did not think this required a rejection of faith in the loving power of the personal God of the Bible. Rather, prophetic black Christianity presented a Christo-drama from the underside of empire. By interpreting Jesus Christ as a sojourner for justice, one who was always searching for the suffering in the world in order to heal them, Truth created the theological architecture for a truly prophetic evangelicalism in America.

Douglass had doubts about the ability of Christianity to redeem itself after its captivity to chattel slavery, but Sojourner Truth and Harriet Tubman saw prophetic evangelicalism as the only hope for liberation from this captivity. Truth and Tubman knew what it meant to experience acute suffering under the slave regime, but they also knew what it meant to experience God's grace and sustaining care. Living their lives as tireless witnesses to the Gospel, Truth and Tubman held up the possibility of a Christianity that was prophetic and egalitarian, extending God's grace to all, regardless of their race, gender, or socioeconomic status.

If Christianity was going to dislodge itself from its white supremacist reign, it would have to be patient, deliberate, disciplined, and stouthearted in opposing the proslavery forces and systems that were so deeply rooted in the very formation of the nation. From the beginning, the wedding of Christian theology and white supremacy sanctified the system of slavery in America. As a result of the faithful, courageous labor of Christian abolitionists, black and white, the theological debate over slavery became more and more intense during the 1850s, eventually reaching the boiling point in war.

In this context of religious populism and partisan politics focused on issues of race, religion, and politics, controversy and division was the rule of the day in antebellum America. Preachers, Bible scholars, and theologians were unable to achieve a consensus, polarizing the church and the nation. Noll writes, "The supreme crisis over the Bible was that there existed no apparent biblical resolution to the crisis. . . . It was left to those consummate theologians, the Reverend Doctors Ulysses S. Grant and William Tecumseh Sherman, to decide what in fact the Bible actually meant."[54] Through four long and bloody years (1861–65), brother fought brother and Christian fought Christian in a struggle to define the nation. At the end of the Civil War, slavery was defeated. Nonetheless, deeper underlying questions emerged, most important the issue of race.

Noll argues that the Civil War provoked a twofold theological crisis.[55] First, evangelicals realized it was increasingly difficult to unify the nation's republican culture around the Bible when there remained deep disagreements about what it meant. Second and more seriously, evangelicals failed to develop a tradition of theological reflection that substantively engaged the social issues of race and economic inequality. Racism, rapidly expanding industrialization, and Christian nationalism remained ethical dilemmas for evangelicals after the war.

Before the Civil War, many evangelicals on both sides of the struggle shared a common belief that America was a Christian nation with roots in a broadly Calvinistic doctrine of Providence. John Calvin's theology was based on the sovereignty of God and the principle of election—some are chosen for salvation and others are rejected. When these notions were applied to nation-states, the idea emerged that particular nations played strategic roles in God's redemptive plan. During the founding of America, a myth of Christian origins was developed that continued to shape evangelical piety through the Civil War. The Civil War challenged the Puritan ideal that the people of the United States stood in a special covenantal relationship with God.[56]

Throughout the Civil War, both sides invoked God's name. From May 1864 to February 1865, as the number of civilian deaths increased, the Union and the Confederacy both began to invoke God and Jesus Christ with more passion and frequency.[57] Revivals in the military grew toward the end of the war. As the Confederacy began to lose more battles, it increasingly held God as its only hope. Many proslavery southern evangelicals identified their struggle with the name of Jesus Christ to theologically legitimate their cause against the "monster heresy" of abolition.[58] Harry S. Stout writes: "Religion would never become more central or affirming than in the final months of the Confederacy's life. In fact, the clergy had no choice. Having already sacrificed a prophetic voice of their own to the sacred cause, their fortunes were linked inextricably with their government's."[59] Now the evangelical churches that had played a vital role in the formation of a common national culture were faced with a great moral dilemma: How could God be invoked by the armies of both the Union and the Confederacy? Was God on the side of freedom or the side of slavery?

After being forced to confront the ethical contradiction of building the U.S. economy on slave labor, evangelicals found it increasingly difficult to theologically understand America as a Christian nation. Furthermore, the fact that the United States did not fully come to terms with the problem of racism until the 1950s and 1960s also demonstrates the theological problem with the notion that the United States had a providential destiny. Noll writes, "The crisis created by an inability to distinguish the Bible on race from the Bible on slavery meant that when the Civil War was over and slavery was abolished, systemic racism continued unchecked as the great moral anomaly in a supposedly Christian America."[60]

In failing to marshal theological and political resources to solve the debate of slavery in the antebellum period, the evangelical Christian tradition proved unable to provide a coherent and sustainable vision for public policy and racism in the postwar United States.[61] A biblically based policy framework was replaced with an increasingly secularized democratic process.

Although nineteenth-century evangelicalism failed to provide a coherent public theology for the nation in the postbellum period, it had awakened an important segment of the population to a radical social ethics through the abolition movement. From Frederick Douglass and Sojourner Truth to Jonathan Blanchard and Charles Finney, prophetic evangelical abolitionists, black and white, led a struggle for justice based on their biblical vision of Jesus Christ as a prophet and king, whose kingdom was a kingdom for all. As Stout writes: "The greatest guarantor of America's claim to global hope as it emerged in the Civil War was surely abolition. . . . Indeed, abolition represented the indispensable prelude to equal civil rights, however long that might take to achieve."[62] Evangelical abolitionism was one of the most important contributions of the evangelical church to the health of the nation and the world.

The Civil War and its aftermath confronted American Christians with three ethical dilemmas: racism, economic injustice, and Christian nationalism. These struggles plagued postbellum evangelicalism in the North and the South. There was a moment after the Civil War when national racial reconciliation appeared to be a possibility, but this possibility was squashed as white racism and Christian nationalism reforged a deadly new alliance readily accepted by many evangelicals of both North and South.[63]

With the emancipation and empowerment of blacks after the Civil War, northern and southern whites were faced with a dilemma: would they stand with freed blacks or would they turn their backs on them? White southern evangelicals who were shaped by the egalitarian tendency of antebellum revivalism tried their best to embody a prophetic evangelical theology of reconciliation, but those who felt threatened by the emancipated blacks slid quickly back into a new form of oppression that reconstituted an institutionalized, racialized social hierarchy. The whites of the North and South converged in the reign of Jim Crow.

Defeated by the Union army, white southerners felt deeply humiliated after the Civil War. Neo-Confederate religiosity developed in the form of "Lost Cause Religion."[64] Many southern evangelical apologists for slavery as an instrument of conversion became apologists for the revivalist conversions of soldiers during the war. Harry Stout writes: "Just as white Christian apologists in the antebellum South had praised slavery as a converting institution for the slaves from paganism to Christ, so these Civil War apologists now praised the war as a converting institution for white soldiers and, in turn, white society. . . . The 'Lost Cause' of the white Christian South would constitute a self-contained region—and religion—isolated from the international community of believers that preserved the sacred memories of the war and the revivals its army produced."[65] Underlying "Lost Cause Religion" was a deep, romantic longing to return to the glory days of the princely plantations, a system of agriculture built on the broken backs of black slaves.

After the Civil War white southern men experienced a great social inversion. Their world was turned upside down. They went from a position of honor to a position of shame in every dimension of their life. As soldiers of the Confederacy they had been defeated by the Union army. As white men they had to accept the liberty of black men, who now walked freely in the streets of their towns. As planters they lost their supply of free labor. Defeated militarily, culturally, and economically, they hung their heads in shame in communities, churches, and homes that were increasingly shaped by a feminized Victorian evangelical culture.

As a result of the social disorientation of the post–Civil War South, white men sought new forums for expressing their anger and aggression. Ted Ownby argues that southern white men in particular had always struggled with a desire for freedom and forums of aggression, for example, in their ritual hunts and in their desire for the social stability found in the home and the church. Southern evangelical men were continually conflicted between a desire for combat and compassion. Ownby writes, "Male culture and evangelical culture were rivals, causing sparks when they came in contact and creating guilt and inner conflict in many southerners who tried to balance the two. The two forces operated against each other in an emotionally charged dialectic, the intensity of each reinforcing the other. It was the tension between the extremes of masculine aggressiveness and home-centered evangelicalism that gave white southern culture its emotionally charged nature. . . . Evangelicals, then, strove to bring men closer to the temperament of women and children."[66] With the end of the slave-based economy, white southern men lost the infrastructure that had stabilized the dialectic of male aggression and evangelical piety. Acutely experiencing postwar self-negation, white southern men often found themselves alienated from northerners, African Americans, their women, and themselves. In this moment of posttraumatic stress, they did what they always did in dire circumstances—went to the woods. In the big country, under the trees, they killed deer, drank whiskey, fraternized, meditated, and began to plot their revenge.

Men may have found temporary freedom and release in the cold, mysterious darkness of the woods, but "the bonds of blood and marriage" in family and the church were the social glue of life in the Deep South.[67] The white evangelical southern vision of reconstruction focused on defending the sanctified home, the last pristine garden of purity amidst a quickly encroaching dark wilderness.[68] Kimberly R. Kellison writes, "Faced with a world that witnessed disorder and immorality in both the secular and the religious arenas, many white evangelicals projected their heightened fears of sexuality onto those who did not conform to their vision of the family."[69] In the evangelical imagination of defeated and humiliated southern white men and a rapidly growing group of northern white men, the single greatest threat to their vision of family was black men. Black men were viewed as sexual predators and a threat to the last bit of territory that the white man ruled—the patriarchal home.

After the war, many whites in the North and South worked hard for racial reunion during Reconstruction (1865–75). Although there were fleeting moments of interracial solidarity that reflected the egalitarian spirit of integrated antebellum revivals, by the early 1880s, racial reform was halted and a new national solidarity based on a reconstituted whiteness was inaugurated. The lynching of black men became a racist ritual that played a role in the forging of a new sectional reconciliation among whites of the North and South.[70]

Lynchings were the public hangings of those identified as enemies within a given community, the overwhelming majority being black men. The lynching of African Americans began in the post–Civil War era, and the numbers increased substantially from 1880 on. From 1880 to 1930, about five thousand African Americans were lynched. Black and white Christians interpreted lynchings differently. Many white evangelicals of both North and South viewed lynching as a "sacrifice" meant to effect the redemption of American culture and Christian civilization; black Christians viewed lynchings as the enactments of persecutions.

If lynchings were considered a religious sacrifice for the nation, then the identity and circumscription of the nation-state was the primary locus of meaning, not the horizon of redemptive history presented in the Bible. The exorcism of black men from the community was asserted by whites to be in the interest of the nation. Whites in the North and South experienced the postbellum period as a time of massive social transformation as a result of emancipation, industrialization, modernism, the rise of black culture, and rise of the new woman. When societies are in flux because of a massive social change, identifying a scapegoat is an easy way to establish social cohesion.

For a postbellum white culture experiencing severe social disorientation, black men became a scapegoat. Since the early days of slavery, the "black man" had been identified as an internal enemy within the bounds of the nation: "In the intrusive mode of representing social death the slave was ritually incorporated as the permanent enemy on the inside—the 'domestic enemy.'"[71] As a permanent evil within the boundaries of the white nation, the "black man" was forbidden to cross a sacred boundary: to touch the flesh of white women. Through this encounter the "black man" became more than a criminal; he was seen as a demon that must be exorcized immediately from white society. Through the violent extraction of this dark-skinned male contaminate, white society is reborn once again. As "the myth of regeneration through violence became the structuring metaphor of the American experience," the culture of white male honor sought its own regeneration through the shameful death of the "black man."[72] The lynching of the "black man" was a working out of the logic of social death to its final frontier—physical death. As the American public continued to accept these sacrifices to the white mob, America as a white nation continued to grow stronger.

Throughout the nineteenth century the white community held a deep fear of black men's threat to the sexual purity of white females. On antebellum plantations, white masters did everything in their power to emasculate black men. They worked them, whipped them, slept with their women, and fathered mulatto children, while children of black men became their personal property.

Within the racialized and gendered sex economy of the antebellum South there was a continual clash of masculinities between black and white men. By sex economy I refer to the complex web of sexual relationships on antebellum plantations. White women were often seen as too pure for lustful sexuality, whereas black women became the object of colonial desire. When the transatlantic slave trade ended, it was up to black women slaves to quickly reproduce the plantation labor force. As a consequence, human erotic longing on these isolated farms was redirected toward almost entirely economic ends.

Black men longed for stable marriages with black women based on romantic love, yet the slave economy constantly broke up these relationships and families. Black men were broken and alienated from sources of stability and strength. Since African notions of masculinity were defined by the number of dependents, including children, the size of the white master's extended family and workforce of slaves was a point of envy and deep resentment in the heart of the black male slave.[73]

Orlando Patterson interprets the psychology of the white slave master through a Hegelian dialectic.[74] Modern slavery was based on "the idea of the slave as *instrumentum vocale*—a chattel, a possession, a thing, a mere extension of the master's will."[75] The white male will to completely dominate the black Other was a distillation of the racial logic of modernity. Although the ideal of the white slave master was complete independence and total domination of the bodies and souls of his slave population, in reality, as the dialectic of slavery played itself out, the white master was deeply dependent on his black slaves at every level. The honor of the white man was the ideal that he wielded over the shameful or dishonored condition of the black male slave, a condition of no manhood. The masculinity of the white man found its basis in the emasculation of the "black man." Patterson identifies three stages in the emasculation of the "black man": the slave is ritualized as an enemy; the master mediates between the life and death of the slave; and the slave when he dies, dies in the master.[76]

Lynchings became a way for white men to ritually enact the actual physical death of black men, re-creating the perverse logic of social death that animated antebellum slavery. These murders were often instigated by the allegation that a "black man" had raped a white woman. Lynchings were a violent response to a perceived attack on white womanhood. Donald G. Mathews writes, "Masking the political functions of their acts, white men invented a 'sexual alibi' for punishing African-American men: the latter stood accused of having 'ravished' white women."[77] Thus, we see a sexualization of evangelical postbellum politics driven by deeply contested understandings of race and religion among white evangelicals, on one hand, and black prophetic Christians, on the other.[78] White evangelicals often sought to sanctify their community and nation through the ritualized murder of black men who inhabited the permanent position of being an enemy of the state.

On a subconscious level, the lynching of black men by a white mob constituted a ritual reenactment of blood sacrifice in the imagination of many southern evangelicals. Lynching can then be interpreted as propitiation for the sin of blackness and expiation for the white supremacist community.[79] In the white evangelical imagination, the bodies of black men were sacrificed to redeem America and defend Christian civilization, two realms that were racialized into whiteness.

According to the white evangelical mythology, the angelic virtue of white women is defended by white male crusaders who see themselves as agents of God's righteous judgment. While they implement an earthly judgment on black men hung to die on a bloody tree with echoes of Christ's crucifixion, the white men's own vocational framing as crusaders places their actions in an apocalyptic Christo-drama in which they take responsibility for enforcing God's will on earth. W. Scott Poole writes, "White Southern Christians, armed with shotguns, bowie knives, and lynching ropes, saw themselves at the heart of a theological drama—not the bloody drama of Calvary but instead the final battle, the apocalypse."[80] White southern Christians become agents of God's action in redeeming the South and sanctifying the nation. The black rapist is beyond a criminal, he is a demon who can never be tolerated, only vanquished. This racist mythology captured the religious imagination of many evangelicals in postbellum America, but it was ultimately unsustainable.

But as the white mob sought to experience collective regeneration through violence, it was sowing the seeds of its own death. Lynchings were anarchist acts committed by a mob outside of the rule of law. The pure evil of these extralegal lynchings began to turn the stomachs of white moderates with a conscience. Although white racists continued to sanctify white culture through these theological narratives of lynching, in actual fact they were desanctifying the white mob. Southern whites who wanted to claim the mantle of evangelicalism through their participation in the lynching of blacks were transformed into the imperial Romans—they became the Pontius Pilates and the Roman centurions who crucified Christ. Through a ritual that they saw as part of their own sanctification as Disciples of Christ, they were actually transforming themselves into Christ's killers. Precisely at the moment when white men sought to gain independence, once again, from black men, they found themselves again dependent on them for their identity construction and meaning-making in a rapidly changing world. The white mob's murder of the "black man" anticipates its own demise.

While the white mob read lynchings as texts of black sacrifice for the sake of a white Christian nation, blacks read them as persecution narratives of an oppressed people. Edward J. Blum writes, "By associating black victims with the biblical Christ, black writers turned this white supremacist cosmology on its head. They sought to reveal lynchings for what they really were—evil mob murders committed against innocent African Americans by bloodthirsty and unchristian whites."[81] Seeing Jesus Christ as a black Messiah who was killed in a manner similar to lynching, hanging on a cross, prophetic black thinkers sought to unmask the logic of violence that provided Christological structure to this supremacist regime.

In contrast to the ritualized racism and terror that animated white readings of lynchings, W. E. B. Du Bois placed lynchings within another Christo-drama, one where Jesus the Messiah is black. In his *Crisis* articles "The Gospel According to Mary Brown" (1919) and "The Son of God" (1933), as well as the short stories in *Darkwater*, Du Bois discusses the cross and Christ to unveil hope in the midst of despair. Black flesh can mediate salvation for the oppressed in a culture of suffering and violence. Du Bois is not seeking to bless or sanctify redemptive violence, rather he is attempting to find a theological way out of the problem of suffering. He does this by reading suffering into the Godhead in light of postbellum black suffering: "God wept; but that mattered little to an unbelieving age; what mattered most was that the world wept and still is weeping and blind with tears and blood."[82] In another short story, "The Crucifixion of God," Du Bois describes man's journey into the wilderness and his eventual death, ending the story with an unfulfilled crucifixion in the heart of God: "Wherefore God called his Son and sent him forth to writhe in the Almighty forest to be crucified and commanded him saying 'Thou shalt be crucified and may not die—behold thy crown of thorns.'"[83] In connecting God's suffering with the suffering of black Americans, Du Bois anticipated the rise of black theology in the late twentieth century. Yet Du Bois's subversive readings of lynchings would find true life only through their embodiment in the political movement to end lynching.

Ida B. Wells distinguished herself as a Christian prophetess in the struggle to end lynching. Wells was a teacher and writer in Memphis, Tennessee. In March 1892, three of her friends were lynched because they started a grocery store that competed with white stores. With time, rumors began to circulate that these black men were sexually involved with white women, allegations she knew were not true. As she began to denounce the rumors, the whites began to harass and threaten her, and she was spirited out of Memphis.

In her stinging indictment of lynching *A Red Record* (1895), Wells documents in gruesome detail the horror of lynching and called the church and the nation to join the struggle to end it. She encouraged African Americans to share with the world the "degree of dehumanizing brutality which fixes upon America the blot of a national crime. Whatever faults and failings other nations may have in their dealings with their own subjects or with other people, no other civilized nation stands condemned before the world with a series of crimes so peculiarly national. It becomes a painful duty of the Negro to reproduce a record which shows that a large portion of the American people avow anarchy, condone murder and defy the contempt of civilization."[84] In her struggle to end lynching Wells encountered stiff resistance from white evangelicals.

Interdenominational movements like Dwight Moody's revivals and the Woman's Christian Temperance Union provided new forums for whites and blacks, southerners and northerners to gather together in the postbellum period. Moody, however, segregated his revivals, reinforcing the festering problem with a conservative evangelical synthesis between white racism and Christian nationalism. Moody perceived segregated crusades as a necessary concession to gain broad acceptance among white southerners.[85] With a gospel message of individual piety, his revival movement was easily co-opted in the project of North-South sectional reconciliation instead of fostering a prophetic evangelical confrontation of institutionalized racism.

Moody's segregated revivals infuriated Ida B. Wells. She launched a frontal assault against Moody's form of individual piety-oriented evangelical revivalism. Wells writes, "I remember very clearly that when Rev. Moody had come to the South with his revival sermons the notices printed said that the Negroes who wished to attend . . . would have to go into the gallery or that a special service would be set aside for colored people only. . . . Mr. Moody has encouraged the drawing of the color line in the churches by consenting to preach on separate days and in separate churches to the colored people."[86] In his final years, Moody began to integrate his crusades, but upon his death the revivalist movement continued on in the ministry of Sam Jones, "the Moody of the South" who supported the practice of lynching.

James Cone rightly argues that the lynching tree in postbellum America should become the standard of judgment for twentieth-century Christian theology. In these brutal murders of black men by a white mob we see a complex set of issues surface from the dark side of American history—race, sex, economics, politics, and religion. During this period as northern and southern whites united around a white racist vision, we witness the birth of a prophetic black church tradition. These two streams—white evangelical and black prophetic—continued on to clash during the civil rights movement but would begin to converge in the aftermath of the Iraq war in the early twenty-first century.

The white evangelical line of Carl Henry and Billy Graham has its roots in the stream of evangelist Dwight L. Moody and Billy Sunday. Carl F. H. Henry and the neo-evangelical movement emerged during the 1940s and 1950s out of revivalist fervor on the airwaves and in the camp meetings of marginalized American fundamentalism. Henry himself was uneasy about racial injustice, but the white evangelicals he led often resisted joining the struggle for racial justice.

Another stream of prophetic Christianity flowed out of the black church tradition. In the postbellum period, the black church tradition consolidated and expanded.[87] Reconstruction proved to be a long and arduous journey to freedom of self-determination for many southern blacks. The ministries of Bishop Alexander Payne of the AME and Pentecostal-Holiness preacher William Seymour continued the spirit of nineteenth-century revivalism but began to transform evangelical religion in ways that were more responsive to the needs of African Americans. Shortly before and during Reconstruction a host of new black institutions were created: the African Methodist Episcopal Church (1860), the National Baptist Convention (1865), followed by the Church of God in Christ (1897). Within this rapidly growing black church tradition, there were both fundamentalist and progressive streams of black public theology.

With roots in the line of Harriet Tubman and Sojourner Truth, W. E. B. Du Bois and Ida B. Wells, a prophetic tradition of black Christianity embodied a third option to the split between liberals and fundamentalists that plagued early twentieth-century American Protestantism. Martin Luther King Jr.'s vision of beloved community and the civil rights movement would emerge as a prophetic Christian theology, permanently disrupting the white theological hegemony that sought to suppress and repress its deepest prophetic impulses.

White evangelicalism, which saw a defense of the nation and redemption of the South in the lynching of black men, mistakenly identified the polis with Christianity. As a result of identifying the polis with the Christian imaginary, white evangelicals read the Christian imaginary racially. In contrast, black Christianity saw living according to the equal and reconciled relations set forth in the Gospels as the primary task of Christianity. The close identification of black victims of lynching with the life and death of Jesus Christ was made by black theological thinkers not to justify suffering, but rather to inspire Christians to struggle together to overcome violence and suffering in the world through embodying an ethic of love and justice. Which one of these models is more evangelical? If you really want to understand the evangelical display of faith in our contemporary midst, in which of these two trajectories do you find it?

3

MARTIN LUTHER KING JR.'S THEOLOGY
OF THE CROSS

Martin Luther King Jr. is the most compelling religious leader of the twentieth century and one of the most difficult to fully understand. He is increasingly considered a moral hero for a new generation of evangelicals, which presents an important question: how does King relate to the evangelical tradition? Debate about this subject has been ongoing within the evangelical world since the 1960s. Two articles that appeared in a 1966 edition of *Freedom Now,* a progressive evangelical publication, centered on two questions: first, was he a fundamentalist, and second, was he a communist?[1] The author of the two articles concluded that King was neither a fundamentalist nor a communist. Avoiding the political extremes of conservatism and radicalism, King labored tirelessly at building a new moral consensus in America, intentionally moving out of the theoretical and cultural contours that divided white evangelicalism and the black church in the 1960s.

Many of King's detractors within white evangelicalism assembled a litany of criticisms. They rejected his doctrine of the atonement, his higher critical view of scripture, his message of direct-action civil disobedience, his socialist leanings, his appropriation of Gandhi's philosophy, his critique of the war in Vietnam, and his extramarital affairs. These criticisms aside, a growing group of evangelical leaders now claims to be actively working out of the King tradition. King is increasingly being used as a theological resource among evangelicals, especially among the younger generation. Furthermore, a growing number of evangelicals freely refer to King as an evangelical. Therefore, a new historic genealogy that features King more prominently is vital for deepening our understanding of the history of evangelicalism, understanding the contemporary configuration of evangelical politics, and cultivating a more coherent evangelical public theology in the future. Despite disagreement over whether King was an evangelical, it is clear that evangelicalism today is influenced by his legacy, justifying further study of how his life, faith, and theological vision fit within a history of evangelicalism.

Many have interpreted King as a black theologian (e.g., James Cone) and as a liberal theologian (e.g., Gary Dorrien), but few have interpreted him in relation to the evangelical theological tradition.[2] Yet King cannot be fully understood without attention to the evangelical features of his theology, practices, and identity. Many evangelical historians and sociologists have settled on the term "black Protestant" to describe King, but one consequence of this approach is a scholastic distancing between white evangelicalism and the black church experience. Many current interpretations of King downplay his evangelical features. An honest look at American religious history, however, helps to clarify the ways in which King's theology resembles evangelical theology and the ways in which he is distinct from it. The King tradition of black prophetic Protestant religion cannot be understood without being in conversation with the white evangelical tradition, and the white evangelical tradition cannot be fully understood without considering its relation to King. Thus a new paradigm of historical and theological analysis is needed.

I propose to read King's vision as a blended theology shaped by three streams: the black church, liberal theology, and evangelical theology. Given the history of slavery and segregation from which King emerged, it is important to acknowledge the Afrocentric roots of his black church tradition since it means (necessarily) that King sings his theology in a different key. When reflecting on the slave songs of the black tradition, Frederick Douglass writes, "The songs of the slave represent the sorrows of his heart; and he is relieved by them, only as an aching heart is relieved by its tears."[3] This musical tradition of slave songs and spirituals that gave birth to King means that his blues-inflected theology will always be one that connects the suffering of the human flesh of Jesus Christ with the suffering of the African American people in the history of the United States.

King's Christology is best understood as a theology of the cross. Interestingly, King's Christology resembles that of the great German theologian whose name he bears, Martin Luther's *theologia crucis*. Luther
launched his ministry through critiquing a Roman Catholic theology of
glory and called the church back to a theology of the cross. So, too, Martin Luther King Jr. called white North American Christians to confront
their theologies of triumph and embrace a theology of the cross. King was
calling white evangelicals back to the Gospels, back to their Savior, and
back to the call to love thy neighbor. According to King, the only place
that we meet Jesus Christ is on the cross. But before considering King's
Christology, we must first explain how King relates to the evangelical tradition.

Many sociologists and historians of evangelicalism have used the term
"black Protestant" to describe African American Protestants. One of the
reasons for this designation is the different social location and cultural histories of whites and African Americans. Historians writing evangelical history first developed the idea of considering black Protestants as a category
separate from white evangelicals in part because of an inability to fully integrate the Afro-Christian story into accounts of white evangelicalism;
standard histories of American evangelicalism do not include a complete
treatment of the African American experience. Following David W. Wills,
my genealogy is part of a new direction in the history of evangelicalism,
one that sees black-white interaction as a central theme in the history of
Christianity in the Americas.[4]

Sociologists methodologically trying to think about how to measure the
denominational affiliation of those in theologically conservative churches
recently adopted the additional designation of black Protestant. Previously, people were grouped according to denominational groupings, for
example, fundamentalist, moderate, and liberal Protestant, without respect to racial differences. The prominent justification for considering
black Protestants as separate from white evangelicals is the fact that "the
social experience of African Americans has subtly shaped their theological
doctrines and has more explicitly influenced the social and economic implications they draw from them."[5] Given the legacy of slavery and segregation in the United States, it is understandable that this distinct designation has been made. Placing black Protestants in a completely separate

category according to their racial identity, however, isolates them from the white Christian experience and does not provide a way of explaining the mutual relationships and influences between black and white Christians.

Separating black Protestants often serves to further problematize the division between the two groups. Although it does acknowledge there is a particular and different experience of religion between white evangelicals and black Protestants, it fails to recognize the ways that "whiteness" impacts white evangelicalism and how white power and privilege have contributed to white evangelical theology and politics. The designation "black Protestant" acknowledges the cultural particularity of the black experience in U.S. history; however, it does not give a full accounting of the *theological* complexity of King's vision, which are informed by the two streams of Protestant theology, liberal and evangelical. While I maintain this designation of black Protestant to categorize King, I am interested in highlighting his evangelical heritage and traits.

Based primarily on his core theological beliefs, King demonstrates significant evangelical traits. He believes in biblical authority, in the salvific mediation of Jesus Christ, and in the power of God that both draws one into faith and leads the people of God into the struggle for justice. Nevertheless, the racial divide has made it difficult for many African Americans to identify with the larger (primarily white) evangelical movement. It has also made it historically difficult for many white evangelicals to identify with King, though this is changing as a new generation of white evangelicals is expressing a strong commitment to racial and economic justice and increasingly looking to Martin Luther King Jr., not Billy Graham, as their moral hero.

Since King was such a complex and multifaceted thinker, his legacy has been appropriated by many different schools of theology. Whereas James Cone emphasizes King's roots in the black church tradition, and Gary Dorrien emphasizes his place in twentieth-century liberal theology, I wish to emphasize the evangelical character of his vision. Although considering these three distinct streams that inform King's thought (the black church tradition, the liberal theological tradition, and the evangelical theological tradition), I will highlight the evangelical features of his theology. Before presenting my interpretation of King, I will consider the interpretations of James Cone and Gary Dorrien.

Building on the scholarship of Vincent Harding, Peter Paris, and Cornel

West, James Cone, the father of black theology, has persuasively argued that King's deepest roots lie in the black church tradition. In particular, Cone sees King's theology as Gospel-centered and embodying the justice-oriented radicalism of the black church tradition.[6] His formation in the black church helped King connect the Gospel with the oppression of African Americans. Furthermore, the black church provided him with the rhetorical tools he needed to reach the nation with his urgent vision of justice and reconciliation.

Cone argues that it was the black church that shaped King's oeuvre. It was the black church tradition that King struggled with intellectually during college, seminary, and graduate school. It was the black church that rallied around him in the Montgomery struggle. It was the black church that sustained him during his most difficult struggles later in his life. King was first and foremost, through and through, a black "churchman."

King grew up in Ebenezer Baptist Church in Atlanta, Georgia, the congregation pastored by his father. He often introduced himself in his speeches and writings as the son and grandson of Baptist preachers. The black Baptist church provided the milieu and motifs for the constructive theology that would emerge as he found his theological voice during his graduate education.

Cone acknowledges the influence of white liberalism on King's thought, but he sees this as a secondary stream, without the force that runs through the mighty river of the black church tradition. Cone writes, "in regard to deepening King's optimism about the elimination of racism, the political philosophy of integrationism and the faith of the black church were much more important than Hegel or any other white thinker."[7] If King is read through the lens of white liberal theology alone, notes Cone, the black church tradition is silenced, weakening the distinctive perspective of black theology that emerges from the cultural upheaval of the 1950s and 1960s.

Cone rightly sees that the black church tradition was a more important influence on King than any of the white philosophers and theologians whom he studied in graduate school. While King was shaped by the metaphysics of the white liberal theological academy, he was able to creatively articulate and embody a theology of reconciliation that was more concrete. King's vision of beloved community was articulated, organized, mobilized, and realized within a movement of black Christian activism.

Cone goes further in deepening our understanding of King's theology and practice through contrasting it with the more radical black nationalist vision of Malcolm X. Malcolm X, who claimed to be "the angriest black man alive," represented a black nationalism that was not opposed to demonizing "the white man" and using violence against him. When Malcolm converted to Islam and traveled to Mecca and throughout Africa, he deepened the Afrocentric architectonic of his theology and his own spiritualized account of blackness and whiteness. Whereas King sought to help the "negro" integrate with the "white man," Malcolm X sought to empower the "black man" through a black nationalism, dreaming of a nation-state led by and populated by African Americans alone. King and Malcolm X shared a common commitment to liberating oppressed African Americans, but they had a different vision of where they were headed and how they could get there. In interpreting King in dialectical opposition to Malcolm X, Cone downplays the black nationalist impulse in King. In the early period, King was interested in integration, but even then he was talking about integration with empowerment. Cone's dialectical approach makes it difficult for his readers to understand that both King and Malcolm X had integrationist and black nationalist tendencies.[8]

We cannot read King exclusively through the black church but must embrace both approaches. This is vital because it is King's black nationalist impulse that illuminates his Christian theology of Jesus and the Kingdom of God. King's understanding of the Kingdom of God goes beyond its earthly instantiation as a beloved community within the confines and corridors of the American nation-state; for King, the kingdom is both within and beyond the American nation. His black nationalist impulse helps him conceptualize a political time and space outside of America. This is precisely why King's theology and Christology can help white evangelicals to envision the demolition of America's resilient racialized order. King's theological vision is compelling because it draws from both the black church tradition and black nationalism to think in and beyond the parameters of the American nation-state.

Gary Dorrien interprets King as an "evangelical liberal," providing an important stepping-stone for my evangelical interpretation of King. Yet King's vibrant evangelical impulse is subsumed into the narrative of liberal theology in Dorrien's magisterial three-volume history, *The Making of*

American Liberal Theology.[9] King's life and legacy represent one of the greatest achievements of twentieth-century liberal theology, and as such he plays a prominent role in Dorrien's third volume. Dorrien presents King's public theology as a synthesis of two earlier movements of liberal theology: Rauschenbusch's social gospel and Reinhold Niebuhr's Christian realism.

Dorrien argues that liberal theology is "the child of two heritages": modernist liberalism and evangelical liberalism.[10] The modernist stream attempts to ensure that theology will be plausible given the conditions of knowing of the modern world, while the evangelical stream attempts to ensure that theology is faithful to the revelation of God in Jesus Christ witnessed to in the Bible.

Dorrien reads King as an *evangelical* liberal because the Gospel-centered character of this form of liberalism, as he defines it, fits most closely with King's black church heritage and vision of beloved community. King's deepest core theological beliefs—Bible, Jesus, Christian experience, and mission—lie embedded in the heart of the evangelical theological tradition. In Dorrien's judgment, it is the evangelical stream of liberalism that is most decisive for King's theological vision and is mediated to him through the rich tradition of earlier white evangelical liberals, including Walter Rauschenbusch, Reinhold Niebuhr, Edgar S. Brightman, and L. Harold DeWolf.

Dorrien's interpretation of King as an evangelical liberal is based largely on King's teachers and studies in formal academic settings. King studied liberal theology in different forms under Benjamin E. Mays and George Kelsey at Morehouse College; George Washington Davis at Crozer Theological Seminary; and Edgar S. Brightman, L. Harold DeWolf, and Walter G. Muelder at Boston University. Benjamin E. Mays and George Kelsey introduced King to the black social gospel,[11] and George Washington Davis introduced him to Walter Rauschenbusch, the father of the white social gospel.[12]

Rauschenbusch's *Christianity and the Social Crisis* "left an indelible imprint" on King's thinking.[13] In a provocative, electric style, Walter Rauschenbusch criticized the early twentieth-century church for having lost its connection to the Kingdom of God. He believed that the Kingdom of God had come to be nothing but an "otherworldly" hope, while the church was a "this worldly," present reality. He sought, therefore, to bring eschatology and ecclesial ethics together in a theology of the social gospel, arguing that the Kingdom of God is humanity organized according to the will of God. Even though King criticizes Rauschenbusch for identifying the Kingdom of God too much with a particular social and economic system, much of Rauschenbusch's theology of the kingdom emerges anew in King's theology of the beloved community.[14]

At Crozer Theological Seminary, King was introduced to another school of liberal theology—Boston personalism—through George Washington Davis. Because personalism was such a central influence on King's theology, Dorrien goes a step further and interprets King as an "evangelical liberal *personalist*."[15] Joining other King scholars, among them Rufus Burrow Jr., Dorrien sees personalism as one of the most illuminating windows into King's life and theology.[16] King's personalism finds its deepest intellectual sources in the personalist theology of Boston University, where he completed his Ph.D. in theology. From his early papers for Edgar S. Brightman to his dissertation, King focused his doctoral studies on historical and constructive treatments of divine and human personality.[17]

King's appropriation and expansion of personalist theology as an African American was unique, developed as it was in the context of the black church and the black intellectual community. King was part of a vibrant African American student community at Boston University. The personalist motifs of Edgar S. Brightman and L. Harold DeWolf resonated deeply with the African American graduate students like King's friends Major Jones, Philip Lenud, Wayman "Mac" McLaughlin, and Daniel Webster Winn.[18] With his magnetic personality and passion for debate, King convened a monthly meeting of his friends called the Dialectical Society. In this supportive and informal setting, they would read and critique each other's papers, often on topics emerging in their studies of Boston personalism.

While affirming many of the themes and practices of King's black church heritage, personalism also provided King with the philosophical vocabulary to give intellectual expression to the faith in which he was raised. Personalists considered the world through the category of personality—the world's most ultimate value. Personality was seen to be the ground of reality and the ground of social ethics. Personalism affirmed that God was personal, that all human life was sacred, and that reality and persons had a communal nature. Like a jazz virtuoso, King introduced, expanded, and interwove these motifs throughout his writings in an amazing display of improvisation, moving effortlessly between the personalist tradition and the contemporary struggle for justice. King's greatest contribution to the personalist tradition was embodying a personalist ethic through his leadership in the civil rights movement. King was able to deploy an evangelically oriented personalist philosophy on behalf of a robust black social gospel.

Dorrien's interpretation of King helps deepen our understanding of the many streams of thought that King was able to weave together in a seamless synthesis. Dorrien argues that King was successful because of his ability to creatively fuse "the transformational aspects of black church religion, social-gospel personalism, Niebuhrian realism, and Gandhian pacifism to change the nation."[19] Given the breadth and depth of King's vision, liberal theology alone cannot account for the various features of King's theology and their development. In placing King in the narrative of white liberal theologians, who often spent more time in their studies than on the streets, Dorrien does not do justice to the populist dimension of his ministry. Although King was influenced by liberal theology, reading him through the history of liberal theology has its limitations.

Evangelical liberal theology experienced its most intense death pangs precisely when King was coming of age in the 1950s and 1960s. Dorrien sees the tradition of evangelical liberalism begin to die with the death of Pit Van Dusen, and Rufus Burrow goes so far as to date the demise of personalism to King's assassination in 1968.[20] Given the rapid decline of evangelical liberal theology in the 1960s, do we read King's theological project as the last gasp of evangelical liberalism or as a vibrant expression of black prophetic evangelicalism?

Dorrien's Niebuhrian perspective misses an important shift in American religion. By reading King as a mainline liberal at the moment of liberal theology's greatest decline, Dorrien misses a major paradigm shift that took place in mid-1950s America. As Mark A. Noll writes, "Public theology is flourishing in the contemporary United States on a scale not witnessed for more than a century. To be sure, American public theology since the mid-1950s has been populist, nonacademic and movement-centered, and so quite different from the kind of 'Niebuhrian' public theology that loomed large in certain academic and national forums during the period 1930–

1955. . . . This more recent public theology has arisen 'from below,' first in the Civil Rights movement and then in right-wing Christian politics."[21] Noll helps us see that King's vision for the civil rights movement was successful because it was able to emerge organically as a grass-roots populist religious movement ("from below"). Furthermore, King's vision and practices are better understood as drawing on the legacy of the abolitionist tradition of antebellum revivalism, bringing form to a prophetic black religion energized by evangelical and liberal impulses.

Dorrien's folding of the black social gospel tradition into the white liberal narration of theology does not adequately account for the ways that this tradition draws deeply in evangelical wells while also working against aspects of liberal theology. In important ways the black social gospel tradition more closely resembles prophetic evangelicalism. Dorrien himself alludes to the importance of King's evangelical heritage, writing, "When King told the story of his life, he emphasized the influence of reputable white theologians and philosophers upon the development of his thinking and said very little about his background in the black Baptist church. But his familial, middle-class, southern, black Baptist background was formative for his thinking and personality. His nurture in the evangelical black church religion featured a fervent belief in a personal God of judgment, grace, and miracles, a gospel of redemption and sanctification, and a strong insistence that the gospel has a social dimension."[22]

Dorrien's reading helps us understand the way that King relates to the liberal theological tradition, and he also begins to acknowledge the evangelical features of King's theology. But Dorrien's desire to read King primarily as a liberal theologian makes it more difficult for him to make historic sense of King's evangelical heritage. Although Dorrien thoughtfully explicates the influence of "liberal theology" on King the evangelical liberal, a deeper explanation of the influence of "evangelical theology" on King is in order. Gary Dorrien emphasizes his training in the evangelical liberal tradition of Walter Rauschenbusch and Edgar S. Brightman, and James H. Cone rightly points out King's roots in the black church tradition of Daddy King and Benjamin Elijah Mays, but there is a third theological stream that informs King's thought: evangelical theology.

In emphasizing King's black church tradition, Cone puts him in closer proximity to the evangelical theological tradition, and Dorrien's reading

King as an "evangelical liberal" provides an important bridge for a more robustly evangelical reading of King. Dorrien shows clearly the multiple lines of liberal theology that influence his thought. The influence of liberal vocabulary, concepts, and motifs saturate King's early writings; however, as his thinking progresses in the civil rights movement, we observe that its most basic theological logic is evangelical—Christocentric, cruciform, and based on a strong faith in a loving, personal God.

A consideration of the ways that King is influenced by evangelical theology is circumscribed by a deep theological division within U.S. theology—the debate between fundamentalists and liberals in the 1920s and 1930s, a debate raging during King's childhood in Atlanta, Georgia. But the black churches on Auburn Street in Atlanta did not fit clearly on either side of the great theological divide. While Daddy King and Reverend William Holmes Border were black fundamentalists, they were reformists who sought to transform the streets and structures of inner-city Atlanta. Although King had some childhood doubts about conservative doctrine, the biblical theology of transformation in the southern black church remained the plumb line of his thought and ministry.

When King attended Morehouse, he found an erudite, engaged black Christianity. Benjamin Mays's winsome and irenic approach to Christianity provided a welcomed alternative to the "whooping" and stubborn dogma that marked King's experience at Ebenezer. Morehouse sent King down the path of studying most of the classic texts of twentieth-century liberal theology at Crozer Theological Seminary and Boston University. The liberal tradition helped King clarify some of his deepest intuitions. For example, Boston personalism's affirmation of the sacredness of all persons helped King bring intellectual precision to the black theology of "somebody-ness." But as the immorality of the Vietnam War shattered King's dream after 1965, a growing distance emerged between King and liberal theology.[23] In King's final phase (1966–68), his thought radicalized, but it also deepened theologically as he sunk his roots deep in the fertile soil of his Baptist upbringing. When King's dream turned into a nightmare, he drew strength from the promises of Scripture and his personal encounters with Jesus.

While acknowledging the significant influence of liberal theology on King, I will consider the impact of the evangelical themes of his black church heritage, from the beginning to the end of his career. The black church's theological orientation is evangelical in character. King's theology fits broadly our five features of evangelicalism: (1) conversion, (2) Biblicism, (3) activism, (4) Christocentrism, and (5) transdenominational populism. I will use these five features of evangelical thought to explain the evangelical character of King's life and theological vision.

As for the first feature of evangelicalism, King, like other evangelicals, began the salvific journey through conversion to belief in Jesus Christ. Although King believed in born-again conversions, he did not have a dramatic conversion experience himself. King did accept Jesus as his Lord and Savior as a boy of six years old but described the experience as a competition with his sister. When she accepted Jesus, King did not want to be left behind, so he decided to join her at the altar.

Evangelicals emphasize born-again experiences, but fewer evangelicals have had dramatic conversion experiences than evangelical theology would lead us to expect. Like King, most evangelicals have several experiences throughout their lives that initiate them into faith in Christ and life in the church. In King's case these experiences include his confession of faith as a youth with his sister, his baptism, his call to ministry at Morehouse, and his "kitchen table" experience in Montgomery.

King's "kitchen table" experience was crucial in the formation of his evangelical identity. One night King could not sleep because the constant onslaught of death threats made him fear he was putting his family in danger. He got out of bed and paced around the house:

> I was ready to give up. With my cup of coffee sitting untouched before me I tried to think of a way to move out of the picture without appearing a coward. In this state of exhaustion, when my courage had all but gone, I decided to take my problem to God. With my head in my hands, I bowed over the kitchen table and prayed aloud. The words I spoke to God that midnight are still in my memory. "I am here taking a stand for what I believe is right. But now I am afraid. The people are looking to me for leadership, and if I stand before them without strength and courage, they too will falter. I am at the end of my powers. I have nothing left. I've come to the point where I can't face it alone."
>
> At that moment I experienced the presence of the Divine as I

had never experienced Him before. It seemed as though I could hear the quiet assurance of an inner voice saying: "Stand up for righteousness, stand up for truth; and God will be at your side forever." Almost at once my fears began to go. My uncertainty disappeared. I was ready to face anything.[24]

King's description of this event is very evangelical—"experiencing the presence of the divine." God's call to him is personal and prophetic, to stand up for righteousness and truth.

For white evangelicals and black Protestants of the South, baptism more than any other practice has been the most visible demonstration of new life in Christ. White evangelicals have often emphasized the individual dimension of conversion and baptism, but King emphasized the collective dimension. Evangelicals can learn from the collective dimension in King's self-understanding of his conversion. King came to faith in Christ through being raised in the church. King's faith was the faith of his people, the faith of black Christians in the Americas. His dramatic kitchen experience confirmed his embodiment of the faith of his ancestors.

Whether conversion is seen as a dramatic individual experience or a more gradual immersion into the life of the church, King affirmed that it must be a personal commitment. Christ's call to conversion was a call to live a life worthy of the calling, embodying a life of love as a sign of the beloved community. As Noel Erskine writes, "As a Baptist pastor, King believes in the necessity of personal conversion; and even if one argues that before 1965 he did not quite understand the endemic and systemic nature of social evil in America, it is clear that after the experience in Chicago in 1965, he began to call for structural change in the society."[25] Erskine rightly points to King's belief in personal conversion, but a conversion marked by a life converted to the cause of peace and justice in the world. King accepts this fundamental tenet of salvation in the Baptist tradition, and he deepens the notion to include a more collective and worldly dimension to salvation: individual salvation takes place in the context of the church and for the world. Christians are called to embody their faith in a life committed to love and justice, including working toward systemic transformation in society. King believes in conversion, but he expands some of the conservative evangelical ways of thinking about it.

Second, King shared evangelicals' deep commitment to biblical authority. King successfully deployed the Bible through an Afro-Christian hermeneutic that also tapped into the myth of American civil religion that united many white evangelicals and liberals in the 1950s and 1960s. It was the Bible that fired the young King's imagination at Ebenezer, it was the Bible that he studied critically at Crozer and Boston University, and it was the Bible that animated his sermons and speeches in the civil rights movement. From the slave songs and spirituals, to sermons and stories, the black church inhabits the drama of the history of redemption narrated in the Bible.

Personal and collective identity within the black church tradition is shaped by the biblical stories of redemption.[26] Within the black church tradition, King interpreted the Bible through the lens of the Exodus and Jesus's proclamation of the Jubilee in Luke 4:18: "The Spirit of the Lord is upon me because he has anointed me; he has sent me to announce good news to the poor, to proclaim release for prisoners and recovery of sight for the blind: to let the broken victims go free, to proclaim the year of the Lord's favour." Vincent Harding argues that Jesus's inaugural sermon from Luke 4:18 "seemed almost literally to inhabit King as he worked his way into the heart of the Southern Freedom Movement, as he testified to its grounding, his grounding, in the most powerful prophetic servant traditions of the Old and New Testaments."[27] Black Christianity is more successful than any other tradition in connecting biblical stories with the contemporary struggle for justice. Prophetic Christian leaders like King are viewed by their community as leading God's people out of oppression just as Moses and Jesus did.

Throughout his ministry King addressed both mainline and evangelical audiences. For the first he would evoke the saints of American civil religion, and for the second he would evoke the saints in the Bible. Invoking Lincoln, Rauschenbusch, and Gandhi helped King reach a white mainstream establishment, but he was forced to plumb the depths of his black evangelical soul where personal faith and prayer reigned, participation in the sufferings of Christ was practiced, and the community was sustained by the Word preached to build the church and embody signs of the kingdom in the world. That a deep well of prophetic Biblicism and piety irrigated King's sermons, speeches, and soul is indisputable.

Third, King's civil rights activism embodies his commitment to the activist impulse within evangelicalism, with its practices of evangelism and social justice. Through King's preaching he tried not only to save souls but to convert the nation. Richard Lischer writes that King's gospel "would either redeem the soul of America or consign it to judgment. In this respect, he was a true evangelist for whom every speaking engagement was a potential altar call."[28]

King's activist politics is biblical in its origin and evangelical in its method. While his method of nonviolence was learned from Gandhi, his method of organizing was shaped in part by Billy Graham.[29] Graham shared with King some specific logistical strategies, which he then used as he organized large civil rights gatherings. After the Montgomery bus boycott, King was having problems reaching a broad audience with his nonviolent movement. King used his preaching ability and implemented mass meetings on a "touring frenzy modeled on the crusades of Rev. Billy Graham, from whom King received quiet encouragement and occasional advice."[30] Taylor Branch points out that throughout King's ministry, he was in periodic contact with Billy Graham, often through communications among their lieutenants. For example, King sent Wyatt Tee Walker and Chauncey Eskridge to speak with Graham's media advisor Walter Bennett and chief of staff Walter Smyth to learn about Graham's organizing strategy and practices.[31]

King and Graham shared a similar faith, but they had different vocations: Graham was an evangelist and King a social reformer. Branch writes that Graham "regarded King's gospel as his own, and King respected Graham's course professionally if not in doctrine."[32] The reason for the affinity between the two ministers was that they worked from a similar revival-style format of evangelicalism and were above all else "proselytizers."[33] King was eager to learn from Graham's success in mass crusades, and Graham, who was gradually accepting a broader vision of racial reconciliation, was (at first) eager to help him. Thus, what we see in King's appropriation of the mass meeting is a translation of evangelicalism into "a method of social transformation" in which the "Ebenezer Gospel" is expanded into a "Gospel of Freedom."[34] While there were some points of contact between King and Graham, both learning from each other, there were some stark differences in their respective public theologies. The evangelical impulses in King's theology took a more radical theological form, but he preached like a passionate revivalist to folks who were very supernaturalist and very literalist in their theological views (i.e., "evangelical" in the most ordinary meanings of the term). Mark Noll writes, "The religion of King and his associates was always more than just black evangelical revivalism, but it was never less."[35]

Fourth, King's theology was Christocentric. Since I discuss King's Christology in more detail later in the chapter, I will comment only briefly here. From singing "Jesus I Love Thee" as a little boy, to writing papers about Jesus in seminary and graduate school, to preaching and speaking about Jesus's concern for the poor and commitment to nonviolence, King had a Christ-centered ministry from beginning to end. King studied the "evangelical liberal" theory of Christ as a moral example, and he deepened his thinking about Christ throughout the civil rights movement. For King, Christ was not merely a human example for us to follow but the mediator of faith in a personal God.[36]

King's Christology was based on a personal union with Christ that expressed itself through caring for the "least of these" (Matthew 25:31–46). Christians were called to be "vicars of Christ," imitating him and following him down the path of radical discipleship. King understood Jesus as an "extremist of love" who lived a life of self-sacrificing altruism that stood in defiance of the "powers and principalities of the world."[37] Jesus Christ was a "transformed non-conformist" who understood that to live in synch with the Kingdom of God meant not conforming to the unjust ways of the world.[38]

King understood Christ as the Son of God who suffered and died so that we could live as prophetic witnesses, redeemed and ready to work tirelessly for the reformation of the world. Since Christians experienced a deep union with Jesus Christ, they must be willing to "shed [their own] blood" for the kingdom cause of love and justice.[39] And as with Jesus, this would sometimes entail losing one's own life in holy martyrdom. King's Christology was fundamentally a theology of the cross.

Fifth and finally, King and his movement fit the understanding of evangelicalism as a transdenominational populist movement. When read through the lens of prophetic evangelicalism with its roots in the Great Awakenings and the abolition movement, King led a populist movement for justice "from below." The black and white evangelical abolitionists in the nineteenth century were King's theological forbearers. Sharing the biblical and cruciform theological contours of evangelical theology, these prophetic evangelicals embraced a broader social justice agenda that focused on racial and economic justice.

Throughout King's life there was a wide variety of responses to his prophetic ministry. Some evangelicals, for example, Bob Jones Sr. and Jerry Falwell, rejected his ministry and methods outright. Others, like Billy Graham, had a more complex relationship with King, including periodic communication and collaboration. Finally, some, like Frank Gaebelein, joined the march from Selma to Montgomery embodying the importance of white evangelical support of the civil rights movement.

Black evangelicals were often more sympathetic to King's cause. William Pannell and John Perkins joined the struggle for civil rights and helped many white evangelicals embrace King's vision of beloved community. Black evangelicals like Pannell and Perkins represented a prophetic evangelicalism that had its roots in nineteenth-century evangelical abolitionists, in Harriet Tubman and Sojourner Truth, Jonathan Blanchard and Charles G. Finney.

During the antebellum period, evangelical Christians had a decision to make. Would they seek to abolish slavery or would they defend it based on biblical teachings and Christian theology? Likewise, in the twentieth-century postwar period (1945–65), evangelicals were faced with another theological and ethical dilemma—would they join the struggle for civil rights or would they resist it? The majority of white fundamentalists and evangelicals were silent or actively resisted King's call for civil disobedience to accelerate the end of segregation. This evangelical resistance to civil rights was based on its deep roots in apolitical fundamentalist thought, often shaped by a nexus of beliefs that included orders of creation, social conservatism, and white racism.

The fundamentalist-modernist controversy of the early twentieth century ran deep in the fabric of American religion, impacting the psyche of the twentieth-century evangelical mind. While some "old school" fundamentalists were apolitical, the neo-evangelicals of the 1940s and 1950s sought a broader social engagement. Some white evangelicals marched with King, but the black evangelicals, men like John Perkins, were the most responsive to his call. Black evangelicals shared with King both a common context of oppression and the resources of black Christianity to help them overcome this oppression.

King develops his understanding of the Bible through a Christ-centered interpretive strategy, but the Exodus narrative of the Mosaic vision and the Hebrew prophets' emphasis on justice, central to the black church tradition, contextualize his focus. King's Christology is grounded in scripture and emphasizes Jesus's humanity, suffering, and identification with the poor. Furthermore, Jesus provides a powerful example of the neighborly love that all Christians are called to follow through the power of the Holy Spirit.

King also affirms that sin, both personal and social, is humanity's fundamental problem. Human history demonstrates the "depths and strength of sin."[40] He writes, "We have to recognize that man has misused his kingly prerogative as a social animal by making others bear the burden of his selfishness. Only the one who sits on the peak of his intellectual ivory tower looking unrealistically with his rosey colored glasses on the scene of life can fail to see this fact. The word sin must come back into our vocabulary."[41] As a Baptist preacher, King preaches that sin is the problem and faith in Jesus Christ is the answer. Only through faith in Jesus Christ can one overcome personal and systemic sin. Faith in Christ begins with the conversion of individuals in the church and works itself out in social transformation.

King expands the conversionist tradition of Baptist theology to include the transformation of systemic sin in society. King illustrates the structural change that he is calling for in an essay titled "Love, Law, and Civil Disobedience," delivered to the annual meeting of the Fellowship of the Concerned on November 16, 1961. According to King, "Sometimes it might be the right thing to not obey laws because it is not the maladjusted human that commits the sin, but the structures of society that are corrupt and suffer from brokenness and therefore are sinful. 'Non-cooperation with evil is as much a moral obligation as the cooperation with good.'"[42] A law is not always a just or a moral law. It is not a moral law if it "does not square with the law of God," or in other words, "an unjust law is a code that the majority inflicts on the minority that is not binding on itself."[43] For King, to follow Christ and act according to the truth means both to dismantle the laws that keep African Americans from having equal rights as whites and also to resist through nonviolence and without bitterness.

Social transformation has to go beyond the redemption of individuals and materializes as a collective struggle for justice implemented through peace. As King states, "Peace is not merely the absence of some negative forces, it is the presence of a positive force." He continues, noting that this is how he interprets what Jesus means when he says "I come not to bring peace but a sword."[44] Christ has come to this world to manifest the King- dom of God as it is on earth. King describes the Kingdom of God that Jesus ushers in as "a positive peace, which is brotherhood, which is justice."[45] Even though Christ is at work in the heart of the individual person, the fight that has to be fought is not against human beings but rather against powers and principalities embodied in institutions. Thus, King's Christology emphasizes Jesus as a redemptive sufferer who suffers with the oppressed and as a prophet who challenges sin both in the human heart and in social structures. It is through prophetic activism directed to- ward alleviating suffering that the church participates in Jesus's suffering.

In the biblical discourse, King sees Jesus as the beloved Son of God. This theology of the beloved Son is at once Johannine, black, and Baptist. King's theology of the beloved Son provides the grounds for his over- arching theological vision of the beloved community. Many King scholars, including Lewis Baldwin and Charles Marsh, have found the vision of "beloved community" to be the very heart of King's vision.[46] I also see beloved community as the strategic metaphor that King deploys to build a Christian social movement.

Just as Christ suffered on his way to and upon the cross, and thereby brought salvation for humanity, disciples of Christ should expect suffering that can only be understood in the shadow of the cross.[47] King writes, "The cross is the eternal expression of the length to which God will go in order to restore broken community. The resurrection is a symbol of God's triumph over all the forces that seek to block community."[48] The love of God through which this happens is a strong, creative love since it seeks to love and to preserve and create community. In other words, "the immi- nent work of God in each and every human being, leads to a universal lib- eration for humanity as a whole, which in its length creates the Kingdom of God, a Beloved Community."[49] Beloved community is the "creation of a society where all men can live together as brothers, where every man will respect the dignity and the worth of human personality."[50]

King also translates the theological concept of beloved community into nationalist discourse, talking about America as a "beloved nation." There was a longing among the participants of the civil rights movement to restore rights and dignity to African Americans so they could achieve the American dream. In a commencement address he delivered on June 6, 1961, at Lincoln University in Pennsylvania, King stated, "America is essentially a dream, a dream as yet unfulfilled. It is a dream of a land where men of all races of all nationalities and of all creeds can live together as brothers."[51] He continued by saying, "The hour is late." It is time for America to wake up and end its exploitation of minorities if it is to remain a "first-class nation and not destroy itself."[52]

King's Jesus is the embodiment of love and justice.[53] Love and justice are at the heart of King's vision of the universe. King writes, "As Christians we must never surrender our supreme loyalty to any time-bound custom or earthbound idea, for at the heart of the universe is a higher reality— God and his kingdom of love—to which we must be conformed."[54] Theocentric love is "at the heart of the universe," and it is embodied in Jesus Christ.

Jesus becomes a living example of a life of love and justice that King is calling U.S. Christians to live out. King writes, "It was the Sermon on the Mount, rather than a doctrine of passive resistance, that initially inspired the Negroes of Montgomery to dignified social action. It was Jesus of Nazareth that stirred the Negroes to protest with the creative weapon of love."[55] Elsewhere he says, "I think I have discovered the highest good. It is love. This principle stands at the center of the cosmos."[56] Only through the love of God is it possible to be both tough-minded and tender-hearted.[57] Love for the Afro-Christians is not a sentimental feeling of community but an active collective struggle to embody Christ's love and justice in concrete ways in the world.

In his essay "An Experiment in Love," King develops a biblical theology of love. He takes the Greek term "agape" to mean the creation of community through the focused vigilance of those who seek to embody it.[58] When King talks about love he means agape. Agape means "understanding, creative, redemptive, good will to all men. It is an overflowing love, which seeks nothing in return. Theologians would say that it is the love of God operating in the human heart."[59] King's interpretation of love is unique because he takes the principle of agape, a selfless divine love, and applies it in the very concrete context of genuine struggle for racial justice. What is critical in King's account of love is its "willingness to go to any length to restore community."[60]

Agape is love, which is at once overflowing, spontaneous, concrete, and creative. It springs from the needs of the other person and it discovers *neighbors* in every person it meets. A good example is the biblical story of the Good Samaritan, to which King always comes back. In the story, a Samaritan helped a Jew on the Jericho road (Luke 10:30–35). The Samaritan, the man who was least expected to help the robbed and wounded Jew, was moved with pity. King explains the act of the Samaritan, saying that he "was 'good' because he responded to the human need."[61] The Samaritan looked beyond his own prejudiced views of the deeds of the Jewish people and saw a neighbor, a brother in need of help. To respond to human need is to manifest the love of God in reality.

The love of enemy is the supreme expression of King's love ethic. King states, "I'm very happy that he [Jesus] didn't say like your enemies, because it is pretty difficult to like some people."[62] He further writes, "When it comes to personal liberation, liberation for blacks is also liberation for whites because when the black man loves the white man, who has oppressed him, just like the Samaritan loved the Jew, the black man helps the white man to be liberated from his tensions, insecurities, and fears."[63] Through the evangelical belief in Christ all life is interrelated and involved in a single process. This interconnection of life is a further reason for loving your enemies because following the dictum "If you harm me, you harm yourself" makes the reality of a beloved community more distant. Instead, humanity should strive toward a common goal, the beloved community.

On the evening of January 30, 1956, King's home in Montgomery, Alabama, was bombed. After the bombing, he internally desired to fight back. He struggled with whether or not he could lead others into a nonviolent response to violence. Would the freedom struggle include violence or not? Against the wishes of some of his more radical followers, King insisted on confronting the situation peacefully. If King or his followers had retaliated, a violent response could have ensued. Instead, King embodied Christ's teaching to love one's enemies.

From that point on Gandhi's philosophy of nonviolence shaped both King's Christology and his methodology. King writes, "Then I came upon the life and teachings of Mahatma Gandhi. As I read his works I became deeply fascinated by his campaigns of nonviolent resistance. The whole Gandhian concept of *satyagraha* (*satya* is truth which equals love, and *graha* is force; *satyagraha* thus means truth-force or love-force) was profoundly significant to me. As I delved deeper into the philosophy of Gandhi my skepticism concerning the power of love gradually diminished, and I came to see for the first time that the Christian doctrine of love operating through the Gandhian method of nonviolence was one of the most potent weapons available to oppressed people in their struggle for freedom."[64] King's appropriation of Gandhi's nonviolent principles helped him cultivate pacifist readings of the Bible emphasizing biblical shalom; however, King's use of Gandhi made many white evangelicals question the orthodoxy of his theology, since almost no white evangelical theologian of the era made use of Gandhi's teachings.

Jesus is both an embodiment and exemplar of love in the world. In this sense, King's Christology is fundamentally incarnational and socioethical. Interestingly, love and justice come together in King's Christology through the motif of redemptive suffering. He does not want to draw attention to his own trials, but at the same time, it is sometimes necessary to "take his [Jesus's] yoke upon us" in our struggle for freedom and justice.[65] To make something creative out of suffering, one must be courageous and Christ-centered. King writes: "It is becoming clear that the Negro is in for a season of suffering. . . . I pray that, recognizing the necessity of suffering, the Negro will make of it a virtue. To suffer in a righteous cause is to grow to our humanity's full stature. If only to save himself from bitterness, the Negro needs the vision to see the ordeals of this generation as the opportunity to transfigure himself and American society. If he has to go to jail for the cause of freedom, let him enter it in the fashion Gandhi urged his countrymen, 'as the bridegroom enters the bride's chamber'— that is, with a little trepidation but with a great expectation."[66] To suffer on behalf of a just cause is to grow into our "full stature" as humans, seeking to be like Christ in his vigilant commitment to justice. King even talks about the transfiguration of African Americans and the nation, alluding to Jesus's transfiguration as a rising up out of the earth in a liminal place close to heaven. King was willing to suffer like Christ and not fight back with physical violence because of Jesus's example of love and peace. Jesus's willingness to suffer is redemptive not because suffering is intrinsically redemptive, but when it inspires people, through his grace, to work to end suffering.

King's Christology emphasizes Jesus's activity in the present, whereas many white evangelicals emphasize Jesus's redemptive activities in the past, especially on the cross and in his resurrection. The focus of belief is on a past event, but King's conception places Jesus's action in the present tense and on a global social stage. King sees himself as following Jesus in a particular freedom struggle, the struggle of African Americans for full civil rights.

The Christ who emerges in King's thought is a living Christ who continues to lead the Kingdom of God in a struggle for love and justice. During his thirteen-year ministry in the civil rights movement (1955–68), the narrative vision of King's public theology is ever guided by one polar star—the person and work of Jesus Christ. King's Christ, however, is not a savior stuck in the past but one we encounter here and now.

King saw Jesus as the only mediator to the personal God of the Bible. As a result of his civil rights activities, King experienced unceasing suffering. He was arrested, thrown in jail, stabbed, bombed, and the recipient of unremitting death threats. Amidst this constant suffering, King found solace in his union with Jesus Christ. Jesus was the source of his strength, salvation, and his struggle for justice. King writes, "There are some who still find the cross a stumbling block, and others consider it foolishness, but I am more convinced than ever before that it is the power of God unto social and individual salvation. So like the Apostle Paul I can now humbly yet proudly say, 'I bear in my body the marks of the Lord Jesus.' The suffering and agonizing moments through which I have passed over the last few years have also drawn me closer to God. More than ever before I am convinced of the reality of a personal God."[67] Jesus said, "Take up your cross and follow me!" The cross, as King understands it, is the cross of the freedom struggle, while many white Christians see their cross as a struggle for individual moral purity. For King, following Jesus means taking up your cross to live a life dedicated to love and justice in personal and political life.

James Cone has consistently lifted up this theme of King's cross-centered theology. Although some womanist theologians have sought to distance themselves from finding any value in suffering and Christ's death on the cross, Cone's black theological vision has plumbed the depths of King's cross-centered theology, where suffering that is the result of persecution for gospel witness is a valid expression of reconciliation.[68] Womanist theologians have expressed deep concerns about King's understanding of redemptive suffering. Dolores Williams writes: "As Christians, black women cannot forget the cross, but neither can they glorify it. To do so is to glorify suffering and to render their exploitation sacred. To do so is to glorify the sin of defilement."[69] Since a logic of domination has often been used in Christian culture to justify the suffering of women, in domestic violence situations, for example, theological accounts of human suffering must engage this reality. King would agree with Williams that suffering encountered through black social agents' engagement in the struggle should not be glorified. The call of Christian social ethics is to work to end suffering and oppression. King does not glorify suffering but works in the theological tradition of the early Christian martyrs to whom suffering is sometimes visited because of their bold prophetic witness for the Gospel. He understands that when suffering comes as a result of a prophetic and righteous life, it should be endured with the courage of Christ and the power of the Holy Spirit.

Like Dietrich Bonhoeffer, King understood that a cross-centered Christian life will mean suffering, persecution, and even martyrdom. As King led the civil rights movement in America, he encountered much resistance and many deep wounds. Yet through his Christology he could give a theological account of the suffering, which both he and his people had to bear. "Bearing the cross" meant confronting the resistance of white separatists with nonviolent love.[70] The only way King could make sense of his suffering and pain was through his deep participation in the suffering and pain of his Lord and savior Jesus Christ.

Like Harriet Jacobs, King inhabited a subversive theological subjectivity, where amidst the suffering of his life, he could see beyond and minister through it, simultaneously participating in the cross and the life of the Resurrection. Like Harriet Jacobs, King was in an in-between place waiting for the matchless power of God to emerge amidst the movement's attempt to embody the Kingdom of God. Beloved community needs to be birthed. With birth comes birth pangs. The birth pangs of the civil rights movement were the physical, emotional, and spiritual wounds that were inflicted on black bodies by the racist movement of white rule, an expression of the deeper racism prevalent in American structures and systems.

In summary, King's Christology emphasized a living Christ who suffered and died for us on the cross. In a deep mimetic spirituality, King called Christians to follow Christ through imitation. The call to Christians to take up their cross meant to live a life of complete surrender to the Kingdom of God, embodying God's love and justice.

By taking up their own crosses, Christian members of the civil rights movement could participate with Christ in embodying justice. Living with the love of Christ meant complete identification with the poor and the oppressed. Although challenging the corrupt system on behalf of blacks and the poor may cost you your life, it was the only cause worth living for.

Martin Luther King Jr. lifted up this distance between white and black experience and considered it unjust. Throughout his ministry he tried to help white moderates, many of whom were evangelicals, recognize the sin of white racism. Disappointed with the lack of white Christian participation in the civil rights struggle, he wrote in his "Letter from Birmingham City Jail":

> I must confess that over the last few years I have been gravely disappointed with the white moderate. I have almost reached the regrettable conclusion that the Negro's greatest stumbling block in the stride toward freedom is not the White Citizen's Counciler or the Ku Klux Klanner, but the white moderate who is more devoted to "order" than to justice; who prefers a negative peace which is the absence of tension to a positive peace which is the presence of justice; who constantly says, "I agree with you in the goal you seek, but I can't agree with your methods of direct action"; who paternalistically feels that he can set the timetable for another man's freedom; who lives by the myth of time and who constantly advised the Negro to wait until a more "convenient season." Shallow understanding from people of good will is more frustrating than absolute misunderstanding from people of ill will.

> Lukewarm acceptance is much more bewildering than outright rejection.[71]

King was "gravely disappointed" that white moderates were not joining the struggle for racial justice. Furthermore, many were often actively resisting it in shrewd or subtle ways. During the 1960s the great majority of white moderates regardless of their theological or ecclesial identity were sitting on the sidelines during the civil rights movement. Their silence, legitimated by a theological commitment to "order," ensured a noticeable absence of participation in this national struggle for racial and economic justice. Whether mainline or evangelical, white moderates (years later) were happy to embrace the positive fruit of the civil rights movement, but history indicates that only a small group of white evangelicals actually did or said anything to usher it in. Given the separation between black and white Christians, does it not make sense to look at streams of the evangelical tradition in both parts of the church?

4

CARL F. H. HENRY'S UNEASY CONSCIENCE

At the time when Martin Luther King Jr. was gaining attention as an international social prophet from a fundamentalist Baptist heritage in the South, another prophet, this one from the white northern fundamentalist Baptist experience, emerged: Carl F. H. Henry. As Billy Graham was evangelicalism's global evangelist, Carl Henry was evangelicalism's theological architect. After Graham's famous Los Angeles Crusade in 1949, his evangelistic crusades drew capacity crowds, becoming a symbol of the spiritual vitality of the evangelical movement during the 1950s. Although fundamentalists had always been zealously evangelistic and missional, these crusades helped to build a movement of conservative Christians who gradually came to desire not only the conversion of individuals but also the transformation of society.

Carl Henry's *The Uneasy Conscience of Modern Fundamentalism,* published in 1947, was a wake-up call, encouraging evangelicals to come out from their cultural hibernation and begin to actively engage in social transformation.[1] Henry called on evangelicals to confront specific political issues of the day, including "aggressive warfare, racial hatred and intolerance, the liquor traffic, and exploitation of labor and management."[2] Henry was calling on fundamentalists who were distinctive in their religious orthodoxy to move toward a more publicly engaged faith. Henry's prophetic message of socially engaged evangelical orthodoxy continues to shape contemporary evangelical politics.

Henry recognized the importance of the struggle for racial justice, but it would be hard to argue that many evangelicals in the 1950s were actively engaged in social issues. Rather, the issue of social justice was a subject of enormous debate within the evangelical movement. Henry felt acutely the need to both report on global injustice and develop an evangelical ethic to respond to global crises. Henry fought hard against strong institutional forces to give voice to the issue of racial and economic justice in *Christianity Today*, but the magazine gave limited coverage to the civil rights movement.[3] His theology of the Kingdom of God, however, opened a new horizon for evangelical theology. While personal conversion remained primary in his political theology, Henry argued that it is vital that Christians engage the great social crises of their day.

Born to German immigrants in 1919, Henry became one of the great theologians and public intellectuals in the evangelical movement that emerged in the 1940s. Henry "has probably done more than anyone, save Billy Graham, to shape twentieth-century evangelicalism."[4] He represents the historic expression of evangelicalism referred to as "neo-evangelical," the post-fundamentalist, postwar school of evangelicalism developed by Edward John Carnell, Billy Graham, Carl F. H. Henry, Harold John Ockenga, and Bernard L. Ramm. With the help of Billy Graham and Harold John Ockenga, Henry played an instrumental role in building two of the enduring institutions of the neo-evangelical legacy, Fuller Theological Seminary in Pasadena, California, founded in 1947, and *Christianity Today*, the magazine of the movement founded in 1956. As a prolific writer and theology professor at Fuller and editor of *Christianity Today,* Henry exerted visionary theological leadership throughout the evangelical world.

Henry's legacy is manifold. In addition to his role as an evangelical institution builder, he was an important systematic theologian and political thinker. Henry wrote a six-volume systematic theology titled *God, Revelation and Authority* that has been translated into five languages and remains a central theological text in many evangelical seminaries.[5] Henry's theological vision also continues to play a vital role in the conservative resurgence within Southern Baptist seminaries.[6]

Theologically, Henry was a tough-minded conservative who sought to faithfully defend the five fundamentals: "the divine authority and inerrant inspiration of Scripture, the virgin birth and sinless incarnation of Christ, His substitutionary atonement, bodily resurrection, and final personal return to glory."[7] In the spirit of early church apologists, Henry passionately defends the inerrancy of scripture and a propositional notion of doctrinal truth. He sees scripture as revelation in the form of "rational communication conveyed in intelligible ideas and meaningful words, that is, in conceptual verbal form."[8] Henry's thoughtful defenses of biblical inerrancy and propositional doctrine are important because these are the central planks of neo-evangelical theology.

In addition to Henry's institution building and scholarship in systematic theology, his political thinking made an important contribution to the evangelical church in the United States. In his deep desire for evangelical Christians to become creative and active participants in public life and cultural transformation, Carl Henry was a prophet before his time.[9] His recovery of Jesus's teaching of the Kingdom of God has played an important role in evangelicals beginning to deepen connections between Jesus and justice. Yet since Henry came of age during the rise of the white neo-evangelical establishment in the postwar period, his call for racial justice would not be heeded until decades later in the wake of the civil rights movement. White racism proved to be a particularly deep-rooted systemic sin within the mainstream evangelical movement and the institutions that it birthed.

The Uneasy Conscience of Fundamentalism, Henry's theological manifesto, was a passionate call to social action for evangelicals in the late 1940s and 1950s. Henry writes of his purpose: "I voiced a plea to then-beleaguered conservative Christians not to abandon society to the forces of Modernism, but to take a bold initiative in penetrating the social order with the biblical imperatives. The manner of that penetration was not detailed other than a call for evangelical example and persuasion rather than merely confrontation."[10] Throughout his corpus, Henry often contrasts his approach of penetrating and persuading America with the more directly confrontational approach of mainline Protestants.

In his work, Henry laments the great divorce between theology and ethics within evangelicalism.[11] He writes, "For the first protracted period in its history, evangelical Christianity stands divorced from the great social reform movements."[12] Like King, he alluded to the parable of the Good Samaritan, referring to the fundamentalist as "the modern priest and Levite, by-passing suffering humanity."[13] He lamented that evangelical social action has been "spotty and usually of the emergency type" and that churches have become "spiritualized juke boxes."[14] Henry's was a call to fundamentalists to move out of their self-centered cultural isolation, toward a more others-centered ethic of neighborly love.

Henry's commitment to the social implications of the Gospel elicited critiques in 1948 from reactionary fundamentalists in the American Council circles and at more conservative schools, like Biola (the Bible Institution of Los Angeles).[15] When comparing King and Henry, it is vital to keep in mind that from the 1940s through the 1960s, Henry was always in active, critical dialogue with social conservative fundamentalists, whereas King was increasingly in dialogue with theological liberals and political progressives in addition to the fundamentalists of his southern youth. In a sustained and rigorous debate, Henry pushed fundamentalists hard to begin the process of thinking through the social implications of the Gospel, but the acceleration and intensity of the prophetic black social gospel that propelled the civil rights movement proved to be further than Henry and many evangelicals were able to go during the revolutionary 1960s. Yet even during the 1960s prophetic black Christianity was subversively leavening the evangelical movement. Henry shared with King a Baptist revivalist heritage and a strong personal identity as a Baptist preacher and theologian; however, Henry's Baptist framework had a particularly Reformed character to it and his Baptist community was largely white and privileged.

While Henry is often primarily interpreted as a Reformed systematic theologian, the prophetic Baptist stream of his theology is of equal importance and often overlooked. For example, in his history of Fuller Seminary George Marsden interprets Henry as part of the core of faculty that was Calvinist in their basic theological orientation and was seeking to recover the Reformed scholasticism of "Old Princeton" theology.[16] Henry was able to deepen his theological roots when he taught at Fuller Theological Seminary, roots in both the Reformed and Baptist traditions.

Marsden argues that Henry's vision of transformation was shaped by "the broadly Calvinistic vision that the Christian's mission involves not only evangelism but also a cultural task, both remaking the mind of an era and transforming society."[17] Like the Dutch Calvinist theologian Abraham Kuyper, Henry engaged this broader transformational perspective, emphasizing the goodness of creation, common grace, and the universal presence of the *imago Dei* in all humans.[18] There is in his work, however, a strong affirmation of religious freedom and a deep suspicion of the state that reflect Henry's deep Baptist roots. Thus, in H. Richard Niebuhr's categories, Henry is somewhere between the "Christ transforming culture" model often associated with the Reformed tradition and the "Christ against culture" model often associated with the Anabaptists.[19] Affirming the distinctive countercultural witness of the Christian community of regenerate individuals, Henry also argued that Christians should seek to transform the world through public service and public policy work.

"Prophetic" is not an apt descriptor for many fundamentalist Baptists, but it is for Henry because he was attempting to articulate a more radical Baptist vision of social engagement: "For the first protracted period in its history, evangelical Christianity stands divorced from the great social reform movements. . . . This creates the most favorable opportunity evangelicalism has had since its embarrassing divorce from a world social program, to recapture its rightful leadership in pressing for a new world order. . . . An evangelical world program has its timeliest opportunity at the present hour."[20] While Henry lamented the fact that fundamentalism of the early decades of the twentieth century had divorced itself from the social reform movements of the day, at midcentury he saw a strategic opportunity for evangelicals to live into a broader social ethic. But he met the limitations of his theological vision in his encounter with the civil rights movement.

Reading Henry as a prophetic Reformed Baptist opens up a new horizon for understanding his consistent call to evangelicals to wake up and live out a more robust social ethic. Raised by a Lutheran mother and Roman Catholic father, neither of whom practiced their faith, Henry made a decision to become a Christian when he was twenty years old. He went on to study theology at Wheaton College, Northern Baptist Theological Seminary, and Boston University.

During his education and throughout his career he drew on the Reformed theologian Abraham Kuyper, as well as on the Baptist theologian Augustus Strong.[21] Henry writes, "I must confess a desire to turn out the next conservative Baptist Systematic Theology, to replace Strong. In line with this, I expect to write my dissertation under Brightman on the influence of Personalistic Idealism on Augustus Hopkins Strong, and I think I can show how he inconsistently held to his evangelicalism in view of his concessions to personalism. That would clear the field for the next Theology text."[22] In contrast to King's active black Christian personalist philosophy, Henry was more skeptical of personalism, but his unique appropriation of personalist themes reinforced his theological individualism.[23] As Baptist theologians, King and Henry shared a common commitment to the intrinsic value and dignity of every human person who is made in the image of God.

A prophetic Baptist is one who works within the Baptist stream of theology and is vigilant in advocating for dignity of all people, with an emphasis on religious freedom, reformist revivalism, and the separation of church and state. There are three ways that Henry can be read as a prophetic Baptist. First, Henry emphasizes the individual freedom of each believer, a prophetic stand because of its stouthearted repudiation of state religion and violent coercion. This radical Baptist individualism has deep historic roots and casts a long and lasting shadow on evangelical social ethics.[24]

Second, Henry was shaped by the revivalist tradition that sought a broader social reform. The prophetic dimension of revivalism is expressed when strong piety embodies itself in the concrete struggle for justice in the world. Marsden mentions the revivalist impulse in Henry but does not develop the theme in depth, writing of Henry, "Though a leader in reforming fundamentalism, he always remained a true revivalist at heart."[25] We see Henry's revivalism in several of his dreams, including his desire for the evangelization of the world, the founding of a Christian university, and in helping evangelicals become more broadly engaged in public life. Henry thought that spiritual renewal was the basis of society's renewal.

Third, Henry's skepticism of the state distances him from the theocratic tendency within some strains of Calvinism. Through being vigilant in limiting the powers of the state, a new horizon is opened up for prophetic Christian witness. Henry's skepticism of the state demonstrates a radical Baptist stream indebted to the political theology of Roger Williams. As Robert Bellah has argued, it is the radical Baptist Roger Williams, not the Puritan John Winthrop, who is the founding political theorist of America.[26] Williams challenged the Puritan establishment of Massachusetts Bay Colony, arguing that civil authority had no right to rule over the religious beliefs and practices of individuals. Banished from the colony on October 9, 1635, Williams went south to found Rhode Island, where all people, whether they were Christian or not, had freedom of religious expression without the fear of being coerced by the state. In the spirit of Roger Williams, Henry advocated on behalf of the freedoms of all individuals who are made in God's image (*imago Dei*) while remaining cautious about the state's ability to fully meet the common good.

The Baptist view of church and state is that of a clear separation. The church does not look to the state for favors or help, but to provide justice and order, so that the church is free to practice religion as it sees fit. The church can preach about sin, including the sins of the state, but there should be a strict demarcation between these two spheres. Thus, the church should not guide the activities of the state, nor should the state have control over the church.

Although Henry was in theory against the idea of a Christian state, he was still susceptible to the influence of Christian civil religion, often partnering with a number of other groups and theologians, such as Francis Schaeffer, who were pushing for it.[27] These conservative evangelicals understood America's origins as Christian in nature, not honestly confronting the transatlantic slave trade and Native American genocide through which the American empire was built. After World War II, evangelicalism was housed and hosted within the American nation-state that was circumscribed by white racism and proved effective in producing a capitalist citizenry. Although the neo-evangelical vision sought to defend the dignity and freedom of all individuals, it was not equipped to fund resistance against racism and capitalism that was promoted by the state. Furthermore, in the postwar period evangelicalism continued to rise in its public power and persona through a convergence of racism, capitalism, and nationalism.

The paradox of evangelicals' understanding of America as a Christian nation in the context of the separation between church and state is this: evangelicals are willing to inform the state of its moral responsibilities, but they do not want any responsibility or accountability to the state in their own affairs. Many evangelicals want the church to be completely free of state control, but they still expect the nation to conduct its affairs according to the moral foundation of the Judeo-Christian tradition.[28] Furthermore, white evangelicals wanted to take credit for being global freedom fighters in World War II, but often they would not actively join the freedom struggles at home, including the civil rights movement and the women's movement.

Yet even from its insulated position within the American empire, evangelical theology was being renewed through a movement on the underside of modernity, the civil rights movement that was emerging from the places of black suffering from which many white evangelicals had fled. In contrast to Henry's simultaneous skepticism of the state and complicity with its nationalist ideals, King, who was also a Baptist, had a more irenic view of the state and its laws, for a strong, centralized federal government provided the structure and the mechanisms of enforcement through which African Americans could gain and sustain ongoing rights and freedoms. The black freedom struggle would reach its goal only through deep transformation of the church, the government, and the economy. It was not enough to change individual lives; Jesus's call for justice demanded a transformation of all societal institutions.

When thinking constructively about a Baptist vision for evangelical social witness, Henry took some cues from the social gospel tradition. He was sympathetic to the social gospel's attempt to fulfill the commandment of loving the neighbor through concrete social action; however, he strongly opposed certain constructions of the social gospel's rejection of personal regeneration. Henry's critique of the social gospel was that it "immanentizes Christ and the Kingdom";[29] it reduced Christianity to the performance of good works in society instead of seeing positive human social action as expressing the gracious, loving activity of the triune God. In the social gospel tradition, kingdom work is seen to be immanent or "this worldly" instead of transcendent or coming from God beyond this world.

Henry's essential critique of Northern Baptist social gospel theologians, such as Walter Rauschenbusch and Shailer Matthews, was that they rejected the transcendence of God implied in supernaturalist theism as well as salvation understood as the personal regeneration of individuals. His piercing criticism of the liberal social gospel tradition also must be placed in the cold war context that Henry lived within, where communism was focused on "the forced revolutionizing of social structures."[30] Although Henry lamented Rauschenbusch's rejection of some orthodox doctrines, for example, the atonement, he appreciated this prophetic Baptist attempt to bring a social dimension to the Gospel, a concern he shared.

In contrast to the liberal social gospel, Henry sought to develop a theology of the Kingdom of God that affirmed the primacy of divine action in transforming the lives of redeemed individuals. He saw the Kingdom of God as a reign of justice that was inaugurated with the life of Jesus. As expressed in *The Uneasy Conscience of Fundamentalism,* the most important theological key to evangelicals developing a public theology was a renewal of preaching the Kingdom of God, emphasizing both its "already" and its "not yet" dimensions.

Henry's theology of the Kingdom of God produces a "regenerational social ethic."[31] From this perspective, the personal redemption or regeneration of individuals is the primary basis of ethical action in the world. Henry argues that "the indispensable prelude to the kingdom of God is a divine regeneration of fallen man."[32] As humans are redeemed through evangelical conversion, Henry argued that their personal regeneration in Christ became the basis of their social action as individual moral agents. For Henry "both individual conversion and social justice" are indispensable to the church's task of mirroring the future Kingdom of God on earth.[33] The Kingdom of God, however, is never to be identified with any expression of earthly kingdoms, including the state and even the church.

Henry's vision of the Kingdom of God provides a metaphor to guide evangelical political and social action that is both biblical and realistic. Henry was deeply concerned that some forms of the liberal social gospel had so misrepresented the Gospel as a liberal political agenda that it was virtually unrecognizable from scripture's vision of redemption. According to Henry, evangelical theology should not try to change the meaning of redemption, but should give "the redemptive word a proper temporal focus."[34]

The Kingdom of God bears witness within all spheres of life. The inaugural issue of *Christianity Today* proclaimed on October 15, 1956: "*Christianity Today* will apply the Biblical revelation to the contemporary crisis, by presenting the implications of the total Gospel message for every area of life."[35] Henry defended "an evangelical conviction that nothing is so essential among Fundamentalist essentials as a world-relevance for the Gospel. Whatever in our kingdom views undercuts that relevance destroys the essential character of Christianity as such."[36] One of the important manifestations of "world-relevance for the Gospel" is the church's work for peace and justice in the world. The Kingdom of God is manifest when the church helps others at their place of greatest need.

Henry believed that the church, in mirroring the kingdom, must be engaged in the struggle for social justice. The prophetic witness of the church is both confrontational and evangelistic, "condemning with redemptive might the tolerated social evils for the redemptive message [is] to light the world and to salt the earth."[37] The notion of salt is especially apt for evangelical ethics as it helps individuals to preserve the three orders of creation: family, economy, and government. Henry called evangelicals to flesh out the logic of Christ's Lordship seeking to apply this reign of love and justice to all aspects of society.

In Henry's vision of the Kingdom of God, Jesus is conceived as the redemptive king. Henry writes, "The extent to which man centers his life and energy in the redemptive King *now* determines the extent of the divine kingdom in the present age."[38] Henry's commitment to world evangelization is emblematic of the neo-evangelicals, of whom George Marsden writes, "While their agenda had expanded to include the rehabilitation of both scholarship and Christian's social consciousness, evangelism remained the *sine qua non*."[39] While fighting all different forms of social evil, the evangelical "ought to be counted upon to point to the redemption that is in Christ Jesus as the only adequate solution."[40] The motifs of Christ's Lordship and redemption are interlaced throughout Henry's corpus.

Fundamentalism's primary focus on evangelism, however, was also one reason it struggled to develop a coherent social ethic. Henry writes, "Fundamentalism concentrated its energies on personal evangelism and foreign missions. It consequently offered no cohesive program of attack on social evils. The solution of all problems was sought by simply intensifying evangelism. It offered no incisive critique of totalitarianism, secular education, racial tension, labor-management controversy, international conflict, or other social evils."[41] The challenge of a post-fundamentalist neo-evangelicalism was to develop a social ethic that went beyond "simply intensifying evangelism" to developing an integral missiology that included social justice work. In order to flesh out his theology of the kingdom, Henry turns to the teachings of Jesus.

Henry builds on Jesus's teaching that the Kingdom of God is both here and not here. This "already, not yet" eschatology has become a standard way for evangelicals to speak about the last days or end times. The basic idea is that Jesus Christ inaugurated the Kingdom of God through his earthly life. This doctrine of the end times is sometimes referred to as inaugurated eschatology. Since the Kingdom of God has been inaugurated, it is now up to Christians to open themselves up to the Holy Spirit as they seek to follow Christ's call to love the neighbor, with the hope that their collective social action will become a parable of the kingdom, bearing witness to Christ the King.

Because part of the Kingdom of God—the transcendent coming kingdom—is not here on earth, the kingdom cannot be identified with the state. Henry writes, "The kingdom which Jesus introduced, it appears, was quite compatible with earthly government which did not interfere with the realization of the *summum bonam* in the lives of regenerate believers, but it could hardly be identified with any government in which the redemptive reference was not central. The main difference between the kingdom of God *now* and the kingdom of God *then* is that the future kingdom will center all of its activities in the redemptive King because all government and dominion will be subjected to Him."[42] Because of the dialectical logic of this form of eschatology, "the kingdom of God *now*" cannot "be identified with any government" in the present. Any earthly manifestation of the Kingdom of God is always provisional. We see throughout Henry's writing a strong critique of an overly optimistic vision of the Kingdom of God being manifest on earth, whether it be of the postmillennial evangelical variety or the mainline liberal social gospel variety. According to Henry, we should never be deceived into thinking that sinful humans and sinful institutions can be so transformed as to actually achieve God's reign.[43] This hope is left for heaven, which will "center all of its activities in the redemptive King."

Henry believes that the church and state inhabit two different worlds: "Nowhere does the New Testament provide the institutional church any authority, jurisdiction, or mandate to wield direct pressure upon government and public agencies for commitment to specific ecclesiastically-approved policies and programs. The church had no revelational solution to secular specifics; nonetheless it encouraged all Christians to fulfill their duties as citizens of two worlds in devout obedience to the commandments of God."[44] The church and the state have two very different and distinct roles. While the state's mission is to preserve justice by supporting the creation orders of society, the church has primarily a redemptive mission, that of inviting all people to new life in Jesus Christ.[45]

Henry explains further that the future kingdom "does not displace an interim world program. That contemporary program in evangelicalism is (1) predicated upon an all-inclusive redemptive context for its assault upon global ills; (2) involves total opposition to all moral evils, whether societal or personal; (3) offers not only a higher ethical standard than any other system of thought, but provides also in Christ a dynamic to lift humanity to its highest level of moral achievement." The church is at its best when it reflects the future Kingdom of God. Henry writes, "The new man and the new community called into being by the gospel of redemption anticipate the new creation as the climax toward which God is daily moving history and the cosmos. Where the church is truly the church, she mirrors that coming new society of the Kingdom of God in miniature."[46] Thus the church can become a window to the kingdom for the onlooking world. By sharing the Gospel with people in word and deed, the church sees individuals and communities transformed to become more like the coming Kingdom of God.

The sin of white racism became an important test case for the viability of Henry's evangelical ethic. Although Henry was not visibly active in the marches of the civil rights movement, he continued to advocate for racial justice through his writing and reporting. Henry saw Graham's integrated crusades as an important example of evangelicals working for racial reconciliation. During the Billy Graham Crusade in Jackson, Mississippi, in 1952, Graham said: "There is no scriptural basis for segregation. It may be there are places where such is desirable to both races, but certainly not in the church. . . . The audience may be segregated, but there is no segregation at the altar. The men and women who come down to accept Christ stand as individuals. And it touches my heart when I see white stand shoulder to shoulder with black at the cross."[47] Graham stopped segregating his crusades by cutting the dividing ropes at a crusade in Chattanooga, Tennessee, in 1953. The tearing of the veil of separation between blacks and whites in the evangelistic crusades marked an important recovery of the egalitarian ideal of many antebellum revivals, an ideal that was buried during D. L. Moody's segregated revivals in the age of Jim Crow. From 1953 on, Graham understood his integrated crusades as his primary gospel witness for racial justice and reconciliation.[48] Michael G. Long writes, "Rather than supporting King's tactical strategies and goals, Graham frequently redlined himself far outside the inclusive, just, and peaceful community that the civil rights leader died trying to achieve."[49] Graham focused on his vocation as a "New Testament evangelist" seeking to convert individuals to Jesus with hope that they would then naturally join the struggle for justice. While integrated crusades were only the beginning of a journey toward an antiracist, intercultural neo-evangelicalism, the evangelical movement was beginning to think more carefully about racism.

Pushing beyond Billy Graham's populism and apocalyticism, Carl Henry sought to more clearly articulate the "world relevance" of the Kingdom of God for inspiring Christians to respond to the great global ethical crises of the day, including the civil rights struggle. Henry had tried to cover the civil rights movement in the 1960s in various ways. In 1965 Henry sent Frank E. Gaebelein to cover the march in Selma, Alabama. An associate editor of *Christianity Today* and the founder and headmaster of the Stony Brook School, New York, Gaebelein went to Selma and was so inspired that he wired Henry in Washington, DC, that evangelicals needed to join the march. But Gaebelein's stories of the Selma march never saw the light of day. The resistance at *Christianity Today* was coming primarily from two people: J. Howard Pew, the Texas oil man and the financer of *Christianity Today,* and L. Nelson Bell, Billy Graham's father-in-law and an editorial advisor at *Christianity Today,* who still had segregationist views. Pew and Bell did not want *Christianity Today* to speak out too critically against racism and capitalism, because they thought it would alienate important segments of the magazine's constituency. Pew and Bell understood white power and privilege and were not eager to see it unveiled and dismantled. They insisted on running more articles on communism, which accelerated the production of white male capitalist citizens who increasingly placed their trust in their "Christian nation."

Openly critical of capitalism and racism, Carl Henry was in ongoing conflict with Pew and Bell over the editorial decision-making policy at *Christianity Today*. Henry's public calls for social justice and racial equality were juxtaposed with tough "in-house" institutional fights with conservative evangelical and fundamentalist leaders. When thinking through the problem of racism Henry tried to offer a third, "evangelical moderate," approach to the poles of fundamentalist political apathy and progressive civil disobedience. Henry writes: "The persistent integrationist question, 'After all, what's wrong with racial intermarriage?' perturbs the evangelical moderate as much as the provocative slogan on letterheads of the White Citizens Council: 'Let's keep white folks white.' He hesitates to rely upon propaganda and compulsion to improve race relations, to the Church's neglect (even disparagement) of the mission of evangelism, regeneration, and sanctification to motivate Christian social impact."[50] For Henry the question of racial justice must be understood as part of the mission of the church, part of God's work of redemption in the lives of individuals. Evangelicals are called to work for racial justice because all people, including people of color, are made in God's image.

Henry's mention of "racial intermarriage" also discloses discomfort in the white evangelical ranks over the prospect of biracial relationships. While Henry thought evangelicals should work to "improve race relations," his comments about biracial marriage reflect a lingering cultural racism that remained linked with issues of marriage, family, and sexuality. Henry and his largely white evangelical audience remained part of the unified Caucasian race that was constructed after World War II to absorb all European immigrant groups within a generic category of "whiteness."[51] Thus, postwar neo-evangelicalism as reflected in the NAE and *Christianity Today* was constituted as a Caucasian reality. These white evangelicals gained collective identity in contrast to nonwhite ethnic groups primarily referred to as "black." Although white evangelicals sought to get along with African Americans better interpersonally, there was still a deep resistance to full cross-cultural fellowship, including biracial dating and marriage. The "black man" remained an ethical and theological problem for neo-evangelical theology.

Henry's "evangelical moderate" position in which he advocated a patient integration was problematic. He tried to paint evangelicals as the reasonable middle path between segregationists and "radical integrationists," but his evangelical moderate proposal for race relations did not include a structural analysis of racism. He did not have the tools of social analysis at his disposal to understand racism as an institutional phenomena and to identify normative whiteness within the evangelical world. His insistence on the term "evangelical moderates" also meant "moving slowly," as in the clergy who wrote to Martin Luther King Jr. in the Birmingham jail and told him to slow down the rapid advance of the civil rights movement. While Henry increasingly deployed a rhetorical call for a patient integration from his editorial office, King hit the streets organizing marches to achieve immediate integration in particular cities throughout the country. After confronting the power of social death that had plagued African Americans during slavery and segregation, King's passionate pursuit of racial justice was a daily life and death struggle.

In closing, Martin Luther King Jr. and Carl Henry shared a common heritage in eighteenth- and nineteenth-century revivalism. They both drew on rhetorical and political themes in their tradition of Baptist revivalism to "reform" the deeper cultural and political isolationist tendency within their respective Baptist traditions. They were prophetic Baptist preachers who believed that the Gospel of Jesus Christ challenges the church to have a prophetic social witness in society. Revivalist rhetoric quickly raised their profile as public speakers and great communicators. Henry's manifestoes and editorials and King's sermons and speeches galvanized two important social movements because they communicated in ways that tapped into the deepest roots of American populism and revivalist spirituality.[52]

King drew on the traditions of republican democracy and biblical Christianity in forming his clear and compelling message of love and equality. He skillfully organized and mobilized the civil rights movement, drawing on different organizing traditions, including the black church tradition and organized labor. King was also shaped by the tradition of American revivalism embodied in the ministry of Billy Graham. Graham was an important influence on the style and strategy of both King and Henry as they sought to implement a broader social agenda that went beyond Graham's crusade strategy of world evangelism.

Although King and Henry shared a common revivalist ancestry, this ancestry took very different historic expressions during the decade of crisis, the 1960s. William Pannell argues that while the black and white churches share a common evangelical heritage embodied particularly in nineteenth-century Baptist and Methodist theological streams, after the Civil War there was a divorce between these two traditions.[53] Henry's heart desired to bring these two streams, black and white, together. Racial reconciliation was viewed by Henry as an important expression of the healing of theology and ethics within the evangelical world.

In order to break open the steel-clad doors of the American evangelical modernity, Henry deployed a theology of protest. The first paragraph of *A Plea for Evangelical Demonstration* (1971) is a manifesto for a prophetic evangelicalism. Henry writes: "This is a call for authentic evangelical protest. A sensitive Christian conscience must openly confront enduring and intractable social injustices. Biblically concerned Christians need not forego a moment of open identification with those of other faiths and alien views in protesting what all together recognize to be unjust."[54] From the lead sentence of the book we see that it is "protest" that Henry is really interested in, though Baker Books opted for the more sedate and apologetic "demonstration" for the title. It is fascinating that in these two first sentences Henry reclaims that language of "protest" and "confrontation," a language he had always reserved for the opponents of his earlier writing, particularly the mainline social gospelers. Here he reclaims the discourse of protest for a prophetic evangelical ethic. Not only should evangelicals protest, but they should do it with people of all colors and faiths. This is a gesture toward the church-based coalition politics that drove the civil rights movement. Finally, and most important, Henry claims that we need to protest "what all together recognize to be unjust," echoing King's comment in the Birmingham jail that "injustice anywhere is injustice everywhere." The Henry of *A Plea for Evangelical Demonstration* is a Henry on fire for lasting social change as a vital expression of our gospel witness.

When reading Henry's work through the lens of a prophetic reformed Baptist theology, we can see a new Carl Henry emerge, one whose passion for defending the Bible, classic doctrine, and objective truth includes a passion for defending the poor and the oppressed. Henry turned to the doctrine of the Kingdom of God to connect a complacent evangelical establishment with a suffering of humanity. Henry's uneasy conscience found form in Christ's kingdom that expressed Christ's heart and his *pathos* for humanity. Jesus's teaching of the kingdom expressed the Christian focus on loving and caring for the Other who is made in the image of God.

Henry forged a kingdom doctrine as a dialectical alternative to the one-sided emphasis of the personal gospel of the fundamentalists and the social gospel of Walter Rauschenbusch. He sought an understanding of the kingdom that affirmed both its present and future dimensions. Yet in the end, his kingdom doctrine still gave priority to a personal gospel, including a social dimension that was seen as a secondary concern.

Postwar evangelical theology and ethics reached a crossroads on the issue of race. After World War II, evangelicals who had played an important role in spreading global freedom during the war had a strategic opportunity to actively join a prophetic indigenous freedom movement at home, the struggle for black civil rights. White evangelicals could turn and actively embrace fellow black Christians as sisters and brothers or remain silent and complicit in a regime that treated them as non-citizens. A conscious choice had to be made.

Although Carl Henry saw racism as a sin that evangelicals should address, his own theological vision did not prove fully adequate for the task. Without realizing it, Henry was ensnared in the logic of the "half-Gospel" that characterized twentieth-century white evangelicalism, focusing its primary energies on personal evangelism and relationships, never able to fully integrate ministries of social justice. Rugged individualism seemed impossible to be extracted from Henry's evangelical dogmatic framework, and racial justice seemed to be an ideal that was impossible to achieve. For Henry, Christianity was fundamentally about the salvation of individuals. This meant that personal evangelism was the primary task of the church, followed by social transformation. Sin was seen primarily as an individual state of immorality, taking precedence over social disorder. Racism was viewed as a problem of the human heart and human relationships, not an institutional social sin. The church was seen as a community of regenerate individuals called to social witness but without a clear theology of public engagement to direct them.

With time, Henry's narrative vision of the Kingdom of God began to gradually resemble King's vision of beloved community, but Henry struggled with how to show white evangelicals a clear path to achieve racial justice. While Henry understood the Kingdom of God primarily in personal terms, he increasingly sought ways to integrate his interpersonal ethic with social transformation, which was the heart of King's vision of beloved community. Yet dominated by a cultural and theological individualism, Henry's social ethic lacked an acute systematic social analysis, a communitarian ecclesiology, and a theology of prophetic citizenship. Henry's inability to integrate the personal and the political remains a challenge for twenty-first-century evangelical theology.

Since there was a fundamental dichotomy in Henry's gospel, his legacy remained open-ended. Would the next generation of evangelicals continue to think of political ethics primarily in terms of personal piety, or would they seek to embody the kingdom's social dimension in the struggle for peace, justice, and creation care? From the "traditional family" politics of James Dobson and the Religious Right to what David P. Gushee calls the "centrist politics" of Richard Cizik and the National Association of Evangelicals, Henry's theology of the kingdom would take different forms. Yet after Carl F. H. Henry, one thing was certain—evangelical politics would have to give a theological account of race.

PART

II

EVANGELICAL POLITICS

I choose to identify with the underprivileged. I choose
to identify with the poor. I choose to give my life for the
hungry. I choose to give my life for those who have been
left out of the sunlight of opportunity. I choose to live
for and with those who find themselves seeing life as a
long and desolate corridor with no exit sign. This is the
way I'm going. If it means suffering a little bit, I'm going
that way. If it means sacrificing, I'm going that way. If
it means dying for them, I'm going that way, because I
heard a voice saying, "Do something for others."
Martin Luther King Jr.

5

FOCUS ON THE FAMILY:
NURTURING AND DEFENDING THE FAMILY

"Tell us about your recent trip to Alaska," Tony Perkins asked James Dobson in the opening session of the September 22, 2006, Vote Values Forum in Washington, DC. Dobson demurred at first, saying, "Tony, I told you not to bring that up," but then told the story of going on a bear hunt with his son, Ryan. They were alone in the woods when a big old grizzly charged, and in a split second Dobson raised his rifle and killed him. Dobson turned to the audience and said, "Those of you who don't like hunting, *deal with it!*" In this introduction to a Religious Right rally, Dobson presented himself as a strong warrior, both as an adept hunter in the Alaskan frontier and, more important, as a seasoned and strong leader on the conservative side of America's belligerent culture wars.

Maligned by the media for being a militant, homophobic conservative power broker, Dobson has been consistent in his public defense of family values—disciplining children, ending abortion, and protecting marriage. Dobson is a part of what Tom Brokaw has called "the Greatest Generation," women and men who came of age during World War II. With old-fashioned values and the stubborn tenacity of Winston Churchill, Dobson is not scared to fight long and hard for the family values he holds so dear.

During the past thirty years, his ministry, the organization Focus on the Family, has grown into a mammoth evangelical empire.[1] Beginning as a ministry to men in 1976, Focus incorporated as a family ministry in 1977. Focus employs 1,300 people and receives 10,000 e-mails, 50,000 phone calls, and 173,000 letters a month. It has a sprawling eighty-one-acre campus in Colorado Springs, Colorado, and its own zip code. With a mailing list of more than six million names and an annual budget of more than $150 million, Focus is a major social force.

In order to extend his political influence, Dobson formed an extensive network of organizations that further the agenda of the Religious Right. Focus is a nonprofit organization with a 501(c)3 designation. Since all donations to Focus are tax exempt, it cannot legally lobby for individual candidates or political parties. As a result of its 501(c)3 designation, Focus is limited in how much money it can spend on its public policy work, which now accounts for less than 10 percent of its overall budget. To strengthen its political activities, Focus has established two legally distinct political organizations located in Washington, DC: the Family Research Council (FRC) and Family Research Council Action. The collective strength of Focus on the Family's public policy arm, the Family Research Council, Family Research Council Action, and Focus on the Family Action, their political action committees, their radio advocacy strategy, and their statewide affiliate organizations—coupled with successful Vote Values campaigns to mobilize conservative evangelical voters concerned about abortion and gay marriage—represents a vital national evangelical social movement.

The organizational mission of Focus is based on the proclamation of Jesus Christ as Lord and Savior of the world. In addition to this core evangelical affirmation, embodied in Henry's theological vision, Dobson's Nazarene heritage, with its particular focus on Jesus Christ as healer, has shaped his Christological vision and his work through Focus. As a child psychologist, Dobson has dedicated his life and the resources of his organization to heal broken families. These two impulses—Jesus as Lord and healer—come through in the mission statement of Focus "to nurture and defend the family." Defending resonates with Christ's Lordship, and nurturing resonates with Christ's ministry of healing.

The evangelical pro-family movement embodied by Focus on the Family is expressed in three ways: its narrative vision, its practices, and its identity. Focus's narrative vision of Jesus as Lord forms the basis of the evangelical pro-family movement's defense of Christian values. Dobson's colleague Tom Minnery has played a critical role in directing Dobson's blend of theology—Nazarene theology coupled with Henry's evangelical vision—into a conservative evangelical public theology. Focus implements this narrative vision through many practices, including an extensive media ministry, participating in Vote Values campaigns, and fighting against liberal political tendencies within the evangelical world.

James Dobson has been a self-proclaimed reluctant political warrior in the most recent round of the U.S. culture wars. He began his career as a child psychologist on the faculty of the University of California medical school. He has continued in this work in marriage and family counseling through Focus, which has made providing practical advice to couples about how to be better spouses and parents one of the staples of its ministry. Founded at the same time that the evangelical pro-life movement was gathering steam, Focus was politicized from its inception. In the 1980s Dobson became more involved in politics, focusing on a cluster of issues related to family matters, including abortion, pornography, and the women's movement.

Dobson is not a "reverend" and claims not to be a theologian, but evangelical theology frames, guides, and motivates the ministries of Focus. Dobson's positive message of maintaining strong families has resonated with millions of people across religious, racial, and national lines. Focus has helped and continues to help women and men be supportive spouses and loving parents. In the age of divorce and broken families, the Focus call center provides free counseling and support for all people, no matter what the problem.

The evangelical pro-family movement, symbolized by James Dobson's Focus on the Family and Family Research Council, is best understood as a white male conservative power movement. Focus on the Family grew out of Dobson's men's ministry that began in 1976. From the beginning up to today Dobson's chief focus has been to support men in their roles as husbands and fathers. His defense of the family is also a defense of male authority. Although he has expanded the focus of his ministry to include wives, mothers, and daughters, his focus on ministries to males has remained unwavering.

Many commentators, including Dobson himself, have argued that the pro-family movement is a reaction to the radical feminist movement of the 1960s. Less noted is that it is also a reaction to the civil rights movement.

The issue of race played an important, yet often underestimated, role in the rise of the Christian pro-family movement in the 1970s. When we consider Dobson's defense of male authority in the church, family, and society through the lens of the civil rights movement, the "whiteness" of his political project begins to emerge. The Religious Right's romantic myth that America was founded as a Christian nation blinded it to the fact that America was founded as a "white" nation. Yet while, on one hand, members of the Religious Right want to defend the Christianness of the American nation-state, on the other hand, they do not want the federal government to dictate how the church and Christian organizations are run. Pro-family evangelicals have a deep suspicion of the expansive powers of the federal government, in addition to their politics of gender and race. Concerns about sexuality, race, and the expansive powers of the federal government provide the framework of this evangelical social movement.

"The pro-family movement symbolized by Focus on the Family and Family Research Council has always been inspired by William Wilberforce, Carl Henry, and Francis Schaeffer," noted Gary Bauer, the founding director of the Family Research Council and current president of American Values, based in Arlington, Virginia.[2] The power of the pro-family movement can be explained only if we uncover the central theological themes that propel it. Dobson's public theology is shaped by Carl Henry's regenerationist social ethic, yet it is driven by a Wesleyan dialectic of discipline and delight.

Henry's notions of the family as a creation order and his emphasis on the Lordship of Jesus Christ are integral to Dobson's public theology. A strong commitment to the integrity of the family was always at the forefront of Carl Henry's public theology. In *The Uneasy Conscience of Modern Fundamentalism*, Henry writes of evangelicalism's theology of marriage as being one of its most important contributions to the moral renewal of the nation:

> In mentioning the typical ethical insistences of Fundamentalist churches, it would be unfair not to allude to the strict attitude taken toward divorce, as contrasted with the increasingly loose secular view of family relations. The insistence that only death or adultery can sever the marriage bond is maintained nowhere today

with such a conviction of absoluteness as in Fundamentalist circles, although there are here, as everywhere, exceptions. The contribution of this viewpoint to the integrity of the family, and its significance in precluding juvenile delinquency, is of no small moment in its social consequences. From a certain perspective it can be said that the effort to remedy the disintegration of the American home, pressed by social reformers, does not get at the heart of the problem as directly as the Fundamentalist proclamation of the divine sanction of a monogamous family life.[3]

In this passage we see a number of themes that reemerge in Dobson's theology of family, including "the strict attitude taken toward divorce," "the integrity of the family . . . precluding juvenile delinquency," "the disintegration of the American home," and "the divine sanction of a monogamous family life." Although Henry took issue with certain foci and tactics of the Religious Right, he always interpreted the leaders of the movement, men like Pat Robertson, Jerry Falwell, and Chuck Colson, as an important embodiment of a socially engaged evangelicalism, the theological tradition from which Dobson's own ministry emerged.[4]

Tom Minnery has played an important role in mediating between the Henry tradition and Focus's public policy work. Founding editor of Focus's public policy magazine, *Citizen*, Minnery has been the principal architect of Focus's public policy strategy. He was shaped by many of Henry's virtues, including Henry's theological depth, cultural conservatism, entrepreneurial creativity, and journalistic clarity. Minnery attended Trinity Evangelical Divinity School, where Henry taught theology, and he represents an important continuation of the Carl Henry school of evangelical religious journalism. Minnery worked as a senior editor at *Christianity Today*, where Henry served as founding editor. Minnery met Dobson while he was writing a story for *Christianity Today* on the Reagan administration's Committee on Pornography, which Dobson served on during the 1980s. Because of Minnery's previous connection to *Christianity Today*, I see *Citizen* magazine as a continuation of Henry's publishing legacy. Minnery's manifesto, *Why You Can't Stay Silent*, echoes Henry's *Uneasy Conscience*, arguing that ministries of social justice are an integral part of the mission of the evangelical church.

The imprint of the Henry legacy is also illustrated in Dobson's political collaborations with the Southern Baptist Convention (SBC). Dobson works closely with Southern Baptist church leaders, especially Albert Mohler, president of Southern Baptist Theological Seminary and a member of Focus's board of directors, and Richard Land, who serves as president of the SBC's Ethics and Religious Liberty Commission.[5] "It would not be going too far to say that Henry has been a mentor for nearly the entire SBC conservative movement. Indeed, he helped officiate at the installation of Richard Land at the Christian Life Commission, Albert Mohler as president of Southern Seminary, Timothy George as dean of the Beeson Divinity School, and Mark Coppenger as president of Midwestern Baptist Seminary in Kansas City," writes historian Barry Hankins.[6] Henry's defense of biblical inerrancy and his Reformed Baptist vision for shaping public life were two important elements in the conservative resurgence in the Southern Baptist Convention.

Carl Henry encouraged the evangelical movement to codify the Lordship of Christ as the only sure foundation for an evangelical public theology: "The extent to which man centers his life and energy in the redemptive King *now* determines the extent of the divine kingdom in the present age."[7] Henry's emphasis on the Kingdom of God here and now is an explicit critique of the premillennial dispensational specter that hovers over evangelicals with its seductive idea that the messianic kingdom is solely a future reality.

In addition to the themes of Christ's Lordship and the creation orders put forth by Henry, Dobson was further inspired by his apocalyptic imagination. Henry names our era as a late hour in the culture wars, coming at the twilight of America's Christian civilization when the barbarians are storming the gates. Pessimistic narratives of cultural decline, like those of Henry, Francis Schaeffer, and Chuck Colson, served as a wake-up call for Dobson and the pro-family movement in the 1970s.[8] One of the reasons that Focus has become such a vibrant network in the evangelical pro-family movement is because of the deep collective sense that something is wrong with American culture.

To generate concrete social change, Dobson also tapped into some of the deepest roots of his Nazarene heritage. Born in Shreveport, Louisiana, James Dobson is descended from three generations of Nazarene ministers with strong roots in the Deep South. Growing up as the son of a Nazarene preacher, Dobson was immersed in deep streams of Nazarene theology and piety. His Nazarene formation continued at Pasadena College, now Point Loma Nazarene College, where he roomed with his first cousin, H. B. London.

The Church of the Nazarene was founded by Phineas F. Bresee, an Iowan Methodist circuit rider, in 1895 in Los Angeles, California.[9] Its theology is based on the thought of John Wesley as embodied in the nineteenth-century Holiness movement. When Dobson moved to Southern California, he was getting close to the epicenter of the Nazarene Church, a region whose evangelicalism experienced a rapid southernization after 1940.[10] The southern stream of Wesleyan/Holiness theology runs deep in the river of Dobson's public theology.

John Wesley's theology was driven by a dialectic of discipline and ecstasy whose destination was social holiness. Wesley's rigorous holiness club, strict "methods" of church life, precise articles of faith, and meticulously edited collections of Christian classics expressed his understanding of discipline, while furious circuit rides, lusty hymn singing, lavish love feasts, comforting camp meetings, and passionate revivalist preaching expressed the ecstasy of Wesleyan religion. Full of energy and exuberance, Wesley's gospel ignited a wildfire on the nineteenth-century American frontier. Wesley's dialectical theology produced a dynamic evangelical movement that inspired and nurtured people into social holiness. From his *Dare to Discipline* to his passionate speeches at Vote Values rallies, Dobson embodies this Wesleyan dialectic of discipline and ecstasy. Earnest and emotional, Dobson embodies Focus's laser-like mission—compassionate care for and defiant defense of the family—with this Wesleyan dialectical fervor.

Three themes in Nazarene theology play an important role in Dobson's public theology: human responsibility, social holiness, and Jesus as healer. Dobson's politics are an expansion of Nazarene soteriology. Soteriology is the Christian doctrine of salvation. It seeks to answer the question "How is one saved?" While Calvinists argue that God chooses us through the doctrine of election, Wesleyan theology affirms that humans cooperate with God's Spirit in the process of salvation.

Since humans make a decision to follow God in the Nazarene theological vision, human responsibility is the first influential theme in Dobson's thought. The majority of the antebellum revivalists called people at the camp sites to actively choose personal faith. For example, Charles Finney used an "anxious bench" where people would sit under the conviction of sin until they were prepared to choose faith in Christ. In this tradition of Wesleyan/Holiness theology, an initial faith commitment must bear fruit in the social sphere. Whereas Finney expressed the social dimension of Wesleyan/Holiness faith in the abolition movement, Dobson expresses it in his leadership of the pro-family movement.

The doctrine of entire sanctification (holiness) provides the template for the public dimension of Christian faith in the Wesleyan/Holiness tradition. The Holiness doctrine is a Wesleyan conception of sanctification that describes how a Christian deepens his or her union with Christ and becomes more like Christ. Although holiness is often thought of in individualist terms, this has not always been the case historically.

Social holiness, the second Nazarene theme, emphasizes that the pursuit of personal holiness must make a concrete difference in the life of the community. From John Wesley's early concern for the poor to the present-day work of the Salvation Army in the slums of America, the Wesleyan/Holiness tradition has always had a robust social witness. Susie C. Stanley describes the expression of social Christianity that encompasses the social impulses of Wesley and his followers in the Wesleyan/Holiness movement as "social holiness."[11] The Nazarene doctrine of social holiness provides a fundamental theo-logic for Dobson's pro-family politics.

Phineas F. Bresee once said, "There is no holiness without social holiness."[12] Bresee's vision of social holiness was embodied in founding a Nazarene church that was a multiethnic, multiclass, and gender-inclusive transformational community located on skid row in downtown Los Angeles. All were seen as equal in the shadow of the cross. Some of Dobson's deepest roots lie within this prophetic Southern Californian Nazarene communitarian ethic, but he, like many within this denomination, has forgotten the radical egalitarian vision of the early Nazarenes, an echo of the egalitarian impulse embodied in the prophetic evangelical abolitionists, black and white, in antebellum America.

The Nazarene doctrine of social holiness in part drives Dobson to political action. Dobson writes, "I do believe that someday I'll kneel before the Lord, and I want to hear him say, 'Well done, good and faithful servant!'

What I do and how I live is important. In Matthew 7, Jesus said there will be those on [Judgment Day] who confess to him but whom he never knew. Why? Because they didn't do—D-O—the work of his father. It's an emphasis on attempting to walk the walk."[13] Human responsibility and social holiness converge in Dobson's social ethic in his view that the evangelical political struggle is an everlasting struggle. The logic of free will salvation means that Christians are free to join the fight for defending the family, but no one knows how this struggle will turn out in the end. This Nazarene soteriology means that everything—both our salvation and the "salvation" of America—is uncertain, so we need to fight long and hard to save ourselves and save America. Dobson is passionate about politics and the defense of the family because he sees the outcome as a matter of life and death, and believes the outcome is in human hands.

Jesus as healer is a third theme that emerges as important in Dobson's public theology. Wesleyan/Holiness circles are shaped by a fourfold pattern of Christology: Jesus is savior, baptizer, healer, and coming king. Aimee Semple McPherson, who founded the International Church of the Foursquare Gospel, captures these four roles of Jesus well: "Jesus saves us according to John 3:16. He baptizes us with the Holy Spirit according to Acts 2:4. He heals our bodies according to James 5:14–15. And Jesus is coming again to receive us to himself according to I Thessalonians 4:16–17."[14] This Wesleyan Christological template includes the classic trope "Lord and Savior" and also Jesus as "Baptizer and Healer." It is Christ as healer that ends up playing a strategic role in the Dobson corpus.

Dobson's public theology is a synthesis of his evangelical and Nazarene heritages. Christ as healer and Lord correlate with Focus's mission to nurture and defend the family. Jesus's healing ministry expresses his desire to nurture people into wholeness, and his Lordship is often associated with his victorious power over sin, death, and the devil. Christ's Lordship and healing ministry converge in Dobson's theology with the idea of the family as an order of creation.

The family is the unifying center of Dobson's theological vision. He writes: "The concepts of marriage and parenthood were not human inventions. God, in his infinite wisdom, created and ordained the family as the basic unit of procreation and companionship."[15] Dobson understands the family at its most foundational level to be a marital union between a man and woman for the purpose of companionship, having children, and providing stability for society.

In American politics, the family has become a critical site within a larger struggle that includes issues of abortion, infanticide, euthanasia, and stem cell research. For Dobson, publicly participating in the life of Christ entails preserving the family as the most fundamental order of creation and healing it when it is broken. As a child psychologist, Dobson has sought to bind the broken hearts of individuals and families. His understanding of the ideal state of the family is drawn from creation narratives in the book of Genesis. Throughout his ministry, Dobson has expressed a sensitive heart for the vulnerable, especially children, expressed in Focus's extensive counseling ministry. Personal and familial healing is the realm in which the restorative power of Jesus Christ is implemented.

In summary, Dobson's understanding of Jesus maintains the emphasis on the transcendent Lordship of Jesus Christ that is a common theological foundation in the Reformed, Wesleyan, and Baptist traditions. Christ's Lordship undergirds God's creation orders, such as the family. But because of sin, the family structure has been rapidly disintegrating, in Dobson's worldview. Signs of this disintegration include the rise of abortion in the 1970s, the broad dissemination of pornography in the 1980s and 1990s, and the normalization of the "gay lifestyle" in the early twenty-first century. In order to respond to the family's disintegration, Dobson invokes the narrative vision of Jesus as healer. This focus on Jesus Christ as healer taps into Dobson's Nazarene roots and offers the possibility of a more holistic vision of the Christian life.

Focus's participation in Jesus's ministry of healing is an embodiment of Carl Henry's prophetic call to "penetrate and persuade" society with the Gospel. As a child psychologist, Dobson's heart has been consistently attentive to healing children from broken families; healing families remains his ongoing pastoral passion. His focus on Christ as healer and Lord can be read in correlation with Focus's mission to nurture and defend the family. Christ as healer resonates with the desire to "nurture" the family, healing broken marriages and broken families. Christ as Lord resonates with the desire to "defend" the family. There is a symmetry between Dobson's Christology and Focus's vision statement: Dobson's view of Jesus Christ plays a formative role in shaping both the vision and mission of Focus on the Family. The narrative vision that shapes the Focus movement is one that emphasizes Christ's Lordship and healing.

Within this theology of the family, Dobson's Jesus plays both a nurturing and defensive role. In addition to being a personal savior, Jesus is a healer who helps to heal broken children and families. Dobson's affirmation of the Lordship of Christ resonates with Focus's mission to "defend the family." Dobson's understanding of Jesus as Lord is also reflected in his emphasis on Jesus's masculinity. Dobson argues that Jesus "went after the men. He was a man's man. He simply called them and said follow me and they came."[16] By viewing Jesus as a "man's man" he frames Jesus's ministry in the same way that he framed his own family ministry, which began as a ministry of men in 1976.

During a panel discussion on men's ministry in a 2004 radio broadcast, Dobson told the story about how God called him to start a family ministry focused on men:

> It goes all the way back to 1976 which was a year before Focus on the Family was started. I was getting hundreds, if not thousands of speaking requests, and I was running all over the country and I was praying. I was on the way to Children's Hospital one day in a little Volkswagen. And I was saying, "Lord, it doesn't really make any sense for me to say what I want to say to all these people who are coming to hear me. Why should I depend on my short-sighted view? Why don't you tell me what you want me to say?" So I am praying along that line and I said, "Just give me your message with regard to the family and the Gospel of Jesus Christ." And as clearly as the Lord is ever going to speak to me, not in audible words, but he said to me, "If this country is going to make it and if the family is going to survive, it will be because husbands and fathers begin to accept their responsibilities for leadership, and especially spiritual leadership in their own families and convey that message!" which is a centerpiece of the film series that I did two years later called "Focus on the Family," and it really was the start of this ministry. I know that women are extremely important to the family. No one can take anything away from the women, but they tend to be more motivated for the family. If you get the husband in-

volved, you get the whole family and if you lose the father and husband, then you lose a certain percentage of the kids as well.[17]

Dobson started his ministry with a divine call, the strongest and clearest of
his entire life; he was to focus his ministry on helping men be good husbands and fathers.

Beginning as a men's ministry, it framed itself against the women's
movement from its earliest days. Dobson proclaimed: "There is a femi-
nization of masculinity in the Western world at this time. Men do not
know what it means to be a man. What they thought it meant is now being
mocked and vilified on television, and men are the fools. The men in the
commercials are stupid guys doing adolescent, crazy things. I think men
get to church and they do not know who they are to be in Christ either."[18]
Dobson saw the feminist movement as a threat to society because of its
commitment to sexual freedom and to abortion. A deconstruction of male
identity was one of the consequences of the feminist movement. From its
earliest days, Focus on the Family was a defender of what Dobson calls
"biblical manhood."

The issue of abortion was also particularly important in Focus's political mobilization. Francis Schaeffer played a pivotal role in galvanizing
Dobson and other evangelicals.[19] In 1975 Schaeffer joined Billy Graham,
C. Everett Koop, and Harold O. J. Brown in forming the Christian Action
Council, an anti-abortion congressional lobbying group. The evangelical
pro-life movement began to show strength in the campaigns and out-
comes of the 1978 midterm elections.[20] In 1979, Schaeffer, his son Franky,
and Dr. C. Everett Koop, later surgeon general of the United States, produced *Whatever Happened to the Human Race?*, a film series devoted to
the complexities and challenges of the issue of abortion. The compelling,
cinematic narrative mode of the film series mobilized a new generation of
young evangelical activists. H. B. London, vice president of outreach to
churches at Focus, recounted: "While Carl Henry helped shape Dr. Dobson's theology, it was Francis Schaeffer who really captured our theological imagination on the issue of abortion. I will never forget the impact that
Schaeffer's film, *Whatever Happened to the Human Race?* had on us all. Its
images of babies floating in the waters of the Dead Sea were imprinted on
our imagination as we realized the horror of this sin."[21] Motivated to ac-

tion by Schaeffer's films and inspired by his *Christian Manifesto,* Dobson began a lifelong crusade to save as many children as he could, working to repeal *Roe v. Wade* and to reduce the number of abortions in the interim.[22]

Traditional interpretations of the Religious Right have emphasized that abortion was the central issue that galvanized the movement, but Randall Balmer argues that the true origins of the Religious Right are more complex and include the component of white racism as represented, for example, in the segregationist admissions policies and ban on interracial dating at Bob Jones University, a fundamentalist evangelical college in Greenville, South Carolina.[23] The Internal Revenue Service, seeking to enforce the Civil Rights Act of 1964, investigated the university because of its racially discriminatory policies. On June 30, 1971, the United States District Court ruled in *Green v. Connally* that a segregationist institution could not be considered a charitable organization and be granted a tax-exempt status. In 1975 the Internal Revenue Service attempted to take away Bob Jones University's tax-exempt status, as the institution would not allow interracial dating.

When Bob Jones University filed suit to keep its tax-exempt status, conservative evangelicals from around the country came to its defense. Their stated concern was that the federal government should not dictate how their religious organizations should be run, setting aside the subterranean dynamic of white racism and the fear of miscegenation, which was the central issue in this case.

When Bob Jones University began to admit African American students in 1971, it accepted only applicants who were married. Since its founding in 1926, Bob Jones University has been dominated by a segregationist evangelical theology, exposing the strength and depth of segregationist thought in southern evangelicalism. Its ban on interracial dating illustrates the institutionalization and normativity of whiteness in the evangelical educational subculture. As evangelicals affirmed white skin power and privilege through this segregationist dating policy, they unmistakably denied African Americans a sense of human dignity, trampling on their constitutional freedoms and rights.

By pointing to the segregationist policies of Bob Jones University, Balmer highlights the constitutive role that the politics of race played in the origins and rise of the Religious Right. The pro-family movement is

not solely a reaction to the sexual revolution of the 1960s; it is also a reaction to the civil rights struggle in the 1950s and 1960s. In fact, during the
civil rights movement, in many pockets of white evangelicalism, there was
a deep resistance to integrationist policies. Although the Religious Right
in the 1970s focused primarily on issues of sexuality, in the context of
American history sexuality must be considered in light the problem of
race.

Interracial sex was the last taboo for many in the white Religious Right.
The underlying reason that Bob Jones University did not want to admit
African Americans and banned interracial dating is because they did not
want blacks and whites to socialize, have sexual relations, get married, and
have children. This incident demonstrates the stubborn legacy of segregationist thought in the southern evangelical imagination. The white citizens of Greenville County refused to celebrate Martin Luther King Jr. Day
until 2004. The Bob Jones affair demonstrates how difficult it was for
many southern evangelicals to dislodge their Christian theology from an
ideology of white supremacy. The evangelical pro-family movement was
"racialized" into religious thought patterns and institutional structures
that separate the "life experiences, life opportunities, and social relationships" of blacks and whites.[24] As the movement grew in the 1980s, these
racial practices became more covert, often invisible, through the daily op-
erations of white evangelical institutions.[25]

As white racism hovered over the movement as a specter of the tragedy
of American history, Dobson saw that abortion was the headline issue that
was quickly gaining political traction. Dobson was irate when legislation
passed allowing young women to have an abortion without parental
notification. He attributed the push to increase access to abortion to radical feminists. Radical feminism worked against his pro-life convictions as
well as against his concept of biblical manhood. Different understandings
of gender became one of the underlining fault lines, alongside race and nationalism, that galvanized the culture wars of the 1980s.

Since its inception, Focus provided resources for churches and families
to help strengthen and preserve the family, but it became increasingly apparent to Dobson that Focus would also need to defend the family against
societal institutions that were actively working against it. Dale Buss writes,
"As the enemies of everything that he held dear became more powerful—

the abortion industry, the homosexual lobby, radical feminists, the main-stream news and entertainment media, and sundry other secularists—Dobson was hounded by the conviction that maybe it wasn't enough for him to help shore up the family one household at a time. He wondered if his voice could also have some influence in the arena of politics and policy, where he believed antifamily forces had become increasingly en-trenched."[26] Dobson decided to use the extensive international network that he had developed through his family ministry as a platform for his po-litical advocacy.

In addition to opposing the civil rights movement and the gay rights movement, Dobson and the pro-family movement remained concerned about the encroaching powers of the federal government. Mark Noll writes, "National attention to race and civil rights was the doorway through which evangelicals marched in their determination to rescue the nation from the gay rights movement and other movements they believed were leading to the destruction of the traditional family."[27] This fear of government intervention echoed the fear of federal enforcement of civil rights legislation among many southern evangelicals in the 1960s and 1970s, where white racism continued to be a strong factor. Racist impulses can be clearly illustrated in the career paths of such evangelical leaders as Jerry Falwell and political leaders like Jesse Helms, but they are much more difficult to detect in James Dobson and Focus on the Family. Many Focus employees see the Bob Jones University case as a sincere and princi-pled stance in defense of religious liberty against government interference, yet they do not acknowledge the problem of educational inequities among races given the legacy of segregation.

Focus approaches the problem of racism as it does all issues—through the rubric of the family. Daniel Patrick Moynihan's report, "The Negro Family: The Case for National Action," still factors in contemporary dis-cussions at Focus about the black family. As an undersecretary of labor in the Johnson administration when the Great Society programs were initi-ated, Moynihan argued that the heart of the deterioration of the fabric of Negro society is the deterioration of the African American family. While Focus sees the problems in the black family, its primary strategy for ad-dressing it is through outreach to the black community with print materi-als containing practical advice on parenting; however, it shies away from endorsing policies that would benefit the African American community: for example, affirmative action, a higher minimum wage, federal day care programs, better prescription drug benefits, and strengthened inner-city schools. Focus's model of ministry to the African American family continues to be an interpersonal model, one less interested in addressing structural issues and policy formation that would directly affect the African American community.

Focus's deployment of the civil rights discourse also works against its aspirations to reach out to the African American families. Rhetorically, Focus on the Family treats abortion as a new civil rights movement and compares the pro-life cause to the abolitionist and civil rights movements. The logic of this linkage is that the movement for black civil rights was positive and just and should now be applied to the protection of the lives of unborn children. Simultaneously, the pro-family movement vehemently opposes as illegitimate civil rights for gays. Within the pro-family movement, the civil rights legacy has come down to a debate between the value of the lives of the unborn and the rights of gays. But what about African Americans, for whom the civil rights movement was historically intended? The contemporary conservative attitude toward the civil rights movement is that it succeeded and therefore there is no need to continually stir up race-based grievances. We have achieved racial equality, and it is now time to move on to more pressing social issues like abortion and gay marriage.

The contemporary debate on race comes down to how we understand the origin, nature, and extent of the problem of racism. Many in the pro-family movement see racism as personal prejudice, but racism is, in reality, institutionalized white supremacy. From this perspective, we must consider the mission, personnel, policies, and practices of the institutions in this country, including Focus on the Family, in order to fully understand their view of racism and practices of racial justice. Focus's rise to political power was due to its work on family issues; however, it was able to capitalize on the political clout of the Religious Right, a coalition propelled in part by racist energies.

Dobson's ascent to political power can be charted from its very beginning in 1980 through his service to four of the last five U.S. presidents, but his intentional engagement on the issue of racial justice emerged through his work with black evangelicals, including Bishop Harry Jackson, the senior pastor of Hope Christian Church in Bowie, Maryland, in the 2004 and 2006 campaigns. President Jimmy Carter appointed Dobson to a select, small task force to summarize the findings of the White House Conference on the Family. Edwin Meese, President Ronald Reagan's attorney general, appointed Dobson to an eleven-member commission on pornography in April 1985. The commission studied the effects of hard-core pornography on the family in the United States, including the criminal links to the industry. In addition to giving Dobson free access to the Reagan White House, membership on this commission also gave him the opportunity to meet with Ted Bundy on death row before his execution. When Bundy confessed to Dobson that pornography had contributed to the rapes and the murders he had committed, Dobson experienced another dramatic turning point in his desire to see Focus become more influential in the public square.

During the Reagan years, Dobson became close friends with Gary Bauer. Bauer had authored an important report on the family for President Reagan, arguing for the necessity of an intact, two-parent family for a child's well-being. As a result of their common work advocating for the family, Bauer began to appear as a regular guest on Dobson's radio show. Toward the end of the Reagan administration, Dobson asked Bauer to lead the Family Research Council in Washington for the purpose of defending the family.

It was the issue of gay marriage that drove Dobson into a high-profile role in politics in the 1990s. Dobson and his political allies were disappointed in Clinton's positions on matters of the family, gay rights, and abortion. On February 7, 1998, Dobson delivered a passionate keynote address to the Council for National Policy in Phoenix, Arizona. The Council for National Policy was a group of Republican Party insiders that Dobson had joined in its infancy. This night, Dobson was indignant. With all eyes and ears hanging on his every word, Dobson came out breathing fire like a prophet emerging from a long sojourn in the wilderness. He lambasted the Republican Party and the Council for National Policy for not having the courage to stand up for the pro-family agenda. Dobson provocatively asked: "Does the Republican Party want our votes—no strings attached—to court us every two years, and then to say, 'Don't call me. I'll call you'? And not to care about the moral law of the universe? Is that what they want? Is that what the plan is? Is that the way the system works? And if so, is it going to stay that way? Is this the way it's going to be? If it is, I'm gone, and if I go—I'm not trying to threaten anybody because I don't influence the world—but if I go, I will do everything I can to take as many people with me as possible."[28] In this speech, Dobson laid down an ultimatum: he had had enough, and if the Republicans could not do a better job, he was ready to walk and take a major Republican constituency with him.

With the election of George W. Bush, Dobson thought the pro-family movement had found a brother in Christ in the White House, someone who would help transform American political culture. As Al Gore, Bush's opponent, struggled to emerge as a strong voice from lingering questions about the Clinton White House, President Bush's message was simple and strong: strengthen the military, cut taxes, and restore dignity to the White House. Bush's "compassionate conservatism" became an important part of his strategy to restore dignity to the White House. In Bush's inaugural address he lifted up the parable of the Good Samaritan, committing himself and the U.S. government to helping the poor and the suffering: "America, at its best, is compassionate. In the quiet of the American conscience, we know that deep, persistent poverty is unworthy of our nation's promise. And whatever our views of its cause, we can agree that children at risk are not at fault. Abandonment and abuse are not acts of God, they are failures of love. . . . And some needs and hurts are so deep they will only respond to a mentor's touch or a pastor's prayer. Church and charity, synagogue and mosque lend our communities their humanity, and they will have an honored place in our plans and in our laws. . . . I can pledge our nation to a goal: When we see that wounded traveler on the road to Jericho, we will not pass to the other side."[29] Within a week the Bush administration had a faith-based initiative office up and running. Bush's faith-based initiative helped him show a humanitarian side to mainstream America while shoring up his American evangelical base. Evangelicals hoped that Bush would appoint conservative judges and join their struggle to end abortion and prevent gay marriage.[30]

Dobson became increasingly concerned with "judicial tyranny." In Montgomery, Alabama, site of the bus boycott that started the civil rights movement, another national debate was taking place. Judge Roy Moore, elected chief justice in Alabama in 2000, had commissioned a monument called "the Ten Commandments." In 2003 a federal judge decided to move the monument from the public view. In August 2003, Dobson accepted an invitation to deliver a keynote address in front of the state courthouse in downtown Montgomery. Describing the event, Dobson said:

> When I saw what that [federal] judge was trying to do despite the will of the people of Alabama and I participated in that rally, that's where my determination to try to make a difference in the 2004 election originated. . . . I saw the excitement of the people. I saw how they longed for a voice and how frustrated they were by having their views overridden by leftist judges and by the inability of the Congress to get anything done to protect their values. It was an exhilarating experience. While we were still in Montgomery, I said [to aides] that I have tried to remain out of the political arena for twenty-six years, because I didn't want to drag Focus into the mucky-muck of presidential elections and all that that means. I had never endorsed a presidential candidate in my life. But in Montgomery, I said that's got to change. For the first time, I felt an obligation to do what I could through direct involvement in an election. I didn't know what influence I could have, but I was going to use whatever God had given me, because I simply couldn't sit this one out.[31]

Dobson made a declaration in Montgomery. He was taking the next presidential election personally. He was willing to do whatever it took, including retiring as the president of Focus on the Family, in order to devote his time and energy fully to the reelection campaign of President George W. Bush.

Dobson's new focus on the 2004 election was in part inspired by a meeting of Religious Right leaders in Arlington, Virginia, in June 2003, including Paul Weyrich and Don Wildmon.[32] The issue that rallied all these leaders was the idea of working for an amendment to the U.S. Constitution that would ban same-sex marriage. Matt Daniels of Alliance for Marriage had begun discussions for a federal marriage amendment in 2001.

In April 2004, Dobson formed Focus on the Family Action, a tax-distinct organization from Focus on the Family, which would provide a platform for informing and inspiring American citizens who care about the family to get more deeply involved in political action. It was a pivotal year. In May 2004, Dobson called the first day of the issuance of licenses for same-sex couples to marry in Massachusetts a "dark day" that would be remembered unfondly by many.

Gay marriage would become a critical issue in the public debate during the 2004 election cycle. Focus worked with Rod Parsley, a white evangelical pastor, and Ken Blackwell, the African American secretary of state for Ohio, to help get out the evangelical vote in Ohio, a swing state that, along with Florida, became decisive in President George W. Bush's 2004 victory. Gay marriage became such a focal and motivating issue for Dobson and Focus because it, even more than abortion, was considered a threat to the structure of the traditional family. Four "talking points" written by Glenn T. Stanton, senior analyst for marriage and sexuality at Focus on the Family, provide a telling glimpse into Dobson's and Focus on the Family's views about how gay marriage will upset God's creation order:

1. Same-sex families *always* deny children either their mother or father.
2. Same-sex family is a vast, untested social experiment with children.
3. Where does it stop? How do we say "no" to group marriage?
4. Schools will be forced to teach that the homosexual family is normal; Churches will be legally pressured to perform same-sex ceremonies.[33]

These four points illustrate the overarching concern of Dobson and Focus—that if gay marriage is allowed, there will be no end to the ways in which the traditional family can be attacked. Focus, through its materials, declared that homosexuality is not an intended part of God's created order and that homosexuals are not born inherently gay. The organization was quick to point to hundreds of cases of "cured" homosexuals, people who had left their homosexual lifestyle because they recognized that homosexuality is against God's creation. The organization maintains some of these former gays and lesbians on its staff, living embodiments of the organization's successful efforts.

In July 2004, in part a response to the issue of gay marriage, Focus launched an extensive voter registration drive by activating ivotevalues .org, with the goal of registering one million voters for the 2004 election. Focus conducted this campaign in coordination with Richard Land and the Southern Baptist Convention. Southern Baptist minister Kenyn Cureton, pastor of First Baptist Church in Lebanon, Tennessee, worked with Richard Land in creating the 2004 iVoteValues.com Voter Resource Guide. This guide was adapted and distributed by Focus on the Family. Cureton had good instincts and keen insight into how to motivate and mobilize evangelical pastors around the pro-family agenda. Tony Perkins rewarded Cureton's grassroots efforts by appointing him as vice president of church ministries for the Family Research Council. Cureton has played a vital role in a broader FRC strategy to reach out to pastors more actively, encouraging them to join the evangelical pro-family movement.

Focus had always had strong ties to the SBC. Together these two evangelical networks simultaneously represented a southernization of American politics. Focus's ties to the SBC continued in August 2005, as Dobson appointed the Southern Baptist Theological Seminary president Dr. Albert Mohler as a member of the Focus board of directors. In October 2004, Dobson and other Focus on the Family executives joined other Christian leaders in signing a public letter urging Christians to vote their values in the 2004 election. Throughout October and November, Dobson called on "pro-Family America" to go to the polls in the 2004 presidential election.

Since the Reagan years, evangelicals had often voted Republican in large numbers. But between 2000 and 2004 the estimated number of evangelicals voting for Bush witnessed a significant increase. A Pew Research Center study estimates that while 68 percent of evangelical voters in 2000 cast their vote for Bush, this number jumped to 78 percent in 2004.[34] Dobson's work in mobilizing voters in 2004 did help direct the outcome.

In exit polls after the 2004 election, the majority of voters (22 percent) chose "moral values" as the most important issue that influenced their vote. Of the people who chose moral values, 80 percent voted for Bush. The Vote Values campaign showed an unprecedented form of political coordination between Focus on the Family, the Southern Baptist Convention, and other conservative evangelical organizations. After Bush's victory, Dobson provided a theological explanation: "I think God has honored Bush. The president did acknowledge Jesus Christ."[35] Bush's victory for a second term was celebrated by many conservative evangelicals as a divine blessing.

Dobson often used the ultimatum in his speeches and letters as a strong-arm tactic to influence Republican Party politics. This was illustrated in Dobson's 1998 Council for National Policy speech and again in his 2003 speech defending the "Ten Commandments judge" in Montgomery, Alabama. In this way, Dobson was using tactics deployed by Billy Graham in the 1950s. During the crusade in Jackson, Mississippi, in 1952, Graham warned that the winning party in the 1952 election must "clean up the country" by 1956 or Graham would lead the sixteen million voters he influenced to the other party.[36] Ultimatums and power politics are nothing new to American evangelicals.

With his Nazarene roots, Dobson's politics are animated by a social holiness impulse to engage society, but he has a more conservative agenda, less concerned with transformation than preservation, less concerned with feminist empowerment than patriarchal politics. Dobson wants men to fight, fight for their women, fight for their children, and fight for their families. Dobson is a representative of a revivalist form of patriarchal politics. He works out of a tradition of American nationalist revivalism embodied in the evangelist Billy Sunday with an emphasis on piety, patriotism, and manliness. White male identity has been the currency of American identity. After World War II, white male identity was coupled with American nationalism. Thus, patriarchy, racism, revivalism, and patriotism produced a unified capitalist citizenry. Outsiders—be they communists, blacks, gays, or Islamofascists—are all seen as threats to the social stability that the white male-led family provides.[37]

In Dobson's apocalyptic imagination, the male-led nuclear family became a battleground in secular modernity's attack on traditional values. Dobson records a gradual decline of moral values in the United States since the 1960s and asserts that Christians must respond through political engagement. Among the younger evangelicals, there is a higher degree of tolerance for sexual immorality, an attitude attributable to moral decline and the breakdown of the traditional family, according to Dobson.

In the 1970s, as women became more educated and entered the workforce in larger numbers, liberated women became a threat to the traditional family. James Davison Hunter sees the new woman of contemporary feminism as an expression of hyperindividuation: "The *individual* woman (her rights, her needs, her occupational and political interests) is now emphasized over against every social context in which she finds herself. In the context of the family, her identity and rights are redefined independently of her spouse's authority (previously absolute); her identity and rights are defined independently of the culturally defined needs of her children (previously all-encompassing). This can even extend to a priority of her independence over that of a fetus/unborn child—in this case, a right to control her body."[38] In order to deal with these independent women and their abortions, Dobson reinscribes the nineteenth-century construct of the Victorian family.

The family that Dobson is defending is the bourgeois family of the nineteenth century. As industrial economies began to replace agrarian economics, the home became a new refuge. We see the rise of a "cult of domesticity," where women nurtured their men and children in the warm world of the family as an antidote to the cold world of the factory.[39] In this nineteenth-century construct, the true woman is marked by four virtues: piety, purity, submission to men, and domesticity.[40] "In the nineteenth-century Anglo-American culture, the home was a sacred place. Outside the home, individuals were exposed to sinfulness and temptations of many kinds, but home life was, in theory, safe, morally pure, and affectionate. . . . More important than the heavens and earth, the family was God's primary method of spreading his influence over humanity. The family was the central institution from which all other human institutions originated."[41]

The family structure in the antebellum and postbellum South helps to illustrate why Dobson's family message and political vision resonated so deeply in Middle America. In the typical model of the family in the American South in the nineteenth and early twentieth centuries, the man was the head of the white family. He worked in farm or factory while his wife cooked and raised the children in her sphere, the home.

Dobson's patriarchal family model is intelligible in the context of this southern religious history. Men are in charge and women submit because this is the way God ordered the family in creation. In this traditional marriage, the men and women have different emotional needs and different gender roles. Dobson writes, "men derive self-esteem by being respected: women feel worthy when they are *loved*. This may be the most important personality distinction between the sexes."[42]

The male is the decision maker and the primary disciplinarian in the home. A man is "the ultimate decision maker" in his family.[43] Through his decisions he controls the family's business. By "daring to discipline" he has a small forum for strict moral discipline, including corporal punishment, seen as vital for child rearing.[44] For example, Dobson indicates that spankings should be "administered with a neutral object" like a "switch or belt."[45] Spanking children at a young age cultivates a religiously approved pattern of violence for both parent and child. If you spare the rod, you will spoil the child. Dobson argues that it is only through physical punishment that strong-willed children can be tamed. Strong authoritarian parenting styles that use corporal punishment lie deep in the fabric of evangelical family practice today.

Dobson's construct of masculinity emphasizes men as warriors who conquer their women and the land they decide to cultivate. Men need to conquer women through courtship, have regular sex in marriage, and require constant respect from their women. Dobson writes, "Masculine self-esteem is more motivated by a desire to 'conquer' a woman than in becoming the object of her romantic love."[46] "A man derives his sense of worth primarily from the reputation he earns in his job or profession. He draws emotional satisfaction from achieving in business, becoming financially independent, developing a highly respected craft or skill, supervising others, becoming 'boss,' or by being loved and appreciated by his patients, clients, or fellow businessmen. The man who is successful in these areas does not depend on his wife as his *primary* shield against feelings of inferiority."[47] According to Dobson, men have a stronger need for sex; women's sexual needs are "less urgent and pressing."[48]

In Dobson's model, the wife is to be a "helpmate" to the husband. She should put her husband and children ahead of her own educational and career goals. Women are more "complex and vulnerable" than men and long for "stability, security, and enduring human relationships."[49] Women are more "emotionally invested" in the home and care more than their husbands about "the minor details of the house, family function, and such concerns."[50] This division of labor is beneficial for both men and women, according to Dobson.[51]

Many women buy Dr. Dobson's books and listen to his radio program so they can learn how to be good wives and mothers. Men are given purpose through offering strong leadership in the family. Dobson writes, "If

American families are to survive the incredible stress and dangers they now face, it will be because husbands and fathers provide loving leadership in their homes, placing their wives and children at the highest level on their systems of priorities."[52] Mothers also play a vital role in family and social formation, shaping what happens in the family, educating children, and preventing their men from going astray.[53]

For many evangelicals, Dobson's appeals to the traditional family resonate. Some, like W. Bradford Wilcox, have argued that many people do desire such traditional families, and his recent work argues that women are in fact happiest when they exist in what he calls neotraditional marriages, where women are freed from not having to work in the paid labor force.[54] Christian Smith's extensive survey of evangelicals across the country finds that although most evangelicals do not believe in male authority and headship in all cases, most do believe in ideas of male headship and equality in the family; as a result, he argues that most would be able to affirm a message from the Southern Baptist Convention that claims wives should submit to husbands and husbands should provide for their families.[55] The research of Wilcox and Smith demonstrates that Dobson's vision of the family rings true to many evangelicals.

Dobson is effective as an evangelical political leader because of his credibility in child psychology, his family focus, and the great trust that many Americans have placed in him. Since Dobson is not a minister but a psychologist, he has gained respect and recognition both within and without the evangelical world. A poll of Protestant pastors conducted by Barna found that Dobson was considered "the most trusted spokesperson for Christianity" by 20 percent of pastors, ranking behind only Billy Graham. Further, this support came from mainline and evangelical pastors, such that when mainline pastors were analyzed separately, Dobson was third on the trust list.[56] Finally, his family focus brings an authentic face and strong brand image to U.S. politics. The family is a "symbol of social stability and traditional moral virtue"; for the Religious Right, the family is its "cause célèbre."[57] In both mainstream and evangelical circles, James Dobson is the embodiment of the family man.

James Dobson is a popular but subtle public theologian. Dobson is a different kind of evangelical. Interdisciplinary and innovative in his approach, Dobson has crafted a political strategy that is more sophisticated than that of Jerry Falwell or Pat Robertson. From the beginning Dobson's family ministry has been based on a synthesis of theology and psychology. Joel Carpenter writes, "Much of fundamentalists' driving force came from their belief that their movement had been raised up by God to preserve the evangelical foundations of American civilization."[58] The politics of Dobson and Focus on the Family are driven by their belief in Jesus as Lord and the preservation of the family as the chief world evangelistic strategy.

Its focus on family matters to the exclusion of other societal ills raises important questions about the way Focus deals with the problem of racism. Although Focus draws a lot of attention to the issue of abortion at the level of political advocacy, it has not done as much as it could to address the problem of unwed mothers in minority communities. The most common reference to the civil rights movement in Focus on the Family discourse is referring to the struggle against abortion as the new civil rights movement of our day. The struggle to preserve unborn children is different from advocating against more than two hundred years of slavery and one hundred years of segregation.

Abolitionist William Wilberforce (1759–1833) is a prophetic evangelical who influenced Dobson's narrative vision. Wilberforce was a British parliamentarian who struggled for the abolition of slavery in England for twenty years. Dobson appreciated Wilberforce's commitment to securing the freedom of African slaves in England. He believed the abolition of slavery was both a victory for the individual dignity of all people and a victory for the family. Wilberforce's status as an icon in Focus's lineage is notable: Focus appropriates the abolitionist struggle in its struggle against abortion. For example, Tom Minnery appeals to American abolitionist Theodore Weld's crusade against slavery. When Minnery lists six lessons learned from the abolitionist movement, however, he applies them immediately to the pro-life struggle. By doing this, the injustice frame that says "slavery is wrong and the slaveholder is the enemy" is transvaluated to become "abortion is wrong and the woman who commits it, the doctor who performs it, the judges who uphold it and the activists who work to uphold *Roe v. Wade* are the enemy." In contrast, prophetic evangelicals like Jim Wallis and John Perkins would see the ongoing struggle for civil rights and racial justice as being the direct successor of the abolitionist movement.

Focus was founded in 1977, after the era of active civil rights protest. Although it was founded at the height of the white evangelical modernity in America, its family-centered message resonated with communities of color. Tom Minnery writes, "We are constantly surprised at the number of African Americans in our radio audience, which exceeds their percentage of the overall population. Our radio programs seem very relevant to black families, since the principles we teach come from the ancient and enduring wisdom of the Bible. We have an extensive Hispanic outreach, both in the United States and throughout Central and South America. Our *Enfoque a la Familia* office in Costa Rica has seventy employees. Our Spanish-language programs are recorded there and they air on Hispanic stations throughout the United States, Central and South America. We strive to better the lives of ethnic minority families by our radio and print advice. That is more central to our mission than merely addressing 'racism.' We are constantly surprised at how relevant our advice is across cultures, by the growth of our radio and print outreach. Our advice now circulates in thirty-three languages around the world, with thirteen regional offices worldwide. Every day, some 200 million people hear Dr. Dobson's advice in some format around the world."[59]

The problem is not with the political application of Dobson's family model, but with the model itself. James Davison Hunter writes, "The Evangelical family specialists (including many ministers) advocated and defended a model of the family that is said to be traditional but in fact has no real historical precedent (in Christendom or anywhere else) in the name of a constituency that has largely abandoned it in favor of an androgynous/quasi-androgynous mode."[60] The message of a male-led family goes over well with Dobson's audience across racial lines. Within American evangelicalism there is a strong emphasis in many conservative churches on the importance of male leadership in the family and church. When viewed through the historic lens of antebellum revivalism, Dobson's defense of the traditional family in the context of the culture wars has historical resonance with the southerner's defense of the "social order" before and after the Civil War. The links between male-led families and churches have become more apparent as Dobson has enacted a patriarchal politics in American public life. But the particular construction of the

Judeo-Christian social order that he is defending, while including families and churches, is not fully responsive to the history and current needs of people of color.

Focus's family message successfully reaches communities of color, but it does not deal with structural poverty and institutional racism. Even though they profess concern for all families, Focus on the Family's programs address issues that primarily concern middle-class white families. Historically, the issues affecting the black family are largely ignored—starting with the impact of racism, lower unemployment rates among black men, and increasing single parenthood in minority families—in Focus's programming and publications.

Beginning in 2004 and again in 2006, Focus began to turn its attention to the African American community with a laser-like focus. As it prepared to defend marriage amendments around the country it knew that it needed substantial support from the black evangelical community. To this end, on May 30–June 1, 2006, Dobson assembled a panel of black evangelical pastors on his daily radio broadcast to discuss the state of marriage, which he perceived as under attack in the world and especially in the United States and in the African American community. Dobson wanted to project a consensus in the black evangelical community on the importance of a marriage protection amendment to the United States Constitution to define marriage as a union of one man and one woman. Dr. Ken Hutcherson, Bishop Phillip Porter, Bishop Larry Brandon, and Bishop Harry Jackson participated in this broadcast and continue to exercise leadership in the Religious Right movement. Ironically, Dobson and the pro-family movement lost the fight for a federal marriage amendment but through their new black evangelical friends gained a new appreciation for the vital importance of engaging issues of racial and economic justice. Black evangelicals are redirecting the Religious Right agenda.

Bishop Harry Jackson, in particular, is a symbol of the ways in which black evangelicalism is reconstructing evangelical politics from the outside in. In addition to pastoring Hope Christian Church in the greater Washington, DC, area, Jackson also serves as the founder and chairman of the High Impact Leadership Coalition and has been the regional bishop of the Fellowship of International Churches since 1999. Since Jackson met Dobson and Tony Perkins through the struggle for a marriage amendment, he has challenged them to take on other issues, such as racism, poverty, and the environment. Jackson is a regular guest on Dr. Dobson's radio show and serves on Tony Perkins's Pastor's Council, advising the Family Research Council on its strategies in policy advocacy and church outreach.

In a recent manifesto for the Religious Right, *Personal Faith and Public Policy,* Bishop Jackson and Tony Perkins argue that in order for the Religious Right to continue to gain political influence it must supplement its core values while holding firm to those that have defined the movement (the sanctity of human life, preservation of marriage, and the defense of our Christian faith) through reshaping its "message and agenda to include other important issues that face our generation—issues like immigration, poverty, the environment, and racial reconciliation."[61] These social issues are new to James Dobson and Tony Perkins but are daily realities for Harry Jackson, a black evangelical who has written on these topics throughout his life.[62] While Dobson and Perkins see Harry Jackson as a symbol of their commitment to racial reconciliation, Jackson brings a whole different set of issues and questions for the pro-family movement to engage if it is serious about Jesus's kingdom, God's reign of love and justice that should be present in all aspects of life.

Jackson has pushed Focus and FRC to embrace a broader social agenda. As a black evangelical, Jackson sees that concerns about the family, society, and the environment need to be tackled together as part of the one mission of God. On the issue of the environment, Jackson persuaded Tony Perkins and Family Research to begin to consider environmental sustainability as an important part of the pro-family policy agenda. Jackson overcame some of his own doubts and questions about what he originally saw as an "environmental hoax" through participating in a scientist-evangelical expedition in Alaska in August 2007, led by a minister and a medical doctor: Rev. Richard Cizik, vice president of the National Association of Evangelicals (NAE), and Dr. Eric Chivian, director of the Center for Health and the Global Environment at Harvard Medical School.

The scientists and evangelicals had an immediate experience of environmental upheaval when they visited Shishmaref, a traditional Inupiat Eskimo village with six hundred inhabitants located on an island in the Bering Strait. Global warming, rising sea level, storm damage, erosion, and melting permafrost are causing the Inupiats' island to disappear into the sea. Throughout the journey, Bishop Jackson joined the other evangelical leaders in posing his questions on climate change and the Alaskan environment to the trip's resident scientists: Eric Chivian, James McCarthy, Camille Parmesan, Peter Raven, and Carl Safina. Gradually, through the course of the expedition, Bishop Jackson became increasingly convinced of the gravity of the problem and the need to get the evangelical church more involved in creation care. As a result of his environmental conversion, Jackson persuaded Tony Perkins that they should coauthor a chapter on the environment in their Religious Right manifesto, informed by the expedition.[63] Jackson and Perkins are now more amenable to the cause of evangelical creation care. Although they may disagree with evangelical environmental activists like Jim Ball and Richard Cizik about the causes and extent of global warming, they now affirm the importance of environmental activism as part of the political mission of the Religious Right. Even the Religious Right is part of an evangelical spring, a new ecological consciousness that is rapidly growing throughout the evangelical world.

On the issue of racism, Jackson has helped Dobson and Perkins engage a specter that has haunted the Religious Right since its constitution in 1980. Jackson and Perkins begin with a confession of evangelicalism's failure: "As compelling as we may find this language now, on the whole, evangelicals failed to support blacks in their struggle for civil rights. This lack of support put a wedge between the strongest branches of the Christian movement. In retrospect we can see that God used the civil rights movement to free many blacks from second-class citizen status."[64] Confessing that evangelicals, by and large, failed to support African Americans in the civil rights movement is the beginning of a process of redirecting the warrior politics of the Religious Right toward the prophetic politics of a prophetic evangelicalism with roots in slave religion, the abolition struggle, and contemporary struggles for social justice.

Jackson's vision for racial justice is a conscious recovery of Martin Luther King Jr.'s vision of beloved community, especially focused on its spiritual underpinnings, a mystical, nonviolent commitment to reconciliation and racial justice. Harry Jackson writes: "The civil rights movement was, from the very beginning, a spiritual movement. It started with a prophetic mantle . . . , [as well as a] community activism mantle, and a political engagement mantle. Those are three separate things. The initial influence that mobilized the black church was a spiritual movement of justice that grew out of King's prophetic vision. It was a movement ordained by God, calling His people to live out the true meaning of justice. The civil rights movement took off at that time, not because of the powerful personalities involved, but because this was the issue on God's heart."[65] Jackson argues that the white evangelical church has emphasized personal righteousness while black Christianity has emphasized social justice. When these two streams of Christianity converge, Jackson thinks we will see the holy materialization of the Gospel in black and white. Through renewing the spirituality of the civil rights movement, Jackson hopes to rekindle the spirituality of the black and progressive church and inspire evangelicals to a more deliberate ethic of racial justice and reconciliation.

While the Religious Right is waking up to the problem of racism, because of the individualism behind its theology it still considers the problem to be primarily one of interpersonal reconciliation. Referring to a book titled *The Biblical Illustrator*, Jackson and Perkins identify three key prerequisites as essential to healing the nation's racial divide: "1. True freedom comes from God. 2. Equality among believers comes from Jesus Christ. 3. True brotherhood is achieved only in Jesus Christ."[66] Following the theological logic of freedom in Galatians 3—that before Christ our gender, race, and economic status does not matter—Jackson and Perkins argue that it is only through faith in Jesus Christ that "true brotherhood" is achieved. In their view, this brotherhood is something that only Christians can share and primarily an attempt to achieve "racial harmony" among individuals. Is the "brotherhood" they hope for the same that King envisioned in his "I have a dream" speech when he said, "One day . . . the sons of former slaves and the sons of former slave owners will be able to sit down together at the table of brotherhood"?

In contrast to King's dream, which demanded the systematic changes of institutions, including governmental policy, Jackson and Perkins dream of "racial harmony" primarily through personal achievement and the charitable actions of individuals and churches. Jackson and Perkins argue that churches "can be the place where the divided can be unified to advance our mutual cause as a nation. Imagine our combined efforts creating millions of dollars of assets; transferring thousands of ethnic prisoners back into society as healthy contributors to their community; saving thousands from contracting AIDS, cancer, heart disease, or diabetes; and seeing thousands being born again in the process."[67] Churches are called to charitable giving and outreach to prisoners and the sick as part of the process of evangelization. With its singular focus on evangelization, Harry Jackson's and Tony Perkins's form of evangelical politics continues along in the broad contours of the neo-evangelical public theology of Billy Graham and Carl Henry. In contrast, evangelicals who work more explicitly in the tradition of Martin Luther King Jr. call for systemic changes—John Perkins calling for "redistribution" of resources and Jim Wallis calling for racial restitution and reparations.[68] In order to interrogate the modern racial logic of the evangelical pro-family movement in America, we must take a more honest look at white racism's legacy, the institutions that gave it birth, and the Christology that undergirded it.

Bishop Jackson is helping the evangelical pro-family movement to engage its racism through gradually transforming its understanding of Jesus and justice. Jackson and Perkins write, "Jesus was quite clear in His declaration in Matthew 25:42–45 that His true followers will help the poor, the stranger (the foreigner or oppressed), the sick (those in need of health care), and the imprisoned. Voting for a tax increase on your neighbor to fund government programs to help the poor across town does not fill the mandate of this scripture. Nor does the opposite of pushing for tax cuts on business for the purpose of creating more jobs. Jesus wants each of us to be hands-on in meeting the needs of others. Government should supplement the charitable work of Americans."[69] Jackson and Perkins now acknowledge a Jesus committed to the poor, the stranger, the sick, and imprisoned, but they still emphasize a conservative politics that stresses personal responsibility and charitable giving instead of intentional, sustained systemic change.

The corporate culture of Focus on the Family is white, male, and hierarchical, making cultural diversity and racial reconciliation an ongoing struggle within the organization. Through the help of Bishop Jackson and other black evangelicals, many Focus and FRC staff members, such as H. B. London, Tony Perkins, and Kenyn Cureton, have been deliberate in reaching out to communities of color through outreach programs and collaborative public policy initiatives. Harry Jackson has joined H. B. London in challenging Focus and Family Research Council to hire more people of color, arguing that Focus will continue to struggle with racism until it includes people of color in the inner circle of decision making. Jackson and Perkins write, "We understand why many people are offended at the quota system of specifying how many blacks, Hispanics, or women should be hired in a specific job. On the other hand, the sinful nature of man being what it is, there is sometimes a reluctance on the part of majority employers and supervisors to give unproven minorities or women an opportunity to try their wings—in other words, the inability to push the right guardians of the 'old boy network' to give access to people who don't look like them in many fields . . . [and] open their hearts and their organizational charts to train the next generation of minority and female leaders."[70] Recruiting a more multiethnic leadership is unfinished business at Focus.

As a result of the labor of prophetic voices like that of Harry Jackson, Focus on the Family hired its first African American vice president in July 2007. A former senior executive for Coca-Cola in Atlanta, Terence Chatmon, was appointed as vice president of community impact outreach, and Dobson had high hopes that Chatmon would help Focus with church outreach, including outreach to the African American community. His accomplishments within less than a year were impressive. His team was tasked with launching a church outreach program with a goal of reaching 25 churches, and in ten months they had relationships with over 300 churches. He wrote a booklet titled "Charting Your Family's Spiritual Course" and saw more than 5,000 families go through the course, which provides practical tools to design and implement a plan of spiritual growth for their families.

From Los Angeles to New York City, Chatmon had a heart to reach out to African American families in America's inner cities, quickly forging strategic partnerships with African American pastors. Under Chatmon's leadership a family ministry with a focus on spirituality was bearing much fruit with the possibility of bringing living water to the African American community. Chatmon was a visionary leader who could help guide Focus into an intercultural future, but in less than a year—in June 2008—he resigned. Black evangelicals have found it hard to survive and thrive at Focus, which remains structured around normative whiteness.

Focus's small attempts to move toward racial reconciliation should be applauded, but its racial reconciliation initiatives are still often framed as paternalistic outreaches to communities of color versus genuine collaborations with them. Tony Perkins's and Harry Jackson's work stands as a sign of hope within the pro-family movement. But although they lift up the issue of racial reconciliation, they still view racism as primarily a personal and spiritual problem. Their Reconciliation Referendum's emphasis on prayer, spiritual awakening, pulpit exchanges, and interracial evangelism deeply resembles Carl Henry's individualistic ethic of regeneration. Dealing with personal prejudice through cross-cultural relationships is an important part of racial reconciliation and justice, but it is not enough. In its mission, policy, and personnel, Focus has demonstrated an active resistance to working to dismantle systemic racism. As a result of not being more active in dismantling racism within the organization and within society, the character of Focus's leadership of the pro-family movement will continue to represent primarily the political concerns of white male conservative evangelicals.

During the 2008 elections, Dobson once again encouraged Americans to "vote values," but the question is . . . whose values? His defense of the family is a defense of a particular form of family—the middle-class business family so important to a capitalist culture. Dobson defends "traditional" middle-class, white values and regards Christian evangelicals as those who are persecuted, as opposed to the poor and those subject to racism, sexism, and other types of oppression. The history of Focus lifting up family values while not engaging systemic racism unveils an ethical problem at the heart of the pro-family movement. In the shadow of the lynching tree in the Jim Crow South, Focus on the Family has not shown that it views racism as a serious societal problem.

In light of fallen heroes of the Religious Right, men like Falwell and Ralph Reed, Dobson has gained great political influence in the Arlington Group, the epicenter of the Religious Right. In the process of political involvement, however, Focus on the Family and Dobson lost something. Focus on the Family has sought to be guided by the Lordship of Christ, but given its institutional mission, the family was always the primary center of its attention, while other issues like racism have been carefully avoided.

Dobson deepened Henry's theology of Lordship by focusing on Jesus as a healer. His Nazarene emphasis on Jesus as the one who heals the bro-kenhearted and broken families is a promising perspective for evangelical theology. However, Dobson needs to go further to consider the broken-ness in the African American community, which has suffered through slav-ery and segregation. Until Focus makes the theological connections be-tween black suffering and the suffering of the Jewish flesh of Jesus, it will continue to promote a white evangelical theology of triumph. This in turn continues to produce a Christian conservative capitalist citizenry whose primary allegiance is to the nation and not to the church conceived as Christ's wounded body bearing witness to a more prophetic form of politics.

The pro-family movement is in crisis and its warrior politics is waning. At FRC's Vote Values Summit in October 2007, Mitt Romney, a practic-ing Mormon and former Massachusetts governor, won the straw poll among Religious Right voters, edging out Mike Huckabee, a Southern Baptist preacher and the former governor of Arkansas. Senator John Mc-Cain, no favorite of the Religious Right, finished ninth out of nine. Dob-son threatened that if McCain was the nominee, he would sit out the elec-tion. Dobson was upset that McCain supported stem cell research, did not support a constitutional marriage amendment, had a notorious temper, and was not a true conservative. When McCain won the nomination and chose Sarah Palin, the governor of Alaska, as his vice presidential running mate, Dobson gave his reluctant support.

The maverick message of McCain and Palin appealed to the base of older, white, socially conservative evangelicals in the 2008 election, but it missed a critical shift among the younger, multiethnic generation of evan-gelicals and weakened their ability to move forward into a post–cold war world. Young evangelicals have expanded their social concerns beyond the issues of traditional family and opposition to abortion. The younger generation is moving from a populist, personal politics to a cosmopolitan, communitarian one that engages a broader set of issues through new social networking strategies at both grassroots and elite levels. The culture war-rior ideal of the cowboy politics of Reagan and Bush had lost its allure. Having come of age in a time when the cold war has been replaced by ter-rorism and Iraq, young evangelicals see real-life consequences when they hear their elders use violent metaphors. They are passionately concerned with the environment, AIDS, sex trafficking, and world hunger. Palin's slogan "drill baby drill" and her caribou hunting raised questions among evangelicals who care about the environment. With their defense of neo-conservative foreign policy, neo-liberal economic policy, and the Iraq war policy, McCain's and Palin's warrior politics, a political vision that Dobson had helped foster, represented an age that has passed.[71]

Through its constant battle to defend the family in legal and legislative ways in this time of crisis, Focus saw the family as under siege in the twilight of civilization. As civilization—white, Western, and Christian—stood in the balance, Dobson was prepared to defend it with the courage of a bear hunter in the deep woods of Alaska. No matter how dark the forest gets, Dobson would forge on into the darkness until he killed his bear.

The slaying of a bear has been an important symbol in the American literary imagination. In William Faulkner's short story "The Bear," published in his 1942 novel *Go Down, Moses,* Ike McCaslin, a sixteen-year-old Mississippi boy, goes to the woods to kill the mighty bear, "Old Ben." In the process he learns of the wisdom of the wilderness through the focused guidance of Sam Fathers, a Native American guide. In the midst of a wilderness vanishing as a result of white southern greed, Ike learns that the only way to care for the Other, be they white, black, or Native American, is to care for the whole of creation. Faulkner's novel title—*Go Down, Moses*—invokes the Jewish and black freedom struggle that undergirds prophetic Christianity, from its founding in Galilee to its postcolonial moment in black evangelical witness, to an exile out of the wilderness of black suffering in America. As Sam Fathers gently guided Ike toward a new level of spiritual and political maturity in the postbellum South, Bishop Harry Jackson is subtly and deliberately guiding conservative evangelicals in the early twenty-first century away from a warrior politics of apocalyptic violence and toward a prophetic politics of worldly love and justice.

6

NATIONAL ASSOCIATION OF EVANGELICALS:
FOR THE HEALTH OF THE NATION

In 1947 the publication of Carl Henry's *The Uneasy Conscience of Fundamentalism* sounded a loud wake-up call to political engagement for American evangelicals who had been comfortably lulled into complacency by their increasing cultural power in the wake of the American victory in World War II. Henry was one of only a few prophets calling American evangelicals to move beyond fundamentalism, seeking to transform their fundamentalist heritage by encouraging them to become more educated, cultured, and politically engaged. Henry was also one of the founding fathers of the National Association of Evangelicals (NAE).

The NAE is an important, ongoing locus for evangelical public engagement. The NAE is an ecumenical association of churches and individuals in the evangelical tradition that was officially convened in 1943 around the classical concerns of the broader ecumenical movement, with a particular focus on evangelism. It provided a necessary forum for evangelical churches to discuss common concerns, such as ways of working together for a broader evangelistic and social witness agenda in a global context.

Today the NAE is composed of sixty-one member denominations and associations.[1] The diversity of the NAE's member churches demonstrates the theological breadth of the evangelical movement. Furthermore, these NAE communions represent millions of evangelical Christians in the United States, a constituency that is growing both numerically and in its political influence.

While organizations like Sojourners are social organizations by charter, the NAE is intentionally classified as an ecumenical association. It is an association of ecclesial bodies, not a single-issue advocacy organization. Unlike Sojourners' Call to Renewal campaign to eradicate poverty and Focus on the Family's struggle to preserve the traditional family, the NAE's witness in public policy has always sought to engage a broad spectrum of social issues. Although the NAE does not have the same organizational form as the three other social movements discussed in this book, it represents an important evangelical social movement within the church, one that seeks to help churches cooperate in common public witness.

When it comes to racial justice, the NAE's approach to racism has evolved. In its first stage (1942–90), it could be described as a "personal influence" strategy of racial justice (Christian Smith's term), an attempt to achieve racial reconciliation through personal relationships. In 1990, however, through dialogue with the National Black Evangelical Association, a new paradigm of dismantling systemic racism broadly under the rubric "global justice" began to emerge more clearly in the conversations and policy positions of the NAE (1990 to present). Don Argue had the courage to name the problem of "whiteness" in 1990, but it was Ted Haggard who appointed significant people of color, including Sammy Rodriguez Jr. and Bishop Harry Jackson, to the NAE board. Through these new voices of people of color, the NAE is beginning to tap the prophetic streams of a truly intercultural evangelicalism: African American, Asian, and Hispanic.

In reaction to the fundamentalist idea of cultural separation, the evangelical churches joined together and formed the NAE as the unified voice of a new socially engaged evangelicalism. Carl Henry joined Harold John Ockenga and others in the early conversations that helped form the NAE, and he was present when the NAE officially convened in Chicago in 1943. A first-year seminary professor at Northern Baptist Seminary and a former reporter from Long Island, New York, Henry coordinated the newsroom for the first convention.[2] He not only reported on the early theological debates within the NAE but increasingly shaped its theological vision. Through his committee service, writing, and advisement, Carl Henry provided important leadership to the NAE throughout his life, a legacy continued by his son, the late Representative Paul Henry (R-Michigan), a participant in the NAE's Christian Student Leadership Conference, which began as the NAE Federal Seminar, held annually since 1957. Henry's imprint on the NAE is lasting indeed.

The NAE's committed purpose was to help evangelical churches unify in the common task of world evangelization in different ways. In the early days the NAE concerned itself "with (1) evangelism, (2) evangelicals' relation to government, (3) national and local use of radio, (4) public relations, (5) the preservation of separation of church and state, (6) Christian education, and (7) the guarantee of freedom for home and foreign missionary endeavor."[3] After World War II, however, there was an increasing interest in providing a strategic social witness. Bruce Shelly writes, "One of the most significant developments within American conservatism since World War II is its awakened interest in humanitarian causes. Fundamentalism's reaction to liberalism's social gospel left American evangelicalism off balance in its stand on Biblical social responsibility."[4] Instead of churches individually helping in the relief effort, the NAE thought it to be wise to pool their efforts and thus developed the World Relief Corporation (WRC). Evangelicals in the late 1940s began to realize that one of the liabilities of their fundamentalist heritage was its failure to engage in broad public witness.

The success of the Allies in World War II led to a new optimism in American churches. In his presidential address, "Christ in America," delivered at the 1943 meeting of the NAE, Harold John Ockenga argued that although America had not fulfilled the strong role it could play in world missions, he saw great promise for America that had a "destiny comparable to that of Ancient Israel."[5] The American nationalism expressed by Ockenga was a part of a broader cultural ethos that was internalized within the larger theological framework of world evangelization. As the NAE became increasingly concerned with social and humanitarian issues, it began to develop more programs in social affairs, including a Commission on Social Affairs and Relief and development ministries, for example, World Relief. A bullish American optimism coupled with a concern about moral decline in western culture motivated member churches of the NAE to bear prophetic witness to global justice. But since the churches' social witness was housed within the circumscription of the nation, evangelicals were also challenged to think about the ways in which American nationalism and white racism worked against their deepest humanitarian aspirations.

The struggle of the NAE during these early years was to keep evangelicalism unified while taking on a broader social and political agenda. Joel Carpenter writes, "The NAE was a natural haven for the progressives, but it could not promote their more pointed agenda. Critical to the NAE's success was the support of as many fundamentalist leaders and institutions as possible. . . . Still, the NAE had taken a stand favoring two of the new evangelicalism's issues: it stood against divisiveness among evangelicals and it stood for a more positive ministry to society."[6] The NAE represented a fundamentalism that had come of age.

In the 1980s the NAE became more deeply politicized, largely due to its leadership's close ties to the Reagan administration. Throughout his term of office, Reagan wooed the NAE. In his "evil empire" speech, delivered at the NAE annual meeting in Orlando, Florida, in 1983, President Reagan called on evangelicals to support his policies in light of the ever-present threat of communism. Reagan's projection of masculine, military strength through his cold war framing of a Christian America versus a communist Russia proved an effective strategy for capturing the NAE's political imagination; however, it reinforced the white-black dyad of race relations that had emerged clearly in postwar America.

The evangelical base of the Reagan White House set the conditions for the development of a Religious Right Republicanism that was a synthesis of social and religious conservatism leveraged on behalf of the Republican Party, a movement that would sweep national politics in the 1980s. Jerry Falwell's Moral Majority successfully mobilized many conservative American Christians, including fundamentalists, but the NAE possessed a broader reach, including moderates and progressives within the evangelical ranks. In the 1990s, members of the NAE became increasingly interested in engaging a broader set of social issues through more progressive forms of public engagement. When Clinton ran for office in 1992, he received 25 percent of the evangelical vote; in 1996, he received 37 percent.

The NAE's doctrine is based on a high view of scripture. Basing its seven-point statement of faith on scripture as its center, the NAE was able to encompass the myriad values between the Reformed church, for example, and the Pentecostal church. Its triadic statement—in essentials unity, in distinctives diversity, and in all things freedom—exemplifies the way NAE doctrine developed ecumenically.

The Christology that shaped early NAE theological statements followed the form of Carl Henry's own theology with its emphasis on: (1) Jesus Christ as Lord and Savior being the ethical center; (2) the Lordship of Christ reaching out into all spheres of life; (3) Christ's teaching of the kingdom clarifying the creation norms in the spheres of family, government, and church. Christ's kingdom provides the central narrative vision for the NAE's public theology. Following Henry, the NAE's strategy remained one of personal influence until 1990 when it was transformed into systemic transformation with a focus on global justice. From the Jesus who crossed racial boundaries discussed in the NAE's 1990 consultation with the National Black Evangelical Association to the Jesus who suffered and lived sacrificially for others discussed in the NAE's *For the Health of the Nation* (2004), the Christology of the NAE is beginning to focus on Jesus and justice.[7]

The NAE has sought to be a Christ-centered movement from its inception. The constitution of the NAE states that the evangelical churches came together to "organize an association which shall give articulation and united voice to our faith and purpose in Christ Jesus." Unique aspects of the Christology undergirding the NAE's theological vision are characteristic of broader evangelicalism, including belief in the virgin birth and the literal, physical resurrection of Jesus Christ.[8] The NAE's Christology has been able to expand to a wider vision by expanding on the logic of the Lordship of Jesus Christ. The Lordship of Jesus Christ is the organizing principle of the National Association of Evangelicals: Jesus is the Lord of all spheres of life. When considered from this perspective, the NAE's political involvement is an important expression of faith, for it expresses total surrender to the Lordship of Christ through active participation in God's reign of love and justice.

The logic of Christ's Lordship led to extensive institution building by NAE member organizations. In the spirit of nineteenth-century revivalists, mid-twentieth-century evangelicals embodied an entrepreneurial ethos viewed positively as creating the conditions in which signs of Christ's kingdom could emerge. Henry challenged evangelicals to consider their institution building as a vital part of their public evangelistic witness in the world. Evangelicals were encouraged and responded to Henry's passionate plea by developing schools, colleges, and radio stations. They sought

to reach the world with new zeal, lifting up their voices on social and political issues across the airwaves of America.

The NAE's narrative vision of the Kingdom of God provided a theological framework for the NAE's political action, and it also targeted the Federal Council of Churches (FCC), now known as the National Council of
Churches (NCC), as a worthy adversary. The members of the NAE were
never as extreme in their adversarial framing of the liberals in the FCC as
their fundamentalist cousins were, but they did generate more cohesion as
a collective movement in their ongoing fight with mainline liberals over
what the Christian political agenda and strategy should be.

The NAE's opposition to the Federal Council of Churches was in part a
debate over who Jesus Christ really is. Evangelicals and fundamentalists
thought that many of the liberals in the mainline denominations were rejecting fundamental dimensions of Christology (e.g., virgin birth, bodily
resurrection, etc.) and thus had jeopardized the theological truth of Jesus
being the Lord and Savior of the world. The evangelical affirmation of
Jesus Christ as Savior has two important dimensions. First, Jesus is conceived to be one's personal savior. Foundational to an evangelical understanding of salvation is the necessity of a born-again conversion experience. Conversion is understood to be the moment of accepting Jesus
Christ as personal savior and cosmic Lord.

The second important dimension of Jesus being Savior and Lord is the
fact that this message must be proclaimed around the whole globe. Since
its founding, the NAE strongly emphasized world evangelization, with the
exception of a few Reformed denominations that were critical of certain
types of revivals and mass crusades. The NAE's vision of world evangelization is based on the visionary movements of the nineteenth century and
embodied in Billy Graham's mass evangelistic crusades in the late twentieth century. Along with this global evangelistic vision went the conviction
that the best way to transform society was through the regeneration of individuals. According to Carl Henry, Jesus Christ is also Lord over every institution in the world, including the whole public realm. But Carl Henry's
personal influence strategy meant that public witness was always implemented by individuals. Thus, Christians are called to be salt and light
through their social and political witness in the public square.

Henry's social vision was always at war with itself, divided between the poles of rugged individualism and social transformation. Henry wanted evangelicals to embrace a broader social ethic, but evangelicalism's stubborn individualism always limited its theological imagination and its broader social impact. Recognizing this problem, Kevin Manoia and Richard Cizik helped initiate the working group on theology and public policy that would eventually produce the *For the Health of the Nation* (2004) document, an evangelical public policy manifesto. Although this work shared some of the fire of Henry's *Uneasy Conscience,* it also pushed beyond it in some important ways.

In the opening paragraphs of *For the Health of the Nation* the "suffering" of Jesus Christ is mentioned in the same paragraph where there is discussion of the "Lordship" of Jesus: "The Lord also calls the church to practice the righteous deeds of the kingdom and point to the kingdom by the wholeness and integrity of the church's common life. This example will require us to demonstrate God's love for all, by crossing racial, ethnic, economic, and national boundaries. It will also often involve following Jesus' example by suffering and living sacrificially for others."[9] The notion of Jesus as a "suffering Lord" is crucial to working on issues of racial, economic, and environmental justice because it provides a strong connection between the common fragility and brokenness of Jesus's humanity, the human family, and the cosmos. "Jesus's example of suffering" provides a window through which we can see that God cares about the poor and the earth. Because the NAE has recently actively worked for environmental justice, it has embraced a broader notion of the creation orders than Focus on the Family.

In *For the Health of the Nation* three of the traditional institutions of society (family, government, and church) are expanded to other societal institutions. Other evangelical organizations, for example, Focus on the Family, concentrated solely on family, government, and church because institutions like labor unions were seen as too liberal. While the NAE does not question the notion of creation order, it applies it more liberally to other institutions that grow out of the created order—schools and labor unions. This reflects the influence of Roman Catholic social teaching on the NAE's thinking about social structures, including a broader application of the concept of social structures in the NAE's social ethic.[10] Focus on the Family has partnered with Roman Catholics on pro-life issues, but the NAE has deepened its partnership to develop a holistic ethic of life. The NAE's vision of social transformation includes all institutions of society and does not prioritize one above all other, the way Focus on the Family privileges the nuclear family.

The theological streams that flowed into the twentieth-century ecumenical movement have shaped the NAE as an ecumenical association. At points, however, the NAE has gone against these streams to assert its evangelical distinctiveness. Four streams have shaped twentieth-century ecumenism: faith and order, life and works, mission, and Christian education. These four streams represent transdenominational movements that emerged in the nineteenth century; they merged into a greater institutional form after World War II in many of the national, regional, and global councils that we know today. One of the best-known instruments of conciliar ecumenism is the World Council of Churches (WCC), formed on August 23, 1948, a council uniting more than 330 communions from around the world.

Church unity was the polar star of the ecumenical movement that drove the great twentieth-century ecumenical leaders. American evangelicals have historically possessed a deep skepticism of the ecumenical movement. This skepticism derived from several different issues. First, world evangelization, not church unity, was the primary concern of evangelical churches. Second, intense ecumenical discussions emerged in the 1930s and 1940s in the aftermath of the fundamentalist-liberal split within U.S. Protestantism, producing a deep suspicion in the evangelical mind of liberal ecumenists. In the fundamentalist imagination, to participate in the mainstream ecumenical movement would require sacrificing the fundamentals of the faith that had been defended so fiercely in the 1920s.

The fundamentalist rejection of mainstream ecumenism was embodied in the conservative theology and cultural separatist vision of fundamentalist preacher Carl MacIntyre. MacIntyre, a fiery Philadelphian, was an old-school fundamentalist who had a black-and-white imagination and a separatist agenda. In MacIntyre's view, only the fundamentalists truly carried on the unadulterated biblical faith. Fundamentalists could not commune or interact with mainline Protestants (often referred to in fundamentalist literature as "neo-Protestants" and "ecumenists") because only separation could maintain theological purity. In order to form an alliance of separation, MacIntyre created an ecumenical association for fundamentalist churches to join in the struggle for defending the faith and evangelizing the world. His organization of fundamentalist churches, called the American Council of Christian Churches (ACCC), was established in September 1941 as a fundamentalist alternative to the Federal Council of Churches (FCC).

The NAE can be interpreted as a "third way" between the ACCC and the FCC. Although evangelicals genuinely shared the mainstream ecumenists' drive for Christian unity out of the "faith and order" stream of ecumenism, their primary concern has always been world evangelization. Such evangelical leaders as Charles M. Fuller, Carl Henry, Harold John Ockenga, J. Edwin Orr, and J. Edwin Wright, who helped organize the association, wanted both to build on a fundamentalist heritage and to push out to a broader public engagement. While they shared the fundamentalists' passion for an apologetic defense of the faith in light of the general trends of secularization and liberalization, the evangelicals' approach was more generous, irenic, and world affirming, rejecting a narrow model of separation.

The NAE's primary purpose was always evangelistic in intent and global in scope. Although many of the churches that joined this movement sought to distance themselves from the more separatist wing of the fundamentalist movement, the fear that liberal Christians would be internalized within the organization forced fundamentalists into maintaining a separatist stance with new ecumenical breadth. This is evidenced in a policy that was formulated at the organization's inception: any member church in the NAE could not also be a member of the FCC and WCC. Thus, Carl MacIntyre's and the fundamentalists' concern for denominational and doctrinal purity were built into the NAE's membership policy.

Even though the separatist impulse of MacIntyre lived on in the NAE positioning itself against the FCC, it moved beyond separatism in several important ways. Within fundamentalism there is a "tension" between its separatist impulse and its transformational aspirations. Some interpreters of American religious history have depicted American fundamentalism as a dying movement after the late 1920s, a consequence of its public humiliation in the Scopes monkey trial of 1925. After this defeat, the story goes, fundamentalists withdrew into an isolated cul-de-sac of Bible schools and churches. In contrast to this account of the early death of fundamentalism, Joel Carpenter has argued that fundamentalism was alive and well in the 1930s and 1940s, but it was being transformed in important ways.[11]

In the 1950s the NAE became more interested in social issues and established a Commission on Social Affairs, on which Carl Henry served. With the prevalent racial strife of the 1950s and 1960s, the NAE was unsuccessful in integrating black evangelicals into the movement. Because of white evangelicals' unresponsiveness to the needs and dreams of black evangelical churches during the civil rights movement, a group of young African American evangelicals saw the need to found the National Black Evangelical Association (NBEA) in Los Angeles in 1963.

The formation of the NBEA demonstrated that the NAE was not responsive to the needs of black evangelicals, who were subjugated under a unified postwar evangelical Caucasian culture. Thus, the NBEA would function as a shadow side to a mainstream evangelicalism shrouded in whiteness. Since postwar neo-evangelicalism was so white, black evangelicals had to develop a counter-identity. As a result, the black evangelicals of the 1960s played a vital role in the emergence of black consciousness movement years before it became publicly recognized during the March against Fear in 1966. These prophetic black evangelicals included William H. Bentley, Herbert Daughtry, Carl Ellis, Anthony Evans, Vincent Harding, Michael Haynes, John Perkins, Ron Potter, Wyn Wright Potter, John Skinner, and Tom Skinner. With time the prophetic witness of black evangelicals, from the underside of a white evangelical modernity, would begin the process of transforming that NAE from the outside in.[12] But the NAE's transformation on the issue of racism would take time.

The NAE took no official position on the civil rights movement, but it did issue this statement on civil rights: "We believe that the Biblical solution to the problem of race prejudice is through the transformation of the individual by the power of the Holy Spirit resulting in a love for all men." The emphasis in the 1960s was still on the "transformation of the individual" with no corresponding acknowledgment that sins like racism are ingrained within systems and institutions. Thus, the NAE continued to see racism as only a problem within the human heart. Dialogues with black evangelicals and the NBEA throughout the 1960s, however, began to call into question some of the basic planks of neo-evangelical social thought, including the dichotomy in its understanding of the Gospel between personal faith and social transformation.

Building on the work of the black evangelicals of the 1960s, a new group of white prophetic evangelicals—including Ron Sider, Jim Wallis, Tony Campolo, Donald W. Dayton, and Wesley Granberg Michaelson—emerged to carry on Henry's call for an integral evangelical ethic.[13] This group of progressive evangelicals was not at the center of the NAE constituency, but it represented the opening of a broader evangelical social ethic within a growing white American evangelicalism. In the late 1970s robust traditions of evangelical social thought were emerging across the ecumenical spectrum in the writings of Richard Mouw, James W. Skillen, and Nicholas Wolterstorff in the Reformed tradition; Donald W. Dayton and Stephen Mott in the Wesleyan tradition; and Ron Sider and John Howard Yoder in the Anabaptist tradition.

In 1977, Ron Sider's *Rich Christians in an Age of Hunger* sounded a wake-up call for the evangelical world, echoing Henry's call three decades earlier.[14] Although many heard his cry for justice in the 1970s and 1980s, it would have an even greater hearing among evangelical youth in the early twenty-first century. While completing his doctoral studies in theology at Yale University in 1969, Sider became involved in organizing evangelicals for social justice, using the mailing list for Evangelicals for McGovern to contact an initial pool of people for Evangelicals for Social Action (ESA). This organization, founded in 1978, became a consistent vehicle for prophetic social witness within evangelicalism, challenging conservative and individualistic tendencies within the broader evangelical movement. Sider would play a vital role in helping to deepen the NAE's social thought.

The passing of *Roe v. Wade* in 1973 marked an important moment in evangelical political life, but it was not until the end of the decade that evangelicals fully mobilized around the issue. After issuing a statement on Christian families in 1970, which emphasized that families need to be committed to Christ, the NAE issued a statement rejecting the practice of abortion in 1973, except in instances when a mother's life was in jeopardy.

President Jimmy Carter was a self-identified evangelical and Southern Baptist, but the evangelicals quickly lost interest in him because of his perceived weakness and liberal politics, including his acceptance of the Equal

Rights Amendment and abortion. Through the late 1970s the evangelical political movement grew in power, emerging as a major force in the 1980s. The perceived moral decline of the nation in the late 1970s and 1980s motivated evangelicals to increasingly engage in politics. President Reagan quickly became a symbol of the new evangelical political movement, speaking at the NAE conventions in 1983 and 1984. Through this marriage Reagan ensured his reelection, and evangelicals raised their political profile and influence.

There was a deep, deep individualism that lay at the heart of the evangelical project. This individualism is best exemplified in the doctrine of personal regeneration. From the Los Angeles crusade on, the purpose of Billy Graham's crusades was to convert individuals. When translated into a social ethic, this meant that the conversion of individuals led to the transformation of society. But as the history of the black freedom struggle shows, racism can be redressed only through confronting the systems that give it life (see chapter 2). Why did white evangelicals in the early twentieth century join temperance campaigns but fail to actively participate in anti-lynching campaigns? The white evangelical absence in the anti-lynching campaigns was repeated in their absence in the civil rights movement. Although some evangelicals, for example, Vincent Harding, John Perkins, and Frank E. Gaebelein, did join the movement for racial justice, most passively watched events unfold from the comfort of their homes. With a theology that emphasized a direct, personal relationship between Jesus the Lord and each individual, there was a failure to give an adequate theological account to the community and social justice. This theological weakness reflected a flawed Christology. Jesus Christ was seen as an object of individual reflection and experience but not as organically connected to the community, church, and creation. It was precisely because of this Christological failure that the majority of white evangelicals of both the North and South neglected to fully engage the problem of racism.

The 1990s ushered in an important theological paradigm shift in the NAE's theology of public engagement. In the 1990s the NAE continued to grow numerically and in ethnic and gender diversity, and it intensified its treatment of political and social issues. The individualism of an earlier era was challenged by a new emphasis on community, church, and creation. During this decade the NAE addressed more intentionally the issues of racism, poverty, and the environment. The NAE statement "Heeding the Call of the Poor," drafted in 1997, included support for welfare reform. There was an increasing interest in international issues reflected in the legislation advocated for in the NAE Office of Governmental Affairs, led by Richard Cizik.

Donald Argue played an important role in leading the NAE during the early 1990s. In 1992, he became chairman of the board and in 1995 was elected president. Argue was inaugurated as president at the fiftieth-anniversary celebration of the NAE in Chicago in 1996. George W. Bush attended, and Billy Graham delivered an address. After B. Edgar Johnson, the general secretary of the Church of Nazarene and the outgoing president of the NAE, handed over the gavel, Argue began his presidential address with the provocative statement that the NAE was "too old, too white, and too male."[15] Serving until 1998, Argue tried to diversify the NAE's constituency through recruiting youth, women, and people of color. The early meetings of the NAE in the 1940s were attended by white men only, but the leadership of American religious culture had changed, and Argue was determined to see the NAE more aggressively and positively responding to these changes.

When Argue came into office, two mandates were given to him: first, to raise the public profile of the NAE, and second, to distance the NAE from the Religious Right. Argue traveled all over the country, presenting a nonpartisan, socially engaged evangelicalism as the new progressive face of the NAE. Argue was concerned about the alliance that was formed between evangelicals and the Republican Party in the 1980s and was determined to see it broken. We hear echoes of Henry the prophetic Baptist in Argue's attempt to encourage the NAE to let the church be the church, not identifying itself too closely with the party politics of the nation.

A prophetic Pentecostal theologian, Argue boldly proclaimed a portrait of Jesus Christ as a Spirit-filled prophet who was not beholden to the Jewish religion and Roman nationalism of his day. Likewise, Argue and the leaders of the NAE became increasingly wary of Jesus being a tool of the "right"; they felt that Jesus's gospel message was about more than just politically conservative issues. Their hope was that distancing Jesus and his teaching of the Kingdom of God from the Religious Right would make the gospel message more clear and compelling. Argue spoke with Presidents

Bush and Clinton to discuss the NAE agenda, with much success. Argue's work on the Religious Freedom Restoration Act was one of the important political accomplishments during his administration. Religious freedom proved to be a centrist issue that all evangelicals could commit to working on.

Argue deployed this irenic, broad-minded approach to public engagement as he actively sought more sustained dialogue with black evangelicals from a position of repentance, with an openness to learn about white racism from his black evangelical colleagues. On January 26–27, 1990, Argue and Russ Knight, president of the NBEA, led a consultation on racism, producing a joint Statement on Prejudice and Racism. This statement marked a clear shift from individualist to systemic thinking about the problem of race:

> Racism is a prejudice plus power. Racism is therefore an institutionalized expression of a controlling group's prejudices. . . . Racism is a foundational sin of the United States, fueled by economic greed and the exploitation of human and natural resources. It has corrupted the foundations, institutions and cultural mores of this country. It has prevented formation of a true cultural democracy. Racism has enslaved, impoverished and oppressed people of color in America. . . . Racism attacks the core of the gospel message. It negates the reason for which Christ died. It also denies the purpose of the church: to bring together, in Christ, those who have been divided from one another. . . . The credible witness of the Church and perhaps the deliverance of the United States depends upon the joint evangelical community effort to dismantle the structure of racism and prejudice.

It was through black evangelicalism that white evangelicals began to think systemically about the structures of racism.

Black evangelicals were not only rethinking sin's social dimension, they were rethinking Christ. In the letter that Don Argue and Russ Knight sent to NAE/NBEA pastors about the joint Statement on Prejudice and Racism, they appealed to Paul's egalitarian vision in Ephesians. Paul writes, "But now in Christ Jesus you who once were far off have been brought near by the blood of Christ. For he is our peace; in his flesh he has made both groups into one and has broken down the dividing wall, that is, the hostility between us. He has abolished the law with its commandments and ordinances, so that he might create in himself one new humanity in place of the two, thus making peace, and might reconcile both groups to God in one body through the cross, thus putting to death that hostility through it" (2:13–16). Their invocation of this Pauline Christology in the context of racial reconciliation unveils the Jewish flesh of Jesus as the very site in which the Jew and the Gentile are reconciled. The reconciliation between the Jew and the Gentile in the early church period becomes the theological basis for the reconciliation of black and white in the Americas. For white evangelicals to listen and learn from black evangelicals about racial justice entailed a deeper transformation of evangelical theology. Christologically this meant that Jesus would no longer be viewed primarily as divine, but also as a fully human, earthly prophet whose ministry crossed racial boundaries and whose death and resurrection is the site of redemption for people of all races and ethnic groups.

Argue was a white evangelical leader who was committed to mediating the black evangelical vision of Jesus and justice to the white evangelical world. On February 6, 1995, Argue met again with top leaders of the NBEA, asking "forgiveness for the sins of racism within white evangelical ranks." Argue also worked with ten thousand churches, handing out a racial reconciliation packet to church leaders "outlining practical steps to bridge the divide."[16] Argue was committed to expanding the evangelical table, allowing people who had formerly been forbidden to enter the mainstream evangelical fold. Argue saw that in order for a prophetic evangelical ethic to materialize it would have to reconnect with the deepest streams of prophetic Christianity, first in the black church and then in the ecumenical church.

Desiring to heal the historic division between the evangelical and ecumenical churches, Argue began conversations with the National Council of Churches in 1996, reaching out to both mainline Protestant and Eastern Orthodox member churches of the NCC.[17] The NAE was drawn into conversation with the Eastern Orthodox Church on the issue of engaging in ecumenical evangelism with the Orthodox in largely Orthodox postcommunist countries.[18] Describing his conversations with Joan Brown Campbell, the general secretary of the NCC at that time, Argue stated that he and Campbell had a mutual respect for one another. Argue thought it was imperative for North American ecumenism that the NAE and the NCC be in dialogue and collaborate on projects where they could.[19] Argue was convinced that for evangelicals to make their greatest impact on society they would have to be in strategic partnership with other traditions. He also reached out to other communions, for example, the Worldwide Church of God, whose headquarters are in Pasadena, California. After making a few doctrinal changes in response to their bilateral dialogue, the Worldwide Church of God was accepted into the NAE.[20] A broader intercultural, ecumenical, evangelical coalition was being built.

Argue embodied the egalitarian ideal of the evangelical abolitionists of the nineteenth century. He led the NAE to reach out more deliberately to those on the margins, including African Americans, Pentecostals, and the religiously persecuted. Argue identified religious persecution as a common issue for which this new progressive Christian coalition could be an advocate. Argue worked tirelessly to advocate for Christians suffering persecution. For example, he spoke to President Clinton about helping give religious asylum to Bob Fu, a Chinese evangelical who was arrested by the Chinese government for his evangelistic efforts outside of the structure of the official church. Through Argue's diplomatic efforts, Fu was able to come to the United States and currently serves as president of the China Aid Association, continuing to work on religious persecution issues in China.

The "Statement of Conscience of the NAE Concerning Worldwide Religious Persecution," presented at the fifty-fourth NAE annual conference in 1996, was one of the crowning achievements of Argue's presidency. In this statement the NAE criticized political leaders worldwide for their persecution of churches, regardless of their confessional communion. Surprisingly, the NCC did not endorse the statement,[21] but communions accepted the statement across the ecumenical spectrum, including both Roman Catholic and Episcopalian churches and ministers. Argue viewed the "Statement of Conscience" as the most important policy statement ever passed by the NAE. Staying clear of partisan politics, the NAE under Argue's leadership was able to expand the ecumenical table and continue its prophetic public policy advocacy.

In 1999 Kevin Mannoia, a Free Methodist minister, became the president of the NAE. His primary concern was to shift the NAE toward a more missional agenda. To this end, he convened a commission to draft a theological framework document for public policy issues. *For the Health of the Nation* was produced to theologically frame public policy issues, without making public policy the singular focus of the NAE.

Mannoia accomplished much during his short tenure as president. First, he continued Argue's work on racial reconciliation. Second, he helped to bring together ecumenical partners for the formulation of a Christian Declaration on Marriage in 1999, shoring up relations with pro-family-movement evangelicals and Roman Catholics. Released in fall 2000, this document was written in collaboration with the NCC, the U.S. Conference of Catholic Bishops, and the Southern Baptist Convention. Third, he encouraged and provided resources for church pastors.

As part of shifting the NAE toward a more missional approach to ecumenism, Mannoia sold the NAE headquarters in Wheaton, Illinois, moving the offices to Los Angeles, California, home of Hollywood and the center of the U.S. culture industry. With its headquarters in Los Angeles and its Office of Governmental Affairs in Washington, DC, the NAE would be fully bicoastal. Mannoia thought it was time to declare a new day, to get into missional engagement with culture as opposed to the cultural exclusion and separatism represented by the Wheaton, Illinois, location. Mannoia had a strong conviction that the future of the evangelical Christianity was emerging in growing, influential urban centers around the country and the world. The move to Los Angeles was also seen as opening up the possibility of greater outreach to the Hispanic community.

Mannoia continued the attempt of healing the divide between the black and white evangelical worlds. After assuming office, Mannoia spoke at the 1999 National Black Evangelical Association (NBEA) annual meeting in Portland, Oregon. In spring 2000, Mannoia convened a consultation with NBEA and NAE leaders, inviting John Perkins, John Jordan, and other African American leaders to attend. The NAE sponsored this all-day meeting, called to analyze why the evangelical movement was segregated. At this meeting Mannoia sought to discuss the merger of the NBEA and the NAE. His attempts did not go over well with NBEA members, who remained unconvinced that the NAE was really ready to fully engage in the difficult work of antiracism, proreconciliation activity in order to merge organizationally. Although the NAE was now beginning to use the rhetoric of "structural racism," it had not demonstrated evidence that it was serious about dismantling systemic racism within the NAE, its member churches, and society. The NBEA applauded the NAE's stated commitment to racial justice, but still there was a long road ahead.

As a result of the theological tensions in the black-white evangelical dialogue, Mannoia thought evangelicals needed a more coherent view of public engagement. On this sound theological basis, the NAE could act decisively on social issues, like racial justice, as they emerged. Mannoia convened a committee at the Dallas convention in 2001 to produce a written policy statement that would form the basis of a book, offering a theological framework for political engagement. Mannoia originally asked Ron Sider, director of Evangelicals for Social Action, and Tom Minnery, director of public policy at Focus on the Family, to cochair the committee that also included Os Guinness and Diane Knippers. The resulting book, *For the Health of the Nation,* began to bring new form to a more holistic evangelical ethic, bringing to fruition some of the important new directions that Don Argue has charted for NAE's public engagement.

Another important part of Mannoia's missional paradigm was bridging the old two-party system of American Protestantism that had emerged in the 1920s. In his article titled "What Are We For?" Mannoia's call to "move forward undaunted in our mission" through embodying "the compelling and transformational message of Christ" represented an important development in the public theology of the NAE. Jesus Christ is not just the source of the salvation of individual souls, but his teaching of the kingdom sets a missional vision for transforming societal systems. Within this transformational Christology, the church is the primary vehicle used by God to embody signs of the kingdom. As a result, all denominations and racial/ ethnic groups should seek to be unified, to thus increase their common evangelistic and social witness. Mannoia's missional ecclesiology attempted to push the NAE, some would argue too quickly, beyond the two-party Christianity that had originally divided the NAE from the NCC. To overcome this divide, Mannoia sought to help shepherd the Reformed Church in America (RCA), a member of the NCC and WCC, into membership with the NAE.

Mannoia's missional vision represented a more ecumenical and socially engaged view of Jesus Christ. He understood Jesus Christ as present not just among Christians in evangelical enclaves like Wheaton but also among the urban masses—black, brown, and white—in Los Angeles. He saw the vibrant faith in Jesus Christ in members of the Reformed Church in America, including its evangelical general secretary, Wesley Granberg Michaelson, and wanted this NCC denomination to join the NAE. Mannoia's broad Christological vision helped him dream big; however, he made some poor administrative and financial decisions that prevented him from making further missional reforms of the NAE.

Mannoia's attempt to grant membership in the NAE to the RCA, coupled with financial problems associated with the move to Southern California, turned some within the NAE against his administration. Many of the conservatives within the NAE were opposed to his dialogue and common work with the NCC. In light of Mannoia's friendliness to the NCC, the National Religious Broadcasters (NRB) at their 2001 Dallas convention voted unanimously, 81–0, to break ties with the NAE, stating that the NAE was moving in a different direction than the NRB, politically and to a degree theologically.[22]

Mannoia resigned in early June 2001. He had accomplished much in his short term of office, but his administration's quick decisions, aggressive ecumenism, and financial instability placed his leadership in jeopardy. The NAE opted for an interim president, Leith Anderson, a well-known evangelical pastor and author. Anderson is senior pastor of Wooddale, a megachurch in Eden Prairie, Minnesota, that is affiliated with the Baptist General Conference. Anderson proved to be a judicious and wise leader in a period of turmoil and transition, bringing the organization more public and financial stability, charting a more measured course for its future.

In 2003, Ted Haggard, pastor of New Life Church, the largest megachurch in Colorado Springs, Colorado, was elected president of the NAE. During the executive committee meeting, Haggard had to excuse himself to deliver a lecture at a local Bible college. When he returned to the meeting, the executive committee asked if he was willing to serve as president. Haggard presented several reasons why he was not the best choice, but the committee was not persuaded. Haggard accepted the position.

Moving the NAE headquarters to Colorado Springs was not a strategic decision but rather one that was made because Haggard's church was located there. Interestingly, during the 1990s Colorado Springs came to replace Wheaton, Illinois, as the new "Vatican of American Evangelicalism." A plethora of evangelical ministries and missions moved to Colorado Springs in the wake of Focus on the Family's decision to relocate there in 1991. Currently the town boasts well over one hundred evangelical ministries.

As a megachurch minister, Haggard was interested in seeing how the NAE movement could learn from and grow with the megachurch movement. He was concerned that evangelicalism had often been identified with the Religious Right in the public eye. Haggard stated:

> The problem that evangelicals face is [that] the rise of the ones that I call the Big Four—Jim Dobson, Jerry Falwell, Chuck Colson, and Pat Robertson, who are each leaders of major media ministries—gave the public impression that these men represent evangelicalism. And I guess in some sense they did because they had to. . . . People like the Big Four ended up rising to the top of the Christian Broadcasting world, and they are, in essence, the Religious Right. They along with some others, but they are the strongest public representations of that view. And that's why people are naive to think that all evangelicals are identical to the Religious Right. There is a much higher percentage of the African American community that is evangelical and Democrat than [there] are white evangelicals who are members of the Religious Right. In the last election, for example, 80 percent of white evangelicals voted for President Bush while 80 percent of black evangelicals voted for John Kerry. Just about two-thirds of Hispanic evangelicals voted for John Kerry. And so for people to equate evangelical with Religious Right—it's just phenomenal to me that there would be such incredible denial of the facts. It's so obvious. . . . I think over the next ten years you'll see increased exposure for megachurch leaders. Rick Warren and Bill Hybels will replace James Dobson and Pat Robertson as evangelicalism's public face.[23]

According to Haggard, the future of evangelicalism lies in the future of the megachurch. He saw megachurches as playing a positive roll in helping the United States move beyond the polarization of the culture wars. If

Haggard's prophecy is right, then evangelical politics in the future will be megapolitics.

Although Haggard claimed that church growth and world evangelization were his chief priorities for the NAE, a closer inspection reveals he was leading the NAE toward an increasingly singular focus on public engagement. During his years in office there was limited programming in areas of evangelism, discipleship, resource development, ecumenical issues, equipping churches, or convening pastors and denominational leaders; politics is largely what continued to drive the NAE during the Haggard tenure.

Amidst the ups and downs of the NAE in the 1990s and early twenty-first century, political advocacy was the one area in which it continued to excel. The NAE's narrative vision of Jesus Christ as Lord provided a theological rationale for sustained and active participation in American political life. "The backbone of the NAE for 25 years," Richard Cizik had meticulously honed an irenic political strategy in Washington, DC.[24] Haggard came from a somewhat apolitical, charismatic megachurch background, but he had gradually become more ecumenical and politically engaged in Colorado Springs. He also proved to be a media darling, eager to interpret a rebranded, socially engaged evangelicalism to the American public. Haggard's media savvy and Cizik's political strategy merged into the public image of a unified and politically active evangelicalism. In this sense, the NAE under Haggard focused on what it did well: political advocacy and action. These political activities continued to be led by the visionary and consistent leadership of Richard Cizik.

"The environmental crisis is the new civil rights crisis of our day," Ted Haggard proclaimed in 2006.[25] Haggard admitted that evangelicals blew it on the civil rights movement, and he was committed to doing everything in his power to ensure that evangelicals did not miss their opportunity to fully engage the growing environmental crisis. Yet even in Haggard's politics, there were deep tensions surrounding this greening of evangelicalism. Haggard's own "free-market" faith was in some ways at odds with it. During his tenure he admitted to using his political influence with President Bush to abolish steel tariffs because of his commitment to free-market economics.[26] Haggard's administration left an important question: given evangelicals' lack of strong involvement in the civil rights movement, could they fully join the creation care movement when their movement had in part produced the Christian nationalist capitalist citizenry, which was one of the primary sources of white racism and environmental degradation? Unfortunately Haggard would not be able to answer this question while in office.

Haggard's leadership in the NAE ended abruptly in 2006. In November 2006, Mike Jones, a former male escort, disclosed that he had had a relationship with Ted Haggard. Haggard initially denied Jones's charges and asked New Life Church to hold an independent investigation on the matter. Dobson, his conservative colleague a few miles away on the Focus campus in Colorado Springs, initially offered Haggard support during the investigation. Against the advice of some of his staffers, Dobson issued a press release in Haggard's defense, stating: "It is unconscionable that the legitimate news media would report a rumor like this based on nothing but one man's accusation. . . . Ted Haggard is a friend of mine, and it appears someone is trying to damage his reputation as a way of influencing the outcome of Tuesday's election—especially the vote on Colorado's marriage protection amendment—which Ted strongly supports." Yet Haggard, who initially had told Dobson of his innocence, a day later admitted that the allegations were true, prompting Dobson to claim that he was "heartsick over the allegation" and that Ted would "continue to be my friend, even if the worst allegations prove accurate. Nevertheless, sexual sin, whether homosexual or heterosexual, has serious consequences, and we are extremely concerned for Ted, his family and his church."[27]

Ted Haggard admitted to buying drugs (although not to using them) and to having an inappropriate relationship with Mike Jones. He issued a statement to his church admitting to being a "deceiver and a liar. There is a part of my life that is so repulsive and dark that I've been warring against it all of my adult life." He admitted to seeking help in the past, but said he had stopped and "began deceiving those I love the most because I didn't want to hurt or disappoint them." Perhaps more significant than the incident itself is the fact that Ted Haggard did not change his official stance on sexuality. He made it a point to join with the other evangelical leaders in calling his behavior sexually immoral. The Ted Haggard scandal shocked the evangelical world and American public, but it did not significantly affect its trajectory of public witness.

The board of the National Association of Evangelicals turned again to

Leith Anderson as the organization's interim president. He helped navigate the NAE movement after the resignation of Kevin Mannoia in 2001, so he was a wise, experienced, and trusted person for the job. Richard Cizik continued to lead the NAE Governmental Affairs Office, pursuing a broader evangelical agenda and taking on issues like the environment, poverty, and the Sudanese genocide.

Since issuing the *For the Health of the Nation* document, the NAE has deepened its social engagement on multiple fronts, including the Sudan Peace Act, the HIV/AIDS bill, the Religious Freedom Reformation Act, and the North Korean Freedom Act. Cizik wrote:

> What is it? It is this idea that, as George Bush has put it and keeps repeating it, freedom is not America's gift to the world; it is God's gift to mankind. That is what beats in the heart of every evangelical. We are growing—7,000 megachurches. We are adding a new church every two weeks.
>
> This is a movement that has learned from its failures in the 1980s. We failed often enough to know how to do it right. It is a movement that has honed its techniques to be able to, yes, go to the congressional Black Caucus when it is needed to pass the Sudan Peace Act, and to the gays to pass an HIV/AIDS bill, and to Tibet and the Buddhists to pass the Religious Freedom Reformation Act, and to go to the apolitical Korean Americans to pass the North Korean Freedom Act.[28]

Cizik notes that the numerical growth of the evangelical church needs to be matched with a growth in social conscience. Thinking about evangelicalism as an intercultural revival movement for justice helps explain why evangelicals today have broader humanitarian aspirations and are willing to partner with others seeking to achieve humanitarian goals. Cizik argues that the evangelical commitment to personal and religious freedom is the basis of a prophetic evangelical ethic. This idea taps deeply into the American evangelical psyche. Cizik grounds the dignity of humanity in the image of God, echoing Carl Henry, who argued that evangelicals have an ethical obligation to challenge all ideologies that trample human dignity as a bearer of the divine image. In the spirit of Roger Williams and Henry, Cizik continued to advocate on behalf of the freedoms of all individuals who are made in God's image, regardless of their race, gender, class, or religion.

Most American evangelicals were dissenters from the state churches of Europe. Cizik saw an important connection between evangelicals' history of marginalization and the marginalization of current immigrants and asylum seekers, all focused on our common humanity. An increasing number of immigrants, many of whom are evangelical, are seeking asylum in the United States, but the Immigration and Naturalization Services (INS) is often sending them home.

Samuel Rodriguez Jr., an NAE board member, has led the organization in addressing the controversial issue of immigration. As the leader of the National Hispanic Coalition Leaders Conference (NHCLC), Rodriguez forms an essential bridge between white and Hispanic evangelicals. "The evangelical church must reclaim Jesus Christ's radical teaching of the kingdom. We see signs of the kingdom emerge when we follow the heart of Jesus, a kingdom heart, called to discern the place of greatest suffering and to go to that place and stand with the suffering and the oppressed. Jesus calls us to love the neighbor, love the stranger, and love the enemy. If we are going to claim the name 'evangelical' today, it is vital that we come down on the side of the immigrant in our current immigration debate. We stand with the immigrant because that is where Jesus is standing."[29] Shaped by the traditions of both Carl Henry and Martin Luther King Jr., Rodriguez represents a new face of NAE leadership—young, Hispanic, antiracist, and visionary. He sees that Henry's focus on the Lordship of Jesus Christ has to be enriched by Jesus's teaching of the kingdom. Rodriguez states, "God is using the Hispanic church in America to help mediate Jesus's teaching of the Kingdom to help overcome the black-white divide that has plagued American evangelicalism. Black, brown, yellow, and white—all evangelicals must stand with the immigrant at this important juncture in twenty-first-century global justice."[30] As a prophetic evangelical leader in the Hispanic community, Rodriguez is able to embody the best of the evangelical past, being honest about its weaknesses but boldly pushing ahead to a more radical expression of the Gospel.

Rodriguez is a symbol of the rise in public influence of Latino evangelicals, particularly on the issue of immigration. Many Latinos are Roman Catholic, but Latino evangelicals number close to 15 million in the United

States and are a strong political voice in American public life. Reconciliation has been difficult within the evangelical circle for white and first-generation Latino churches because of the language barrier. Second-generation Latinos, however, usually speak fluent Spanish and English, and a growing group of primarily white evangelical churches are offering Spanish or bilingual services.

The acceptance of the evangelical faith among Latinos in the twentieth century brought with it an acculturation to the American lifestyle. But by joining American evangelical churches, Latinos were in a double bind. On one hand, they were often rejected by their families for leaving Roman Catholicism. On the other hand, they were never fully accepted by the white evangelical church. Thus, many of the early Latino evangelicals lived in the "in-between," a space between an often Roman Catholic Latino past and a white evangelical future, as Juan Martinez argues.

This complex dilemma forced Latino evangelicals to begin developing a new collective identity. Instead of adopting the term "evangelicals" to identify themselves, many Latino Protestants refer to themselves as *evangélicos*. Evangélicos courageously live within the tension of two worlds— one Spanish and one English. Given the history of the Latino diaspora, many evangélicos develop strong communities of resistance and transformation. Together it is easier to resist the white racism still present throughout the evangelical world. As evangélicos find their collective political voice, they can affirm the best of their ethnic identity and embody a faith that is relevant to the political issues most directly affecting them.[31]

Evangélicos are helping the NAE push beyond the black-white evangelical divide. Rodriguez has been shaped by both the civil rights tradition of Martin Luther King Jr. and Hugo Chavez and the neo-evangelical tradition of Billy Graham and Carl Henry. Rodriguez said: "The two men who have inspired me most are Billy Graham and Martin Luther King Jr. I appreciate Billy Graham's commitment to the Kingdom of God, his biblical orthodoxy, his personal integrity, his living what he believes, his concern for the eternal destiny of every soul, and his worldwide preaching of the Gospel that there is room at the cross for all. I appreciate Martin Luther King Jr.'s theology of loving the neighbor as embodied in the question of the Good Samaritan parable, 'Who is my neighbor?' as well as his struggle for social justice, equality for those who can't speak for themselves."[32]

Samuel Rodriguez believes that the narrative vision of Latino evangelicalism can build bridges between white and African American evangelicals. He argues, "We need to bridge relationships with other parts of the church. We have been an isolated cocoon for so long, very happy with our growth, but we have not made viable bridge-building with the African American community a priority." [33]

Cizik and Rodriguez have called on the evangelical church to stand with the oppressed and the marginalized in the United States and around the world. Allen D. Hertzke interprets the NAE's work with the persecuted as living in radical solidarity with the suffering church abroad. Hertzke writes, "Asylum seeking illustrates the vital link between the *suffering church* abroad and the *free church* in the West, which fuels the faith-based movement to harness the tools of American foreign policy in defense of global religious freedom."[34] This emphasis on the suffering of the global church, read through the lens of cosmic reconciliation through the suffering, Jewish flesh of Jesus Christ, symbolizes a transformation of the NAE's theological vision, which now considers human suffering and systemic sin with new gravity.

In his work on religious freedom, Cizik joined with conservative evangelicals deep in the heart of the Lone Star state. In the flat, sandy deserts of Texas, in the hometown of George W. Bush, an important expression of the evangelical religious freedom movement emerged during his administration. Many know Midland as the home of many Bush insiders, including the retired four-star General Tommy Franks and Secretary of Commerce Don Evans, but the town is also known for a vibrant group of ministers and laypeople, the Ministerial Alliance of Midland, Texas, that has embodied a distinctively evangelical public ethic.

No one has captured the spirit of these socially engaged evangelicals from Texas better than Deborah Fikes, an advisor and former spokesperson for the Ministerial Alliance of Midland, Texas. Fikes has played a fundamental role in the religious freedom struggle in several ways. She joined Richard Cizik and other evangelicals in encouraging President Bush to do more to bring peace and stability to Sudan and to end the genocide in Darfur.[35] When the Ministerial Alliance of Midland wrote to Sudan's Minister of Foreign Affairs Mustafa Osman Ismail, Ismail encouraged Khidir H. Ahmed, the Sudanese ambassador to the United States, to talk with

Christians from the "village of George Bush." As evangelicals in Midland lifted up their voice with other evangelicals, mainline Protestants, and Roman Catholics, President Bush began to respond. Bush appointed former U.S. Senator John Danforth as a special envoy to Sudan and began to make progress on the issue.

As the efforts of Cizik and Fikes demonstrate, for evangelicals to be successful in Beltway politics they have to work with broader coalitions of people of different backgrounds, races, and religions. Cizik's tireless advocacy for the religious freedom of those who are persecuted embodies a resurgence of an evangelical ethic of solidarity with the oppressed. There is a direct link between the NAE's advocacy for religious freedom today and the abolitionists' struggle on behalf of enslaved African Americans in the nineteenth century. Still, there needs to be more intentionality and cultivation of a prophetic intercultural evangelical coalition for justice.

By enacting this new evangelical internationalist ethic, Cizik drew a connection to the "let justice roll" tradition of King's civil rights activist tradition, as it is embodied in the ministry of John Perkins. It is no coincidence that both Haggard and Cizik increasingly began to frame their narrative political visions around the theology of Martin Luther King Jr. There is no way for white evangelicals to move forward in social ethics without dealing with the heart of racial justice. Argue called on the NAE to take on a vision of racial reconciliation, and the NAE is gradually living into this new vision. The fact that in its *For the Health of the Nation* document the NAE is moving toward a broader social ethics tradition in closer proximity to King's vision of beloved community begins to illuminate the deep fissure between Dobson and Cizik. Debates over climate change became the new battleground for the future of evangelical social ethics; Cizik saw creation care as evangelicals' hope, whereas Dobson saw it to be their demise.

Cizik's leadership of the evangelical creation care movement is built on a strong foundation of evangelical leaders from Francis Schaeffer to Jim Ball. In 1970, evangelical theologian Francis Schaeffer fired off the initial salvo of the evangelical creation care movement in his book *Pollution and the Death of Man*. In 1972, three young evangelical leaders—Ron Sider, Wes Granberg Michaelson, and Jim Wallis—started a small radical evangelical political movement called Evangelicals for George McGovern. Although McGovern lost the election, these men forged deep friendships that would prove vital to the transformation of evangelicalism from a socially conservative movement with a myopic view of America to a more broad-minded evangelical environmentalism and internationalism. Granberg Michaelson started the Creation Care Institute in Montana in the 1980s, and Ron Sider and ESA launched the Evangelical Environmental Network (EEN) in 1993. The following year, 1994, hundreds of evangelical leaders signed the "Evangelical Declaration on the Care of Creation." Evangelical environmentalism was off and running.

Richard Cizik was a central architect of the NAE's creation care movement in the early twenty-first century. His advocacy on behalf of the environment was based on his theology of the good earth and an ethic of creation care. Cizik has forged strategic partnerships with environmental activist groups and foreign dignitaries to work collaboratively on environmental justice. Leveraging many years of capital city advocacy experience, Cizik was agile and able to build bipartisan coalitions to push through environmental legislation.[36]

While evangelicals have a long track record, Cizik's environmental activism is a recent development. In 2002, Richard Cizik went with Jim Ball, the leader of the Evangelical Environmental Network, to a conference on Christianity and the environment in Oxford, England. Cizik was persuaded by evangelical scientist Sir John Houghton (the first chair of the scientific assessment group of the Intergovernmental Panel on Climate Change) that climate change was a serious global challenge that was being exacerbated by human activity. Cizik left Oxford with a newfound focus on the impact of climate change, habitat destruction, and species extinction on earth. After his heart was "strangely warmed" to the cause of environmental justice, Cizik responded, "I couldn't shirk, shrug, rationalize or escape my biblical responsibility to care for the environment."[37] While Cizik had a dramatic conversion surrounding the problem of climate change and the necessity of the church to respond prophetically, James Dobson did not.

During summer 2006, when Cizik argued that evangelicals should take responsibility for climate change, James Dobson fired back on his radio show, saying, "Evangelicals taking on the issue of environment will divide evangelicalism . . . and destroy the U.S. economy."[38] Dobson's retort demonstrates the limits of his theology of creation. His family focus had demonstrated limited his ability to grasp the environment as a worthy creation cause. Additionally, Dobson's supplemental comment regarding the destruction of the U.S. economy unveiled his underlying allegiance to a capitalist consumer economy.

Focus on the Family emphasizes the family as the primary creation order, chronologically manifest before government and the church. Focus on the Family appeals to the early chapters of Genesis for the theological framing of the institution of family, but it does not emphasize the theme of creation care that is also in Genesis. The creation care theme is, however, developed in the theology and policy statements of the NAE. The environmental issue has been contentious within evangelicalism since the 1970s; however, the NAE has acknowledged human complicity in climate change and sees environmental justice as an integral part of the association's social witness. This demonstrates a broader understanding of the creation orders and a social ethic that includes concern for animals and the earth.

To address environmental issues, the NAE teamed up with the Center for Health and the Global Environment at Harvard Medical School to convene thirty leading scientists and theologians in December 2006 and begin a dialogue. These scientists and ministers gathered at the Melhana Plantation in Georgia to discuss ways they could work together. With a common sense of urgency, they made a pledge to collaborate in addressing the problem of climate change.

The closed conversation at Melhana continued and culminated in a press conference held on January 17, 2007, at the National Press Club, cosponsored by the NAE and the Center for Health and Global Environment at Harvard Medical School. For Cizik, the environmental problem is not a theoretical question to be debated but a concrete problem that requires a practical response. Evangelical activism is a practical issue—replacing incandescent bulbs with compact fluorescents, recycling, driving a hybrid car, doing an energy audit on our houses, and supporting businesses that are creation friendly.

Cizik's involvement in advocacy around the environmental issue became an ongoing point of conflict with James Dobson. Dobson was infuriated that Cizik was leading the NAE to embrace an environmental agenda and fought tooth and nail to remove Cizik from his position, with the hopes of removing the environment from the evangelical social agenda. In Dobson's view, this issue more than any other has the possibility of dividing evangelicalism. After Dobson criticized Cizik in his May 19, 2006, Focus on the Family broadcast, he contacted President Ted Haggard calling for Cizik's resignation. Sharing Cizik's passion for the environment, Haggard stood behind Cizik and did not capitulate to Dobson's demands.

Not rebuffed by this first attempt to remove Cizik, Dobson struck back. On March 1, 2007, a letter was sent to L. Roy Taylor, chairman of the NAE board, signed by twenty-five evangelical leaders, including Gary Bauer, James Dobson, Harry Jackson, Tony Perkins, and Paul Weyrich. Most of the signers of the letter were members of the Arlington Group, a group of religious and social conservatives that meet quarterly in Washington, DC, for off-the-record conversations about the conservative movement. They wrote: "Cizik and others are using the global warming controversy to shift the emphasis away from the great moral issues of our time, notably the sanctity of human life, the integrity of Marriage and the teaching of sexual abstinence and morality to our children. . . . We believe the NAE lacks the expertise to take a position on global warming. That is the essential point of this letter. Richard Cizik also lacks this expertise, and to our knowledge, he has never been asked to speak for the rest of the Association in such areas of controversy."

The NAE board of directors discussed the letter at their spring board meeting at Leith Anderson's church in Eden Prairie, Minnesota, on March 8–9, 2007. The letter to Taylor was released to the press ten days in advance of the meeting. As the annual meeting began, word had begun to percolate about this letter.

After dinner, Richard Cizik delivered the keynote address. Cizik challenged the NAE board members to follow Jesus's courageous example in loving the neighbor: "We have heard Carl Henry's call in *The Uneasy Conscience of Modern Fundamentalism* and responded with our *For the Health of the Nation* statement. Our evangelical faith is no longer divorced from a broader social ethic. We root our activism in the redemptive work of Jesus Christ on the cross. And now with Henry's encouragement we are giving the redemptive word a proper temporal focus. Evangelicals around our country and the world are waking up to the call to love our neighbor and care for creation. This is Christ's call and it is an expression of the unity in Christ that we already share."[39]

In this statement Cizik makes several important moves. First, he grounds the biblically balanced and broad-focused *For the Health of the Nation* statement in Henry's evangelical call for justice. Second, he places Christ's redemptive work on the cross as the epicenter of evangelical public theology. Finally, he connects Jesus's person and work with the call to love the neighbor and work for unity with other Christians. We see in Cizik's Christology deep roots in the theology of Carl Henry, working out the logic of Christ's Lordship in neighbor love, church unity, and creation care. For Cizik, Christ is a paradigm of neighbor love and creation care.

Cizik's address struck a chord with the board. At a time of evangelical disunity, he called for unity. At a time of global injustice, he called for global justice. At a time when the environment was in peril, he lifted up the evangelical responsibility to care for creation. The next day, after a brief discussion, the NAE board reaffirmed its 2004 evangelical call to public engagement and decided it would continue its public ministry of creation care. Cizik had become a lightning rod during the previous year of intense public debate about the environmental problem in North America, and now the NAE board rallied around him. The NAE board's full support of Richard Cizik demonstrated a widening of the evangelical political agenda to include a truly broader agenda.

Will evangelical politics continue to be dominated by a neo-fundamentalist, pro-family politics alone, or will it span out to cover a broader range of issues, including creation care? Cizik's victory on environmental justice unveils a new day in evangelical politics. But given evangelicalism's history of colonial and racist oppression, it will have to integrate its commitment to environmental justice with its stated commitment to racial justice. Its theological commitment to all people being made in God's image, which reflects the image of Christ, the fully human and fully divine Lord and Savior of the world, is an important theological starting point. The NAE will need to spend more time connecting its current work in human rights and environmental justice to the civil rights and women's movements of the 1960s if it is to fully develop a prophetic evangelical ethic.

The evangelical ethic of the NAE has shown itself to be responsive to issues of racial and social justice. It has had a clear vision of being "salt and light" in the world, transforming the culture and creation. This transformational impulse is an important trajectory within contemporary evangelicalism. The NAE continues in the Carl Henry tradition in its ecumenical generosity in contrast to cultural separatism and in its attempt to embody a broader social ethical agenda instead of a narrow conservative political agenda. Because of its ecumenical breadth, the NAE has been able to advocate on a wide variety of issues.

Since the 1990s the NAE has tried to develop a systematic approach to social and political advocacy work, and during each period the president of the NAE has set the pace in its approach. This demonstrates how strong personalities tend to dominate the broader contours of this evangelical social movement. For example, Kevin Mannoia had a clear vision for the NAE's social action, yet he moved too fast for many of the conservatives in the movement. His pushing, in particular on racial justice and ecumenical dialogue with the NCC, met with some stiff resistance. This indicates that thinking systematically about social justice remains an ongoing struggle for the NAE constituency.

The NAE's active embrace of a broader social agenda reflects important transformations in its Christology. In the 1940s the NAE was concerned about defending the deity of Christ to Christianity's cultured despisers, but in the early twenty-first century, the NAE is interested in demonstrating through its collective action how Jesus Christ's suffering humanity is relevant to the needs of the world. The Jesus that drives NAE's politics is increasingly one who is an earthly prophet, a Jesus who cares about the poor, people of color, and the earth. The recent emphasis on the suffering of Jesus and systemic and cosmic sin are positive signs of broader public engagement.

Although many Americans think that evangelical politics is focused on a few issues, the NAE has been quietly working to support public policies dealing with a broad array of issues, including human rights, social justice, and environmental justice. As a result of his public support of same-sex civil unions, Richard Cizik was asked to resign on December 10, 2008. After Cizik the NAE's public theology will continue to be irenic, ecumenical, and socially enaged in the Obama era, but in a new configuration.

The subtle theological shifts represented in *For the Health of the Nation* reflect a new hinge point between conservative and progressive evangelicals. As a growing group of evangelicals who are participating in a broader evangelical ethic, they will be forced to ask themselves how they are different from mainline Protestants. The current institutional weakness in both the NAE and the NCC demonstrates a broader identity crisis across the Protestant spectrum. New ecumenical forums like Christian Churches Together (CCT) present a new problem for the NAE. Will the NAE's broader social ethic lead it into a broader ecumenical forum like CCT, making the NAE irrelevant? Critical to this discussion is the role that megachurch pastors like Rick Warren will play in this new paradigm of social ethics. Will they work within the NAE framework, in their own megachurch associations, or in other frameworks? From megachurch ministers to mainline Protestants, the NAE is working with new partners. Yet with its widening agenda, it is vital that it continues the struggle for racial justice.

In the shadow of the lynching tree of Jim Crow America, evangelicals of the NAE still have a long way to go in embodying racial justice. Because the NAE was founded in the postwar milieu as part of a unified Caucasian race, black and Hispanic evangelicals were marginalized. The NBEA provided a forum for black evangelicals to promote fellowship and work together in a structure parallel to that of the NAE. But after several failed attempts to merge the two organizations, a strategic partnership across racial lines should be furthered.

Sammy Rodriguez Jr. has shown one model of strategic intercultural partnership that can work. He leads the National Hispanic Coalition Leaders Conference (NHCLC), which, like the NBEA, is a parallel structure to the NAE; however, as a board member of the NAE he speaks for both organizations and constituencies on the issue of immigration. The struggle for justice in immigration brings together many important threads of evangelical ethics: Jesus as an immigrant, immigrants as made in God's image, immigration injustice as a social sin, and intercultural coalitional politics. Rodriguez has been able to make these links in part because he has gone beyond the neo-evangelical ethical paradigm of Carl Henry and Billy Graham. Rodriguez has sought to bring together the best wisdom of two vital streams of American religion, drawing not only on the evangelical tradition but also on the theology of Martin Luther King Jr. The new "justice generation" of evangelicals (Gary Haugen) is helping to bring justice to the world in the shadow of King.

7

THE CHRISTIAN COMMUNITY DEVELOPMENT ASSOCIATION: A QUIET REVOLUTION

In the post–civil rights era John Perkins emerged as one of the most important black evangelical leaders, cofounding the Christian Community Development Association (CCDA). Forged in the fires of the racial hatred of Mississippi, Perkins is one of the pioneer leaders of prophetic evangelicalism in the United States. Several generations of evangelical leaders have been inspired by his writings and teachings on the three R's of Christian community development: redistribution, reconciliation, and relocation.

Driven by the egalitarian ideal of antebellum revivalism that informed King's theological vision during the civil rights movement, CCDA is an evangelical social movement with roots in the prophetic evangelical tradition of black and white abolitionism. John Perkins continues King's emphasis on the redemptive suffering of Jesus Christ in the context of African American suffering. Perkins's prophetic vision fully engages the three ethical issues that remained after the Civil War: racial injustice, economic injustice, and Christian nationalism. In all three areas, CCDA continues to work for systemic change in communities throughout the United States. Perkins's emphasis on the suffering humanity of Jesus Christ provides a theological framework for a prophetic, intercultural evangelical ethic.

From its roots in the black evangelical underside of white modern evangelicalism, CCDA has emerged as a clear prophetic voice from the margins of the evangelical world. The organization has promoted embodied values that have historically been challenging for the white evangelical community:

racial reconciliation, community development, and social justice. Its mission is to "inspire and train Christians who seek to bear witness to the Kingdom of God by reclaiming and restoring under-resourced communities." It further asserts, in its statement of faith, "We are called to live out justice, reconciliation, and redemption." CCDA is serious about proclaiming and embodying the Kingdom of God in the most mundane details of community life.[1]

Charles Marsh has demonstrated how John Perkins embodies a black evangelical theology of social justice in the tradition of Martin Luther King Jr.[2] Connecting King's vision of beloved community with the black evangelical communitarian vision of John Perkins has important implications for understanding evangelical politics. Although many evangelicals chose not to join the civil rights movement, some like John Perkins stood against racial injustice with heroic courage. Reading John Perkins's ministry and movement as a prophetic evangelical response to the life and thought of Martin Luther King Jr. marks the beginning of a new genealogy of American evangelicalism, unveiling the ways in which prophetic black Christianity has and continues to reshape evangelical public engagement.

Out of the piney woods of southern Mississippi grew an evangelical prophet, with the roots of a mighty oak tree and the height of a towering redwood. Affectionately known by friends and family as "JP," John Perkins grew up in a family of bootleggers and gamblers. After his brother Clyde was murdered by white men, Perkins fled to California in 1947, where he found Holy Ghost religion. When he returned to Mississippi in the radical 1960s, he encountered the system of segregation that had plagued his youth as a sharecropper. Meeting angry whites in Mendenhall, Mississippi, the fire flowed through his veins rising up in his chest; Perkins was ready! He was ready to be a drum major for justice—to stand up for God's justice, to stand up for God's love, to stand up for the Kingdom of God.

Perkins became increasingly convinced that the Gospel must work come to life in the struggle against institutionalized racism and there was no better place for this to happen than in his native Mississippi. It was there in the Mississippi Delta, from Vicksburg to Memphis, Tennessee, that the most vicious form of chattel slavery was practiced on antebellum plantations. And it was there in central Mississippi that he would successfully embody the beloved community through an intentional community and training center, a small prophetic beachhead in the heart of darkness that would become a vital center of an evangelical movement for justice. Central to his vision of ministry was a strong belief in Jesus Christ as a prophet who was leading a worldly movement for love and justice.

Perkins was a reluctant convert to Christianity. He rejected the emotionalism of the black church and the racism of the white church. Given the violence and oppression of his youth in Mississippi, the idea of becoming a Christian, especially when conceived as a "white man's religion," was almost impossible. Yet, Perkins was definitely on a search for religious truth, exploring the teachings of the Jehovah Witnesses, Christian Scientists, Father Divine, and the Black Muslims. But it was through his son Spencer that John really began to deepen his pursuit of Christianity. Noticing that Spencer was glowing when he returned from his Bible classes, Perkins soon joined him, learning more about Jesus and the biblical stories. Finally, on a Sunday in November 1957 he had a personal encounter with Christ in a little Holiness church in Pasadena, California. Like many evangelicals, Perkins is a born-again believer, and from that day forward he surrendered himself to the ministry of the Gospel.[3]

Perkins's first pastoral call was to minister to children, and he has never lost his passion for youth ministry. In Southern California, John and his wife, Vera Mae, joined the Child Evangelism Fellowship to share the good news with children. At the same time, Bill Bright, one of Carl Henry's Fuller Seminary students, was on the campuses of California state schools sharing the "four spiritual laws" with students, John and Vera Mae Perkins used flannel graphs and Bible stories to share the Gospel with children. This Sunbelt evangelical gospel focused on the conversion of individuals through concrete object lessons from scripture. Teaching children biblical stories has had a lasting impact on the ministry of John and Vera Mae Perkins, whose life and vision are a living performance of the drama of redemption presented in the Bible.

Although Perkins was having a successful ministry in California, he felt a tug at his heart to return to Mississippi. His journey home was difficult, as there were many ghosts in Mississippi that haunted him. The move also challenged his understanding of evangelism, moving his conception from merely personal evangelism to include social transformation. The structures of white supremacy were so ingrained in local communities that converting folks to Christianity would not be enough. The actual structures of the racist society themselves would have to change.

Mississippi, for Perkins, lay under the shadow of the lynching tree. As a young boy, Perkins was brought up dirt poor in a sharecropper's family without a father. His brother Clyde was shot in his youth; Perkins saw him die in a hospital bed from wounds caused by bullets from the gun of a white Mississippian policeman. Perkins felt the wounds that killed his brother and decided to leave the state to heal from the pain. But the ghosts of Mississippi haunted Perkins no matter where he lived.

Perkins went west to California, where he discovered a new life, one outside the Deep South. Under the warm rays of the California sun, Perkins had enjoyed not being defined exclusively as a "black man." He enjoyed the economic opportunities that he found there, a fair wage and the opportunity to purchase a home. He knew returning to Mississippi would mean facing many economic and cultural challenges. Perkins writes, "In Mississippi every move I made was defined in terms of my race. I worked on farms and fields, I behaved in certain ways toward my employers, and I received certain wages—all of this defined in terms of my blackness. And in every one of these areas there were different standards for whites."[4] Living in California was a personal breakthrough for Perkins: there he felt free from the constant constraint of his racial subjectivity of being black, signified in southern racist mythology as being inferior. Having learned what it was like to be free of the oppression of racial signification and its legacies of violence, Perkins went home and began a lifetime journey to dismantle institutional racism. Perkins wanted to share the liberation he had experienced in California with his own people in Mendenhall, Mississippi.

When Perkins returned to Mississippi, he returned to stay. As he and his wife tried to evangelize and minister to the children in his town, he began to realize that their problems were not all spiritual, but also economic, educational, and cultural. Thus, his vision quickly moved from child evangelism to local community renewal. He believed that a realistic ministry to children should include a ministry of holistic community transformation. It was the challenge of realizing the beloved community in racist Mississippi that forced Perkins to begin the process of rethinking evangelical theology and social ethics.

In Mississippi, one of the greatest sources of problems for black youth was segregation. On May 17, 1954, in *Brown vs. Board of Education of Topeka,* the U.S. Supreme Court ruled that "separate but equal" schools were unconstitutional. This case meant that drastic changes needed to be made in the segregated Mississippi school system, which privileged whites. In 1953, the Mississippi Department of Education was spending $23,536,022 on its white students and $8,816,670 on its black students.[5] The disparities between the educations of blacks and whites were appalling. These educational systems would not be changed unless someone stood up and tirelessly advocated to change these policies. In order to minister to children in Mississippi, Perkins's ministry would need to include educational reform.

Given the resilience of segregation in Mississippi, Perkins realized that he would need to work for a renewal and restructuring of the entire community, a project that would require money and infrastructure. So he returned to California to raise money for a school. Dr. Jack MacArthur, the senior pastor of Calvary Bible Church of Burbank, California, became a generous benefactor of Perkins's ministry. In honor of MacArthur's generosity, Perkins named his ministry after MacArthur's radio ministry, "Voice of Calvary."[6]

Voice of Calvary Ministries was founded by John and Vera Mae in Mendenhall, Mississippi, in 1962. Perkins wanted to plant a church that was more than a worshiping community, one that would be a site for ministries to meet the needs of all the citizens of Mendenhall. With time the ministry grew to include a day-care center, youth program, adult education program, thrift store, low-income housing complex, and health center. As the civil rights movement was flowing through Mississippi, Perkins was in the process of thinking through an evangelical social gospel in his daily attempt to develop a holistic model of community development in Mendenhall, Mississippi.

It was through participating in the civil rights movement that Perkins could connect more deeply with the black Christian commitment to the whole gospel, both personal and social. Not all evangelicals were as eager as Perkins to join the struggle for racial justice. Perkins writes, "One of the greatest tragedies of the civil rights movement is that evangelicals surrendered their leadership in the movement by default to those with either a bankrupt theology or no theology at all, simply because the vast majority of Bible-believing Christians ignored a great and crucial opportunity in history for genuine ethical action. The evangelical church—whose basic theology is the same as mine—had not gone on to preach the *whole gospel*. . . . It wasn't a question of what 'team' to join. In terms of social justice, *evangelicals just didn't have a team on the field.*"[7] White evangelicals largely sat out the civil rights movement, while John Perkins helped lead the movement in Mississippi. Perkins lamented that "few individuals equally committed to Jesus Christ ever became a part of that movement. What all that political activity needed—and lacked—was spiritual input. Even now, I do not understand why so many evangelicals find a sense of commitment to civil rights and to Jesus Christ as an 'either-or' proposition."[8] Perkins moved from the "either/or" logic of much of conservative white evangelicalism toward a "both/and" holistic prophetic evangelical theology. Guiding Perkins's vision for justice was the notion of Jesus Christ as a prophet.

Martin Luther King Jr. was one of Perkins's chief theological influences. Perkins writes, "For black evangelicals in the sixties, King was our prophet for justice. He articulated all of our hopes and aspirations in his 'I have a dream' speech. When I heard the speech, it was like Moses calling down from the Mountain to the people of Israel. King's dream has not fully materialized but we are standing at the door of a new day. Things are changing quickly. We can see communities where blacks and whites are worshiping and working together for the Kingdom of God. We can see today that our leaders are no longer judged by the color of their skin, but by their character. Now it is time to move for reconciliation. Now it is time to move for justice. King marched so our generation could fly. Let us make his dream of the beloved community a reality." Perkins's theology of community development carries on the prophetic ethos of Martin Luther King Jr. and the civil rights movement. Like King himself, Perkins found his fundamentalist faith transformed by the activist tradition of prophetic black Christianity that erupted into life during the civil rights movement.[9]

During the 1960s Perkins began to develop a prophetic Christology in the spirit of Martin Luther King Jr.; King's vision of the beloved community and understanding of Jesus as a suffering servant who was a herald for justice provided a theological template for Perkins's social vision. Jesus's messianic manifesto in Luke 4:18–19 "captures the need for the poor to be released from oppression by incarnating Jubilee justice in community through the power of the Holy Spirit. . . . To understand why the evangelical Church in America has separated justification from justice—or, to use James' terminology, to understand why we have been strong on faith but weak on works—we have to take an honest look at ourselves, and at our history. . . . The accommodation of slavery is one of the main reasons that the American evangelical Church never really gained an anchor in strong biblical justice. Old Testament Jubilee justice provided for the release of those who had fallen into slavery, so again, we had two concepts that could not co-exist, and justice was the loser." Thus, in order to bring Jesus and justice back together, evangelicalism would have to give an honest accounting for the role that it played in the transatlantic slave trade. Jesus and justice are brought together in Perkins's theological imagination on the cross, where Jesus bears the sin and suffering of the world. Perkins says, "The image of the cross, Christ on the cross. It blotted out everything else in my mind . . . [he was] nailed to rough wooden planks . . . killed like a common criminal." Given Perkins's multiple arrests and his experience of being tortured by the police in a prison in Brandon, Mississippi, Charles Marsh is right to read Perkins as interpreting Jesus Christ as a victim of torture killed by a lynch mob. This invokes the tradition of black messianism that goes back through King to Du Bois. Perkins is expressing a Christological subjectivity not present in mainstream white evangelicalism, a Christology that connects the suffering of Jesus of Nazareth with black suffering in the Americas.[10]

As a "black man" from Mississippi who witnessed murders and experienced torture himself, Perkins's theology takes black suffering seriously. Chris Rice, who lived and worked with John Perkins and his son Spencer for seventeen years, writes poignantly about the impact that John Perkins's beating had on his psyche and the morale of his family:

> JP's son Spencer told me a part of the story JP doesn't tell. Many know about JP's beating in 1970 by white state police in a jail cell in Brandon, Mississippi. What we don't know, what Spencer told me, is how in the months after the beating—in the months after his daughter saw him in the hospital room and ran out saying, "I

hate white people, I will always hate white people"—during those long months, JP wrestled with God. Those days of spiritual pain matched his physical pain. Why bother? Why not give up on white folks? Why not just work with black folks and turn nationalist? We easily forget how many do that, how many of those scarred by the struggle for justice end up bitter, angry, in despair. What Spencer took from his father's agonizing yet liberating journey to forgiveness is that to be a Christian is a constant showdown between our shallow desires and God's deeper vision of transformation, beauty, and joy. And if JP is anything in the midst of all his activism, he is joyful.[11]

When Perkins lay on the bed of recovery, he had much to meditate on. He encountered firsthand what he calls the "the depths of white depravity." Perkins was left with a decision: would he respond with righteous anger and react against white racism or would he courageously move through his anger to love the mean-spirited white racists of Mississippi? Just as King had prayed at his kitchen table for God's help after the bombing of his home in Montgomery, Perkins prayed from his sickbed for God to give him courage to follow the shalom politics of Jesus, to be one who did not return blow for blow but boldly proclaimed a new order of peace and justice.

Perkins understood Jesus as an earthly prophet. Like King, he interpreted Jesus in the Exodus tradition: as Moses led the oppressed out of Egypt, Jesus will lead the oppressed out of their contemporary bondage. Jesus was a liberator of the oppressed. Black evangelical theologian Tom Skinner's famous "The Liberator Has Come" address at InterVarsity's Ninth Urbana Missionary Convention in 1970 brought national recognition to the emerging prophetic black evangelical theology. What is distinctive in this tradition of black evangelical liberation Christology is that Jesus as prophet is directly identified with the black freedom struggle. Within the context of this sacred drama, great African American leaders take on the role of prophets in the struggle for justice. Thus, there is often a seamless flow from biblical story to contemporary struggle.

Jesus as suffering servant and messianic prophet frames Perkins's vision. Perkins's emphasis on Jesus Christ as a builder of messianic community who meets all people wherever they are, expresses the heart of the black church tradition. It is a vivid illustration of how the black church sees Jesus as the prophetic lord and liberator of the oppressed and as the Savior who redeems us from personal and social sin: "If Christ is Savior, He must also be Lord—Lord over such areas as spending, racial attitudes and business dealings. The gospel must be allowed to penetrate the white consciousness as well as the black consciousness."[12] When the Gospel penetrates black and white consciousness, then we can push beyond the black-white binary toward a Creole consciousness. Jesus seen as an agent of God's justice in the world provides a new axis for twenty-first-century evangelical theology.

Working in the civil rights tradition of King, Perkins is able to draw on these Christological motifs in the black church tradition to create a picture of Jesus who is both the savior and a seeker of justice. Since Jesus resisted sin and suffering in the world, he remains a constant source of inspiration for freeing the oppressed, whether they be the poor of his day or of our own. Jesus's suffering becomes important for Perkins and the black church because of the deep connection between Jesus's suffering and the suffering of African Americans through two hundred years of slavery and one hundred years of segregation and lynching. Jesus is in solidarity with the suffering of African Americans and the poor, and Jesus leads the struggle for justice today.

Perkins's prophetic Christology went through the fires of the civil rights movement. During the Freedom Summer of 1964, students from around the country came to Mississippi to help with the struggle for voter registration. Freedom schools were being started in counties all over Mississippi, including one right in the heart of Mendenhall. The freedom schools taught Mississippi youth about freedom, voting rights, organizing, and public service. In a state King described as "sweltering hot with the heat of oppression," these courageous young people continued to organize, educate, and stand for justice, amidst outbreaks of vigilante violence by the Ku Klux Klan. At first, Perkins took it upon himself to evangelize and moralize the uncouth civil rights workers, many of whom weren't Christians and who drank, smoked, and had sex, offending his evangelical sensibilities. But with time Perkins began to see that joining the struggle for justice with people of other faiths or no faith at all was an important expression of the Kingdom of God. Jesus Christ loved all people, no matter what.

Perkins was glad that black youth in Mississippi could experience the love of white folks, the same love he had experienced from white evangelicals in California, which helped him heal the wounds from his painful Mississippi youth. These civil rights summer schools would provide Perkins with a model of organizing among youth that he would use later in his community and leadership development work.[13]

While Perkins worked with young people from the Student Nonviolent Coordinating Committee or the Congress on Racial Equality, a growing stream of evangelical youth came down to join the struggle for racial and economic justice in Mississippi. For example, Harold "H." and Terry Spees came South from an evangelical church in Glendale, California, to work with Perkins. Spees served as Perkins's assistant for eleven years and helped Perkins start Voice of Calvary Ministries in Jackson, Mississippi, in 1972, which emerged as a prophetic evangelical model of blacks and whites eating together, singing together, worshiping together, and working together across deep divides of race, class, and gender.

The Freedom Summer was a positive experience for Perkins's own children, who were socialized into the quiet revolution, God's righteous reign of love expressed through collective acts of justice-making in the community. Throughout their youth they experienced discrimination, often shunned by fellow white students at school in the mid-1960s. Perkins encouraged his children to join the struggle. They worked for voter registration throughout 1968 at the loading dock of the Mendenhall post office and helped to organize a black voting campaign for William "Shag" Pyron, who promised to hire blacks on the Mississippi Highway Commission. In a time of crisis, Perkins proved to be a calm and skillful organizer. Whenever there was racial injustice in Mendenhall, Mississippi, Perkins was on the scene organizing friends and family to embody God's reign of justice.[14]

On a muggy night in 1969 such a night arose. Perkins, hearing that a local "black man" had been imprisoned, jumped in a van with a friend and drove to the local jail. When they arrived, they tried to free their friend but were locked up because of their agitation. As a crowd of African Americans gathered outside of the prison, John Perkins preached about Jesus and justice from the window of his second floor prison cell. Inspired by her husband, Vera Mae immediately began to organize a boycott in Mendenhall to defy the authorities, gathering family and friends to make posters and phone calls and draft together the demands of the black community. On December 23, 1969, the boycott was announced:

> The selective buying campaign in Mendenhall, Simpson Co., was launched today, Dec. 23, 1969, primarily to secure employment in the business establishments in our town. We demand 30% of all employment in all business establishments as we are 30% of the buying population. We also urge and call for employment of Black citizens in city hall, court house. We call for police brutality to come to an end so that no more Roy Berry incidents will develop. We call for Black deputy sheriffs at the court house. We call for Blacks on the school board. We call for complete school desegregation. We call upon reasonable men, Black and white, to help us in this move to bring justice and equality to Mendenhall and Simpson County. . . . *Selective buying will continue until employment situation is corrected. . . . Final acceptance of a settlement lies with the Black Community.*[15]

Black evangelicals in the South who faced persecution had two choices: to grin and bear it or to prophetically resist. Like Rosa Parks, Martin Luther King Jr., and the freedom fighters of the Montgomery bus boycott, John and Vera Mae Perkins chose prophetic nonviolent resistance. Resistance could mean death; however, a theology of total surrender for a cause greater than yourself was the path that Martin Luther King Jr. had walked down. This was the path that John Perkins chose. When he met racism, he would fight back, but he would do it nonviolently and with the prayerful power of the whole black community behind him. It is from the blues of black suffering, including both his own physical suffering and the experience of his brother's death, that Perkins's prophetic evangelical theology arose.

The following year, 1970, the tensions were high at the annual meeting of the National Negro Evangelical Association (now the National Black Evangelical Association). The young black evangelical militants were pushing for revolutionary action amidst crisis and turmoil in the nation. They were tired of white vigilante violence and white evangelical power politics. They rejected Billy Graham's alliance with President Richard Nixon.

Hearing about John Perkins's brutal beating and imprisonment in Brandon, Mississippi, they sought to publicly stand in solidarity with him against southern racial violence. Perkins's struggle became a site of a growing collective black consciousness within the black evangelical theological imagination in the early 1970s.[16]

Perkins was gradually becoming a national figure and visionary activist within evangelical ranks, both black and white. He was a bridge between the prophetic black evangelical tradition of the South and the white evangelicals of both North and South. Perkins took trips north to proclaim the evangelical social gospel at conferences and colleges, and he brought evangelical students to the South for cultural immersion in the southern black community, helping them experience the piety and poverty of black life in the South.

Perkins's struggle was an inspiration to a growing group of evangelicals who were eager to rethink evangelical ethics. In 1973, Perkins traveled to Chicago, Illinois, to help draft "A Declaration of Evangelical Social Concern" (also known as the Chicago Declaration) to engage a vast array of social justice issues, including racism, materialism, militarism, and sexism. A group of black evangelicals, including Perkins and Bill Pannell, met with white evangelicals, among them Jim Wallis and Ron Sider, at the YMCA Hotel on South Wabash Street in Chicago. The meeting was intentionally organized along diverse gender and racial-ethnic lines.

Originally drafted by Paul B. Henry, Carl Henry's son, the declaration was revised by a team that included Wesley Granberg-Michaelson, William Pannell, Ron Sider, and Jim Wallis. The fact that the Chicago Declaration was signed by Carl Henry and his son Paul, as well as by John Perkins, Jim Wallis, and Ron Sider, who represented a more progressive political approach, was symbolic of the start of an evangelical social awakening that crossed the conservative-progressive political spectrum.

The Chicago Declaration confessed the sin of white racism, and the evangelicals who signed it, including black evangelicals like Perkins and Bill Pannell, committed themselves to working to dismantle white racism in the church and society. The declaration stated: "We deplore the historic involvement of the church in America with racism and the conspicuous responsibility of the evangelical community for perpetuating the personal attitudes and institutional structures that have divided the body of Christ along color lines. Further, we have failed to condemn the exploitation of racism at home and abroad by our economic system." White evangelicals were now joining with black evangelicals in condemning racism, including its presence in "institutional structures" and the "economic system." Prophetic black evangelicalism was transforming the white neo-evangelical establishment, helping it begin the process of decolonizing its theological imagination.[17]

The declaration also confessed that evangelicals had encouraged "men to prideful domination and women to irresponsible passivity." Pamela Cochran, in laying out the history of the evangelical feminist movement, shows that it originated in the Chicago Declaration, with many of the Chicago signers involved in the women's movement—for example, Nancy A. Hardesty and Eunice Schatz.[18] This movement toward "evangelical feminism" is tied to the social justice movement in the evangelical church. In the spirit of the radical evangelicals of the nineteenth century, the evangelicals who gathered in Chicago in 1973 launched a new theological paradigm that sought to be intercultural, egalitarian, and holistic.

In the 1980s Perkins began to think about how he could share his incarnational ministry among the poor with the broader evangelical world.[19] He came up with an ingenious way to share the lessons that he had learned in community development. Instead of starting his own organization and try to spread it around in a top-down model (like Rick Warren's purpose-driven church model), he would use a bottom-up strategy. Perkins was committed to searching in all fifty states for existing community development ministries and organizations that could join together in a loose coalition for information and resource sharing, education and leadership development, and strategic networking for justice. CCDA's focus was community development but its scope was national. In the process, Perkins ignited a not so quiet revolution as intentional communities around the country began to get in touch with each other, creating new forms of community outreach as well as subversive strategies to resist the American empire.

Through this network, Perkins was able to broaden the reach of his prophetic evangelical theology that emphasized Christ's redemptive suffering, racism and poverty as social sins, and the importance of living out the Kingdom of God in intentional community living and advocacy work. CCDA deals with racial issues and sees unjust systems as part of the problem of poverty. It calls on Christians to deal with the racism in both personal and structural ways. John Perkins helped to lead racial reconciliation movements of the 1980s and 1990s because of his early focus on the divisions among blacks and whites, the poor and rich, the powerless and the powerful in the early 1960s. Emerson and Smith highlight four key imperatives of the reconciliation movement: that individuals must be in primary relationships across racial boundaries; that people must identify the sin in social structures, dismantle racist structures, and actively and consistently work for change; that whites must repent of "personal, historical, and social sins"; and that blacks must be willing to forgive whites individually and corporately when repentance occurs.[20]

One white prophetic evangelical who understands what is at stake with evangelicalism's legacy of slavery and racism is Shane Claiborne, the founder of the Simple Way. Claiborne serves on the CCDA board and has intentionally submitted himself to the authority of John Perkins because he is a black evangelical. When Jim Wallis asked Claiborne to join the Sojourners board, Claiborne, while he has a deep respect for Sojourners, declined because of his limited time and his primary commitment to Perkins's black evangelical vision. Perkins is continuing to mentor Claiborne; they are currently writing a book together. The new urban monasticism's commitment to racial reconciliation and justice is grounded in the black evangelical theological vision of John Perkins. Perkins's theology of reconciliation has become the basis for a growing evangelical intercultural coalition for justice.

Reconciliation is embodied in the life of the church, Christ's body poured out for the healing of broken communities. In *A Quiet Revolution* Perkins writes, "The Body of Christ becomes the corporate model through which we can live out creative alternatives that can break the cycles of wealth and poverty which oppress people."[21] Perkins's politics is ecclesial politics. The church is called out of the world to embody a socioeconomic alterative to the capitalist order of the American nation-state, a nation constituted by white racism. Offering a prophetic evangelical intercultural vision of the beloved community, Perkins challenges the church to embody five specific prophetic actions: responding to the call of God, evangelizing, performing social action, working for economic development, and serving through justice and reconciliation ministries. These five prophetic actions serve as spokes that shoot out of the church, expressing the body of Christ's ministry in and for the world. When the church seamlessly performs these five actions like a spinning wheel, Jesus is able to fully offer himself to the world through the concrete ministries of the people of God. Individuals are called to pursue these things, but they must fulfill this call in the context of community. Ministries of social justice are enacted through the church and by living in intentional community. Unlike other social movements that focus in part on changing laws and policies, CCDA focuses on what Christian community should be and serves as a resource for those trying to change society through the church. Its purpose is to strengthen community organizations and individuals engaged in community development work; it is involved in equipping, mobilizing, and training the church. It partners with organizations like Sojourners that are more involved in shaping governmental policy.

In 2006, Perkins joined Shane Claiborne, Tony Campolo, Ron Sider, Jim Wallis, and other evangelical leaders in protesting the immorality of George W. Bush's proposed national budget. Perkins preached a passionate sermon the night before the protest. On the stairs of the Capitol building, at seventy-six years of age, Perkins said this was his last stand. When the police came to arrest the group that day, Perkins turned to Shane Claiborne and shared, "This is how I hope I die." Not since his civil rights days in Mississippi had he been arrested for taking a stand for justice, and something just felt right about it. Following in the footsteps of Jesus of Nazareth and Martin Luther King Jr., Perkins felt there was nothing better to devote your life to than proclaiming and embodying the Kingdom of God.

Something new is moving within evangelicalism. Perkins represents a prophetic black evangelicalism that came of age in the civil rights struggle. He has played an important role in mentoring a new generation of evangelical justice leaders, and his work marks a transformation of black politics. Because of the legacy of John Perkins, prophetic evangelicalism is emerging in a deeper shade of blue. It is bound up with the suffering of a blues people—people of African descent who live in the Americas and all those who suffer everywhere. I affirm Eddie Glaude's call for a "a great community colored a deep shade of blue, a view of community and democracy that takes seriously the complexity of racialized experiences in the United States and instantiates new forms of communication aimed at producing democratic dispositions capable of addressing the challenges of our current moment."[22] But whereas Glaude focused on this theme to rejuvenate a pragmatic vision of black politics that can inform contemporary discussions about democracy, I deploy it to rejuvenate a prophetic intercultural evangelical politics that seeks to incarnate the Kingdom of God locally, catalytically connected to communities of resistance worldwide. Glaude's analysis has deepened my critique of the white racism that undergirds the institutions of a white evangelicalism when he argues that much of the theory and practices of liberal American democracy, too, reinforce a logic of white power and privilege. From Garnett to King, Glaude understands that the Gospel of Jesus Christ refracted through prophetic black Christianity lies at the heart of radical democracy in America. African Americans' singing the blues affirms the tragic dimension of American existence and beckons all Americans, black and white, and every shade in between, to "address explicitly the tragedy of race in America."[23] Glaude's strategy to deepen the shade of blue of the black political community is to deploy a pragmatic framework to analyze black politics, but this subjects black Christianity to being a religious phenomenon that finds its value simply in an actualized political agency and problem solving. What is lost in Glaude's proposal, however, is the theological character of black Christian political identity.

Black Christianity is not primarily a sociological, anthropological, psychological, or even "religious" construct but must be approached first as a Christian theological reality. Black Christianity points to the realities of Christian identity among African-descended peoples who were perceived as the negative anchor in the colonial imagination of a white evangelical modernity's racial imagination. Black Christianity points to the Christian identity lived among a people who are positioned underneath the white modern world. It is from the Christian aspect of the identity they live that true and lasting resistance can be mounted to challenge modernity and the racial imagination at its core.

In Perkins's prophetic black evangelical politics, Christian identity centered on Jesus of Nazareth as the bearer of Israel's covenantal reality with God provides the site to resist the suffering of black folks. In arguing that black suffering is illuminated through the suffering of Jesus of Nazareth, Perkins disrupts white evangelicalism's theology of triumph. For Perkins, human suffering is illuminated in Jesus Christ so that it can be overcome. In the spirit of Ida B. Wells, who sought to end the horrific practice of lynching in the Jim Crow South, Perkins joined with Fanny Lou Hammer in ending the oppression of African Americans in Mississippi who had been denied the right to vote.

In Eddie Glaude's terms, Perkins offers a prophetic evangelical politics in a deeper shade of blue. I am sympathetic to Glaude's critique of the reification of blackness within black theology, but his interrogation of "blackness" never quite breaks through to what is Christian. This is precisely what black evangelicalism at its best accomplishes. It moved through "black consciousness" in the 1960s and 1970s, but it did not stay stuck there like the theology of James Cone. One important challenge for black theology today is to move from a politics of identity toward a politics of intercultural community. John Perkins's black evangelical vision of reconciliation has pushed beyond the black-white binary to demonstrate in CCDA's vast network of hundreds of communities around the country that intercultural communities of justice are not just a dream but living reality—a community of communities that continues to grow as a quiet revolution.

It is what is specifically Christian within black evangelicalism that can help a white evangelical modernity break out of its whiteness and its modernism circumscribed by racial and colonial logics. And insofar as black and white evangelicalism do not make this break, insofar as evangelical modernity's racial imagination cannot be perforated and displaced by the fullness of the reality of Jesus of Nazareth, who is the bearer of God's covenant with the people of Israel, to that same extent such interrogations of black Christianity and evangelicalism remain trapped within, not liberated from, the racial-colonial gaze.

In short, black evangelicalism must be seen as first and foremost a Christian reality. The Christian reality is embodying the Kingdom of God through moving with the Spirit to follow Christ in a radical ministry of love and justice. To do less than this is to settle with, not resist (to say nothing of escape the orbit of), modernity's racial imagination.

Inspired by King's vision throughout his ministry, John Perkins has faced black suffering primarily from his Christian identity. Jesus stood with the disinherited in Galilee and was killed on a Roman cross. Martin Luther King Jr. stood with the disinherited in Tennessee and was shot by a white assassin's bullet. John Perkins is standing with the disinherited in Mississippi, knowing that he too may die a martyr's death. In the 1960s, when few black or white folks were willing, John Perkins was a radical evangelical who advocated for civil rights and stood in the gap between white evangelicals and black Christians to foster practices of reconciliation so all people regardless of race and ethnicity could embody the beloved community.

Perkins's Christological locale is not lost on Chris Rice, who writes, "JP's life—even the scars of his very body—calls us to remember the wounds of Jesus's own resurrected body, wounds which did not disappear. In JP's body and story are both the signs of dying and the signs of resurrection. We cannot choose between the two. His life and his body demand our response." Communities around the world are responding to John Perkins's life and his wounded body, seeking to follow Jesus in politically embodying the kingdom through living in intentional intercultural community in the abandoned places of empire.[24] These communities are the signs of a new order, where God's justice rolls "down like waters, and righteousness like an ever-flowing stream" (Amos 5:24).

8

SOJOURNERS: THE GREAT AWAKENING

September 11, 2001, changed the face of American politics. On the day when the World Trade Center Towers in New York City and the Pentagon in Washington, DC, were attacked by terrorists, America was wounded to the core, but it pulled together with international friends to get through the crisis. When President George W. Bush decided to invade Iraq, the evangelical church was divided. Many evangelicals equated Christian patriotism with unquestioning support of the president's decision to go to war, but a smaller group of evangelicals joined international protests of an American invasion of Iraq.

Jim Wallis was among those protesting.

Wallis's conscience was awakened during the Vietnam War, when he was a young man. During that period he and some fellow seminarians started a prophetic peace community and an alternative Christian magazine called the *Post-American,* the predecessor of *Sojourners.*[1] Because of his lifelong struggle for peace and justice, Wallis was prepared to offer a strategic leadership role in the Christian anti-Iraq war movement. His organization, Sojourners, produced a "Six Point Peace Plan as an Alternative to War with Iraq." Wallis was able to share this strategy with Tony Blair's administration in England, but President Bush refused to meet with him. President Bush's refusal to meet with religious leaders opposed to the war deepened Wallis's resolve to create a culture of peace.

Wallis's commitment to social justice activism is shaped by his evangelical upbringing. A white evangelical minister raised in a midwestern Republican family, Wallis was radicalized through the civil rights and peace movements of the 1960s and started a major late twentieth-century evangelical justice coalition through two organizations: Sojourners, established in 1971, whose mission is to offer a voice and vision for social change, and Call to Renewal, a national network of churches and faith-based groups, established in 1996 to overcome domestic poverty. After the 2004 presidential election, his book *God's Politics: Why the Right Gets It Wrong, and the Left Doesn't Get It,* a *New York Times* bestseller, propelled him onto a broader national stage.[2]

In *God's Politics* Wallis argues that the political right has successfully deployed religious rhetoric, but its policies often do not reflect the values of the Gospel. The political left, in contrast, has sought a broader humanitarian agenda that often reflects Christian values, but it is unable to talk about religion. Wallis seeks to break that bipartisan divide through advocating God's politics—the call to love one's neighbor through local community activism and national public policy work. Fundamental to the argument of *God's Politics* is the belief that Jesus Christ proclaims a vision of the Kingdom of God, a prophetic reign of peace and justice.

The key values and vision of Sojourners are more consonant with Martin Luther King's vision of beloved community than with Henry's concept of the Kingdom of God and its focus on individual regeneration. As with King, Wallis in his understanding of embodying the Kingdom of God is not limited to persuasion but includes prophetic confrontation with the specific institutions that oppress the poor and people of color. Wallis developed an evangelical Christology that emphasizes Jesus as a suffering prophet whose radical teaching of the Kingdom of God entails institutional transformation in this world. When viewed from the lens of antebellum revivalism, Wallis self-consciously works out of the tradition of evangelical abolitionism embodied in the lives of Jonathan Blanchard and Charles Finney, Sojourner Truth and Harriet Tubman. American evangelicalism as an antislavery movement for justice was maintained from its earliest days within black Christianity. The rushing waters of prophetic black Christianity broke forth in the civil rights movement, working for justice for all throughout the land. Growing out of the civil rights and anti–Vietnam War movements, Wallis's prophetic evangelical theology taps into the deep river of black Christianity in order to redirect evangelicalism toward an ecumenical movement for justice.

In this chapter I will consider four matters. I begin by arguing that Wallis's blended theology is a synthesis of four streams (King's vision of beloved community, John Howard Yoder's Anabaptist Barthian vision, the Catholic Worker movement, and the contemplative-liturgical renewal movement). Second, I explain Wallis's understanding of Jesus as a suffering prophet who is victorious over the powers and principalities of the world. Third, I examine the practices of Sojourners focused on race, poverty, and war with a special focus on the period from the founding of Call to Renewal (1996) to the present. Fourth and finally, I argue that the collective identity of the Sojourners movement represents a progressive, ecumenical evangelicalism, in contrast to a politically conservative, individualistic evangelicalism. The Sojourners movement fits squarely within the field of prophetic evangelicalism understood as a biblically based, Christocentric antiracist movement for God's love and justice.

First, Wallis was shaped by King's vision for a racially and economically just social order. Wallis, like John Perkins, works out of the black social justice tradition of Martin Luther King Jr. In *God's Politics,* Wallis looks to King's vision of beloved community for a model of prophetic public engagement: "With his Bible in one hand and the Constitution in the other, King persuaded, not just pronounced. He reminded us all of God's purposes for justice, for peace, and for the 'beloved community,' where those who are always left out and behind get a front-row seat. And he did it— bring religion into public life—in a way that was always welcoming, inclusive, and inviting to all who cared about moral, spiritual, or religious values. Nobody felt left out of the conversation."[3] Wallis embraces and expands King's vision of beloved community, seeking to embody an antiracist, proreconciliation democratic politics.

Wallis left his Plymouth Brethren congregation in his youth because of its white racism. Many of the members of his church separated politics from personal faith. When Wallis raised issues of structural racism, members of his congregation would dismiss his concerns. Because his congregation had rejected him and because of the questions he raised, Wallis was warmly embraced by the black church. Wallis found sanctuary and hope in the black churches of inner-city Detroit. And by entering the African American experience of slavery and segregation, as much as a white man can, Wallis discovered a prophetic evangelical vision that held together evangelism and social justice, unified in the one mission of the church.

Martin Luther King Jr. and the black freedom movement was Wallis's entry point for asking the question of how the Gospel relates to suffering of the poor and oppressed. The speeches and sermons of Martin Luther King Jr. have shaped Wallis's thought throughout his ministry. Wallis respected the way that King seamlessly connected Jesus Christ's suffering; his own personal suffering as a black civil rights activist; and the collective struggle to overcome suffering, racism, poverty, and war. Wallis was particularly moved by King's kitchen table experience in Montgomery, which demonstrated the strong personal faith that gave him courage throughout the civil rights movement. The Kingdom of God is a personal reality, but it is also a social reality. Wallis writes, "The kingdom is the vision, but concrete political priorities and policies bring us closer to it or farther away from it. Martin Luther King Jr. had a dream—a vision he called the 'beloved community,' one completely consistent with the kingdom of God. But he fought for specific goals, such as the civil rights law in 1964 and the voting rights act in 1965." Inspired by King's dream of beloved community, Wallis has led Sojourners to continue to work for parables of the kingdom through the Mobilization to End Poverty, calling on the president and the Congress to achieve the Millennium Development Goals and cut domestic poverty in half within ten years. In the long shadow of Dr. King, the work of the Kingdom of God is an ongoing, concrete political struggle.[4]

Two books inspired by King that sparked Wallis's imagination for racial reconciliation were William Stringfellow's *My People Is the Enemy* (1966) and William E. Pannell's *My Friend the Enemy* (1968). Stringfellow, a Barthian Anglican theologian, wrote a stinging indictment of the stubborn racism of his own white people. Black evangelical Bill Pannell argued that black and white evangelicals needed to form deep and lasting friendships through joining the earthly struggle for justice together. King's deployment of Jesus's teaching of "loving the enemy" was behind the prophetic calls of Stringfellow and Pannell. From blacks in the civil rights movement to Iraqis in the current war in Iraq, Jim Wallis has always sought to call the church to love its enemies, no matter what the cost.

King's dream helped Wallis formulate essential elements for an evangelical political theology: a diagnosis of the problems, a vision to inspire, and a concrete plan to address social sin. King's analysis of America's chief idols helped Wallis see where to focus his movement's attention. Wallis takes on the triplet of King, seeking to exorcise the "visible devils of racism, poverty, and war" from the social structures of the American empire.[5] At the root of their societal presence are issues of violence, injustice, and exploitation. For King and Wallis these sins are not simply desires that need to be rooted out of the human heart; they are unjust systems that need to be dismantled and replaced with more just structures that at their best can be parables of the Kingdom of God.

Sojourners' self-understanding is based on the theme of the Exodus story from the Bible that has animated prophetic black evangelicalism from its earliest days as an antislavery social movement. As David Gutterman has insightfully pointed out, Sojourners' self-identity as a social movement draws on the biblical narrative of Exodus as it was articulated in the public theology of King.[6] Wallis joins King and the black church in seeing Jesus as a new Moses who concretely brings people out of their poverty and prison. Wallis writes, "Like another great prophet of God who led his people to freedom, Martin Luther King, Jr., climbed to the mountain top, glimpsed the promised land, but never got there himself. That is left for us. And one senses that Martin's spirit will remain restless until the great journey that he carried so far is one day completed."[7] In this passage, Wallis shows himself to be adept in the tropes of black Christianity as he lifts up a genealogy from Moses through Jesus to King and on to today. A socially engaged gospel faith that draws on Jesus Christ's second exodus and is embodied in a prophetic community exercising concrete acts of love and justice is the black evangelical faith at its best.

As "post-American," the early Sojourners community was a community in exile, estranged from more conservative evangelicals in the 1970s. Instead of conceiving the Kingdom of God as a set of creation orders to be defended, it saw the Kingdom of God as an exodus community that embodied radical democracy. Gutterman writes, "In identifying itself through the Exodus theme of sojourners, Call to Renewal is seeking to use the resonant scaffolding of Exodus to promote a vision of democratic politics that emphatically rejects the exclusionist ethos of chosen-ness. In making this rhetorical move, Call to Renewal claims the legacy of Martin Luther King Jr. and the civil rights movement and extends the implication of the metaphor of sojourners beyond King's efforts."[8] For more than three decades, Wallis has helped white evangelicals live the story of Exodus through embracing a radical Christian identity within an American empire that often resembles Egypt. Part of the post-American identity involves a stern rejection of "the exclusionist ethos of chosen-ness" that dominates the evangelical politics of the Religious Right. In this sense, Wallis's deployment of Jesus as a new Moses has helped to dislocate white evangelicalism, relocating it in prophetic black Christianity and igniting a new intercultural movement, working together toward a post-white social order of love and justice.

Second, Wallis was inspired by John Howard Yoder, a great Mennonite theologian, who argued that the church should be a distinctive counterculture community that stands against the state. Yoder was the single most important influence on the theology of Jim Wallis. Yoder articulated a prophetic evangelical politics embodied in communities of resistance that stood as contrast communities to the imperial power of the state. The anti-empire ethos of Sojourners is reflected in the title of its first monthly publication, the *Post-American*.

Yoder's *The Politics of Jesus* was a decisive manifesto for the movement, presenting a radical Anabaptist theology moving toward political engagement. *The Politics of Jesus* was a must-read among radical evangelicals of the seventies. Wallis would walk around with a very well worn copy wherever he went. Wallis's friend Wesley Granberg Michaelson said, "Yoder's *The Politics of Jesus* had a huge impact on those of us who came from evangelical backgrounds and believe Jesus's words mattered, because Yoder explained why the teachings of Jesus were important and how they mattered politically."[9]

In *Christian Witness to the State,* Yoder explains how Christians should relate to the political order and provides a model for doing so using middle axioms: begin with biblical convictions and translate them into middle axioms by identifying principles and goals that work with contemporary political discourse, thus operating on a basis of radical biblical faith but also finding a common language that creates an entry for political witness. Christians are free to use imperial language in order to seek to persuade the state to formulate more humane policies. Yoder writes, "If the ruler claims to be my benefactor, and he always does, then that claim provides me as his subject with the language I can use to call him to be more humane in his ways of governing me and my neighbors. The language of his moral claim is not the language of my discipleship, nor the standards of his decency usually to be identified with those of my servanthood. Yet I am quite free to use his language to reach him."[10] Yoder's public theology simultaneously affirms the distinctiveness of the community of discipleship while also providing language to communicate with the state to inspire it to join the church in manifesting parables of the kingdom in light of the coming reign of God.

Wallis has engaged Yoder's Anabaptist Barthian vision in conversation with other theologians who broadly worked out of Yoder's tradition, including Jacques Ellul and William Stringfellow. One of the early columnists of *Sojourners,* Bill Stringfellow, had a profound impact on Wallis and his friends. Wallis was inspired by Stringfellow's *An Ethic for Christians and Other Aliens in a Strange Land,* which expressed the witness of a countercultural community going against the grain of the culture and understood the life of the community as a collective life that is not to be co-opted by the culture.

Third, Sojourners was shaped by progressive Catholic thought, including the Catholic Worker movement. Dorothy Day was a shining star of the Catholic Worker movement. Sojourners was shaped by Day's thought, which also influenced the Fellowship of Reconciliation. Dorothy Day's witness of simplicity and direct service with the poor, while in direct engagement with the political order, was very influential on the early Sojourners movement. The Catholic Worker movement began serving food and offering hospitality in its first houses. It embodied radical faithfulness to the Gospel in intentional community life but made an impact on the political order through direct-action protests, including opposition to the Vietnam War, foreign policy in Latin America, and nuclear warfare. Many members of the Sojourners movement also seek to embrace the tension of living a life of radical discipleship that includes both simple living in intentional community and radical protest against the empire's ways of war.

A fourth and final influence on Wallis and the Sojourners movement was a stream of the contemplative and spiritually rooted tradition exemplified by Henri Nouwen and Church of the Saviour in Washington, DC. The Sojourners community moved to the capital city because it wanted to be around people who had some history of spiritual depth in living as a community. Church of the Saviour provided both a deep spirituality and serious political engagement. Wesley Granberg Michaelson said, "It took a while for this deep Christian spirituality to settle into the community. Early on I took the Sojourners community to my grandfather's cottage on Lake Geneva and taught about the inward contemplative life. It was hard for the political activists like Wallis who were 'wired to politics' to sit in silence and draw wisdom from staring at an apple."[11] Sojourners has thrived as an ecumenical social movement because it has drawn deeply from the wells of Christian spirituality. It is the transformative power of God in Christ that sustained the movement in times of weakness and struggle. This spiritual stream of the Sojourners' vision demonstrates that social justice and inner transformation are inextricably linked.

These four streams of theology—King's vision of beloved community, Yoder's Barthian theology, the Catholic Worker movement, and contemplative communitarianism—would shape this emerging prophetic evangelical movement. These influences demonstrate that from the beginning, while Wallis himself was an evangelical, his community was ecumenical, informed by many streams of the Christian tradition, including Roman Catholic thought and the black church tradition. All of these theological streams inform Wallis's Christology.

As with other evangelicals, Wallis argues that Jesus is the Lord and Savior of the world. However, he places special emphasis on Jesus being "of the world," focusing on the humanity and worldliness of Jesus's salvation and Lordship. He builds on Carl Henry's understanding of the Lordship of Jesus Christ, implying that Christians need to penetrate all arenas of society, including the political sphere. Wallis moves beyond Henry, however, in the way he develops Jesus's teaching of the Kingdom of God. Whereas Henry emphasizes the teachings of Jesus that lead to preservation of creation orders, Wallis emphasizes the teachings of Jesus that call for the disruption and transformation of systems of oppression. For Wallis, the Kingdom of God "is far more than a call to a new inner life, or a rescue operation from heaven. It is an announcement of a new order of life that is intended to change everything about the world, and us with it."[12] This eschatological "announcement of a new order of life" inspires Christians to challenge the kingdoms of this world by collectively embodying God's righteous reign of love and justice. Wallis's emphasis on the suffering and vulnerability of Jesus Christ, the social dimension of sin, and the prophetic and collective nature of kingdom life are all themes he draws from the theology of Martin Luther King Jr.

From the beginning, the Sojourners community has been driven by a vision of Jesus as a suffering prophet. The books of Jim Wallis and the pages of the *Post-American* present a portrait of Jesus Christ as a suffering servant who actively engaged the "powers and principalities" of his day. As sojourners, the call of being disciples entails understanding that the suffering that Christians experience for living the Gospel can be understood only through the narrative of Jesus Christ. The Christological vision that guided the early Sojourners movement focused intently on the prophetic character of Jesus Christ's earthly life and his revolutionary teaching of the Kingdom of God. The plotline of Jesus's life unveils his deep concern for the suffering of others, demonstrated through his miracles and healing as well as his own experience of suffering, as he was tortured and crucified as part of a Roman execution. It is only through the axis of the cross of Christ that human suffering can be fully illuminated.

Wallis and his fellow evangelicals who started the "post-American" community at Trinity Evangelical Divinity School in Deerfield, Illinois, were disillusioned with conservative American Christians who defended the status quo. These young prophetic evangelicals came of age during the marches of the civil rights movement and the protests of the Vietnam War. The majority of evangelicals at Trinity, and also at Wheaton College, were ambivalent about the activist culture of protest and civil disobedience. Yet there was always a small but resilient remnant who kept alive the spirit of the radical evangelical abolitionists of the nineteenth century.

In the inaugural issue of the *Post-American,* the predecessor of *Sojourners* magazine, Wallis wrote: "We described ourselves as a movement from two tribes—student radicals who out of our commitment to justice discovered Christ as an ally, a liberator, a Lord, and longtime Christians who began to see in the gospel a call to radical discipleship. As radical Christians we seek to recover the earliest doctrines of Christianity, its historical basis, its radical ethical spirit, and its revolutionary consciousness."[13] The Sojourners movement drew on the wisdom of an older generation of activists while being fueled by the energy of evangelical youth.

The "revolutionary consciousness" of Wallis and his friends was indebted to the "black consciousness" of black evangelicals of the 1960s, men like William Bentley and John Perkins. As a result of his youth in the black church, Wallis had sensitivity for black suffering and sought to understand it Christologically. Discipleship is radical only when one will let nothing hinder him or her from full surrender to Jesus Christ and his kingdom. These prophetic evangelicals in the 1970s were inspired by a Jesus who loved all people regardless of their gender or race, was on the side of the poor and the suffering, and came to bring shalom to a world riddled with sin and violence.

The portrait of a prophetic Jesus is presented in Wallis's book *Call to Conversion* (1981). In this work he describes Jesus as a prophetic preacher who proclaims the Kingdom of God, a reign of peace and justice. In chapter 1, entitled "The Call," Wallis describes Jesus's call to radical conversion: "The goal of biblical conversion is not to save souls apart from history but to bring the kingdom of God into the world with explosive force; it begins with individuals but is for the sake of the world." Thus, Wallis understands that conversion is not just the redemption of individuals but also includes a transformation of the world.[14]

"God is personal, but never private" has been a leading theological trope in the Sojourners movement. Along with Henry and King, Wallis shares the conviction that God is personal and that Christian faith should be public, but for Wallis, the church's embodiment of the Kingdom of God must include a vigilant confrontation of the "powers and principalities" in concrete societal institutions. Of Jesus and the kingdom, Wallis writes, "Without the Kingdom, the gospel is stripped of its public meaning."[15] By emphasizing the Kingdom of God as a movement of justice and social transformation as well as individual conversion, Wallis moves beyond Carl Henry's theological architecture, which focuses on the sin and salvation of individuals and articulates a vision of the Gospel that demands systemic transformation, along the lines of Martin Luther King Jr.'s vision of a beloved community.

Wallis's focus on Jesus's human suffering and his radical teaching of the Kingdom of God provides the narrative vision that guides a growing evangelical movement for justice. Although not all staff members of Sojourners are self-identified evangelicals, they are all Christians of different stripes who share a prophetic evangelical ethos, including their common concern for Jesus's call for justice to be seen concretely in the world. This call to justice has been expressed in different ways throughout the history of the organization.

In its early days the Sojourners community was a group of disaffected evangelical seminary students. They felt alienated from the U.S. government and their church. Through publishing the *Post-American*, they established an alternative evangelical voice and a community that was on the margins of the empire. Developing an intentional community in Washington, DC, was the next phase of this prophetic evangelicalism. Following in the footsteps of Jesus Christ the prophet, the Sojourners community bore countercultural witness. In contrast to a U.S. culture of racism, war, and poverty, it sought to create a community that embodied the virtues of reconciliation, peace, and justice. Living in community proved difficult. Having to deal with the personal sins and problems of individual members of the community on a daily basis became a challenge for Sojourners. Lofty political ideals often pale in comparison to the personal politics involved when a large group of people live in the same house with limited resources. Yet amidst the complexities of embodied community living, what is theologically significant is how the Sojourners' community discerned the risen Christ in their midst—most often it was in places of suffering.

Like John Perkins, Wallis understands Jesus as one who is in solidarity with the poor, a political view of Jesus that has been forsaken by white evangelicals for a politics of fear.[16] Critical to his vision of God's politics is the way that Jesus stands with the marginalized. "God's politics is therefore never partisan or ideological. But it challenges everything about our politics. God's politics reminds us of the people our politics always neglect—the poor, the vulnerable, the left behind."[17] Subject to famine and cold, the vulnerable flesh of the poor becomes the point of access to the One who is suffering with and for them, Jesus the Jew, who in his very fleshly existence in Nazareth and now through his body, the church carries the poor until they overcome their suffering, finding true freedom.[18]

In the early 1970s a new Christology was emerging within evangelicalism that emphasized Jesus and justice. Forged in the fire of black evangelical suffering, theologians like William Bentley, Vincent Harding, John Perkins, and Tom Skinner began to think about Jesus Christ as a suffering liberator, inaugurating a reign of justice that continues today in the church's ongoing nonviolent struggle against social sin. We see an evangelical expression of the "world relevance" of Jesus Christ expressed in the opening salvo of "A Declaration of Evangelical Social Concern" (1973), which Wallis and John Perkins helped pen: "As evangelical Christians committed to the Lord Jesus Christ and the full authority of the Word of God, we affirm that God lays total claim upon the lives of his people. We cannot, therefore, separate our lives from the situation in which God has placed us in the United States and the world."[19]

It is vital that evangelical faith in Jesus Christ relate to the concrete sites of suffering and injustice within the United States and abroad. In the 1970s the social shape of evangelical ethics was expanding to include the suffering of those on the underside of the American empire. As Mark Toulouse writes, "The Chicago Declaration, if anything, marked a passing of the torch to a younger generation of evangelicals who would fulfill Henry's call in ways he had not really ever imagined."[20] Since both Henry and Wallis were signers of the Chicago Declaration (1973), we can interpret Wallis's ministry as a "natural extension" of Henry's ambition for a robust evangelical public theology. The Chicago Declaration held out the possibility of a truly prophetic evangelicalism, a trajectory that Wallis has continued to travel. Where Wallis went beyond the Henry trajectory of evangelical ethics was through his emphasis on Jesus's path of redemptive suffering that led to the cross, the path that Christ's disciples were to follow. This is a path that had been walked and thought through by black evangelicals, who from their vantage were able to challenge the racial imaginary of modern evangelicalism and point to a new economy, a jubilee economy, where all people could have their debts forgiven and lay their burdens down.

Rooted in the black evangelical freedom struggle, prophetic evangelicalism is an antiracist, proreconciliation Protestant Christianity that affirms the authority of the Bible, the saving Lordship of Christ, and a Kingdom of God ethic embodied in the church's common mission. What distinguishes prophetic evangelicalism from other forms of evangelicalism is that it begins with an acknowledgment of white evangelicalism's racist past. As noted in chapter 2, although the Civil War ended slavery, the problem of racism continued through the civil rights movement to today. Carl Henry had an "uneasy conscience" about many social issues, including white racism, but he was not able to articulate a doctrine of Jesus Christ that was connected to the institutions of the world, including institutionalized white racism. As a result, evangelicalism was left without an honest social analysis of racism and a clear, comprehensive public theology to guide its political engagement. Jim Wallis sought to strengthen these weaknesses within evangelical ethics by viewing the problem of racism from the black underside of a white evangelical modernity, finding there a new Christological architecture to address America's white racial imaginary.

Racial justice has always been an important animating value for Wallis. Growing up in Detroit, Wallis observed the ways in which poverty, racial profiling, and police brutality affected the black community. In inner-city Detroit, Wallis was awakened to the depth of the struggle of the African American community in the crucible of white racism and the hope of Christianity's revolutionary spirit embodied in the preaching and praise of the black church. It was from prophetic black Christianity that Wallis learned that the Gospel had both a personal and a social dimension. Thus, in Wallis's vision, life, and ministry we see a concrete illustration of how black evangelical faith transformed his white evangelical faith, helping him prioritize race in his constructions of social justice and poverty alleviation.[21]

A prophetic evangelical theology must begin with an honest confession of America's original sin: "Racial salvation has not yet come to the house

of America, perhaps in part because the white majority has yet to take responsibility and make restitutions for the sins of slavery and racial discrimination. . . . The United States of America was established as a white society, founded upon the genocide of another race and then the enslavement
of yet another."[22] Given America's very constitution as a nation in whiteness, the Gospel of Jesus Christ provided another story in which black selfhood and subversive moral agency could emerge. Wallis's experiences worshiping in the black church in his youth in Detroit was an initiation into
another world where the new order of Christ's kingdom was breaking into
a nation saturated in whiteness. With echoes of the prophetic black evangelicalism of John Perkins, Wallis's synthesis of Jesus and racial justice provided an important foundation for early twenty-first century prophetic
evangelicalism.

Jim Wallis has done much more than most white evangelicals in his gen-
uine attempt to live out an antiracist, proreconciliation vision. Through-
out his ministry, he has been intentional in working actively with many
African American religious leaders, among them Jeff Brown, Yvonne Delk,
Darren Ferguson, Vincent Harding, Roy Hammond, John Perkins, Eugene Rivers, and Barbara Skinner. More recently he has worked closely with
Bob Franklin, James Forbes, Lisa Sharon Harper, Frederick Haynes III,
Obery Hendricks Jr., Zina Jacque, Rep. John Lewis (D-GA), Otis Moss III,
Tavis Smiley, Romal Tune, and Cornel West. Sojourners has had good syn-
ergy in working with the black church, even some of the more radical, black
nationalist expressions of black Christianity. For example, Otis Moss III, senior pastor of Trinity United Church of Christ (UCC) in Chicago, where
President Barack Obama was a long-term member, used Sojourners' "Voting All of Your Values" guide as a bulletin insert in advance of the 2008
election, encouraging his congregation to get out and vote in that historic
election.

The staff of Sojourners is increasingly multiethnic, with African Americans serving in strategic senior roles. Adam Taylor, a young African American activist-theologian who works out of the King tradition, represents
the new post-white, multiethnic faith of Sojourners. Taylor met Wallis
while he was a graduate student at Harvard University's Kennedy School
of Government, where Wallis taught a course focused on the role of faith
in American politics. The course was a seminal moment in Taylor's faith

and career because it fused his passion for the church with his commitment to social justice and love for politics. At that time Taylor was serving as the second president of Harvard's campuswide chapter of the NAACP, working to galvanize a national campaign focused on educational equity and opportunity. A year after finishing at the Kennedy School, Taylor accepted a call to the ministry at Union Baptist Church in Cambridge, Massachusetts, and co-founded Global Justice, an organization inspired by the Student Nonviolent Coordinating Committee (SNCC) that educates, trains, and mobilizes college students around social and economic justice issues. The organization's first campaign focused on fighting HIV/AIDS in Africa and across the world and was instrumental in driving down the prices for AIDS drugs and pressuring President George W. Bush and Congress to dramatically increase funding for AIDS prevention and treatment programs.

Taylor has served as a younger prophetic black Christian voice within Sojourners, complementing Jim Wallis, speaking and preaching at Christian colleges, conferences, rallies, and other events. Since joining the staff, Taylor has led the expansion of Sojourners' constituency-building and organizing work, seeking to develop a clearer organizing strategy and stronger infrastructure behind a faith-driven movement that transforms U.S. politics. Beginning with the 2006 midterm election and again in the 2008 elections, Taylor led efforts to distribute millions of nonpartisan voter issue guides across the nation aimed at motivating Christians to vote all of their values, inclusive of racial justice, economic justice, peace, a consistent ethic of life, creation care, human rights strengthening families and renewing culture.

In 2007 Taylor was promoted to senior political director and now oversees both the policy and legislative work of the organization and its organizing efforts to build a constituency around the country that consists of online activists, clergy, and community leaders. As a new black evangelical voice, Taylor is deepening prophetic evangelical theology in the tradition of Martin Luther King Jr.: "Dr. King called Jesus the world's most dedicated noncomformist, whose ethical nonconformity still challenges the conscience of humankind. . . . Within his context, Jesus served as an agent of justice through his ministry and teaching, resisting and defying the powers of the religious leaders and the Roman authorities. . . . We are called to follow Jesus into the highways and byways of this world, seeking to embody the kingdom's values and creating kingdom space here on earth."[23] In this passage we see Taylor link Jesus, King, and the contemporary church through the lens of Christians' subversive moral agency and their call to create "kingdom space here on earth." By utilizing its moral agency for the common good, the church is able to more fully participate in the Kingdom of God.

Taylor is currently leading Sojourners' Mobilization to End Poverty, which is based on the notion that racism and poverty are coextensive in the United States. Taylor says, "Sojourners has been intentional about dealing with racial justice. Our work to unite the church to overcome poverty has always recognized the inextricable link between poverty and race in America. While we have our blind spots and room for growth we are making strides to reach out to the next generation of Latino, African American, Native American, and Asian leaders. Nearly half of the participants at our annual Pentecost conference are now emerging leaders between the ages of twenty-one and thirty-five with a growing group from communities of color."[24] Taylor has led Sojourners in reaching out to communities of color. Through Sojourners' leadership on comprehensive immigration reform the organization has built deeper relationships within the Latino church community. It has also worked to develop stronger ties to the black church, particularly through collaboration with the Samuel DeWitt Proctor Conference.

But white supremacy has grown long and deep roots in the soil of American and evangelical institutional life. If evangelicalism is going to become more intercultural, this will mean that many white leaders will need to give up power and political influence to lead in more collaborative ways that empower a broader set of people. Because many white people know primarily white people and are blind to their power and privilege, it is difficult for them to overcome the structural evil of racism. Yet it is vital that evangelicals are pushed to confront this sin. Emerson and Smith argue that white evangelicals do not confront issues of structural sin because they tend to deny them altogether; they argue: "The individualist perspective does not eliminate the ability to see socially structured issues. What it does do, in the context of a racialized society, is eliminate the ability to see advantage, therefore creating a society where all compete for something akin to Bakhtin's most favored victim status."[25] Thus, as Sojourners moves ahead with its new Mobilization to End Poverty, it is vital that it give an account of the ways in which whites have a certain set of social and economic advantages, challenging them to listen and learn from the truth-telling of the poor and people of color, responding through active participation in an intercultural movement for justice.

Even though Sojourners has provided leadership in addressing racial justice within the evangelical community, it can continue to develop a deeper specificity in its analysis of the relation of the oppressors and the oppressed, particularly regarding this dynamic among blacks and whites. When race is on Sojourners' social agenda, it is often sublimated to other issues, like poverty and immigration, so Sojourners can gain a broader hearing, greater cultural legitimacy, and be seen as a consensus builder. Sojourners' poverty alleviation efforts will not be successful unless racial justice is foregrounded in the discussion.[26]

Since the early 1990s Sojourners has gone through a transition from its earlier Anabaptist, communitarian ethos toward a more Reformed public engagement model. Sojourners' discourse has shifted from the particularity of the biblical grammar of discipleship toward the democratic discourse of citizenship. Through Yoder's notion of "middle axioms," Wallis found a bridge between the church and the public square. The church was formed by the language of scripture, but this language would need to be creatively translated into a new language to persuade political decision makers in the public square.

Guided by a narrative vision of Jesus as prophet, the practices of the Sojourners would gradually emerge into organizing, advocacy, and direct-action politics. The logic of the King tradition of theology would become even more apparent in the work of Sojourners in the 1990s: the Call to Renewal and Mobilization to End Poverty campaigns can be read as a continuation of King's poor people's campaign. One of the reasons that Wallis's vision of Christ's teaching of the kingdom has been so well received is that it draws on different streams of America's Great Awakenings, including conservative and progressive Protestant traditions, black church and Roman Catholic traditions. Wallis's public theology has sought to be generously ecumenical, intentionally multiethnic, and committed to a radical interpretation of the life and teachings of Jesus Christ.

During the early 1990s, Wallis saw that the evangelical church stood at the crossroads: would it continue to be dominated by the Religious Right or could prophetic evangelicalism grow into a national movement of justice, tapping into the deep streams of the activist revivalist religion of the nineteenth century? The Call to Renewal Campaign to end poverty launched in 1996 was tasked with presenting a viable public theological alternative to the power politics of the Religious Right, which were grounded in the fragments of a fundamentalist past. During the early twentieth century, evangelicalism was transformed by a number of cultural and theological factors and lost much of its radical social justice edge. The factors leading to a privatized faith were fundamentalist separatism[27] and a focus on personal morality instead of public justice.[28] Wallis sees this privatization of faith embodied in the Religious Right's fundamentalist antipolitical separatism as "the great heresy of twentieth century evangelicalism."[29]

Wallis sees a divide in contemporary evangelical political life: one strategy is the power politics of the Religious Right, the other a more extensive campaign for justice in the spirit of the civil rights movement.[30] In fact, as the Religious Right has defined itself through adversarial framing with the secular liberals, Wallis and his movement define themselves in part through framing against the Religious Right. He argues that some members of the Religious Right have been seduced by President George W. Bush's use of religious symbols to legitimate a "theology of empire" implemented through militaristic warfare against an "axis of evil" and global terrorists, continuing this Manichean heresy.[31] Wallis aligns himself with King's legacy, critiquing the failure of Jerry Falwell's Moral Majority and Pat Robertson's Christian Coalition: "The Religious Right went wrong by forgetting its religious and moral roots and going for political power; the Civil Rights movement was proven right in operating out of its spiritual strength and letting its political influence flow from its moral influence."[32] The thesis of *God's Politics* is that faith in the personal God of the Christian faith demands socially transformative public action conceived as prophetic worship of the triune God. To affirm both the personal and social dimensions of the Gospel means that prophetic evangelical theology will look more weighty and substantial in its work of justice-making, in contrast to the shallow shibboleths of the Religious Right.

Wallis has challenged the Religious Right's Christology, asking, "How did the faith of Jesus come to be known as pro-rich, pro-war, and only pro-American?"[33] Sojourners has distinguished itself from the Religious Right in many ways, including promoting a more internationalist view of U.S. foreign policy. For example, Sojourners does not take an "uncritically pro-Israel position" like much of the rest of the evangelical world.[34] Sojourners' focus on international peace, however, is not disconnected from other evangelicals. The NAE failed to come up with a document in support of the war in Iraq despite the work by Richard Land and others to organize evangelical public commitment to it.[35] Sojourners' persistent and persuasive arguments against the war in Iraq played an important role in preventing the NAE from making a public statement in support of the war.

In 2006, Sojourners was part of a campaign among evangelicals throughout the United States to call for increased action in Darfur. Two dozen prominent evangelicals issued a joint appeal for President Bush to take the lead in sending a multinational, United Nations–backed peacekeeping force into the Darfur region of Sudan. They included not just liberal religious leaders but also several notable conservatives, including Richard Land of the Southern Baptist Convention and Ted Haggard, then president of the NAE.[36]

One of the ways that Wallis has tried to bring a progressive agenda into the evangelical church is through renewed attention to the Bible. Michael Kazin argues, "[Wallis's] point is that conservative evangelicals are misreading the Bible."[37] Wallis argues that he shares some of the same concerns as other conservative Christians. "I actually happen to be conservative on issues of personal responsibility, the sacredness of human life, the reality of evil in our world, and the critical importance of individual character, parenting, and strong 'family values,' writes Wallis.[38] Wallis's conservative convictions have served as a way to try to gain support among conservative evangelicals for the agenda of Sojourners.

In his dialogues with conservative evangelicals, Wallis is always in search of common ground. Wallis writes, "I remember a dialogue I had with leaders of Focus on the Family in Colorado Springs a few years ago. I told them I was completely with them in believing that the breakdown of the family is a major crisis in America, and that the reality of many children falling through the cracks of our shattered family systems is a great danger and tragedy. But then I said that I didn't think gay and lesbian people are the ones mostly responsible for all of this, and I asked why their group's focus was so largely on them. After a long discussion, they conceded that point and said they agreed that the breakdown of the family in America is attributable more to 'heterosexual dysfunction than to homosexuals.' So we have some common ground to build on there." Focusing on what the right and left have in common provides a way out of the culture wars and toward a prophetic politics of hope that is serious about collaboration for the common good. Kazin writes: "To his credit, Wallis doesn't write off right-wing evangelicals as depraved. Sharing the same theological grounding, he addresses them as fellow citizens, as well as fellow Christians, with whom one must debate if one wishes to defeat them. To counter the Right's focus on abortion, Wallis endorses the late Joseph Cardinal Bernardin's concept of 'a seamless garment of life,' in which the countless victims of war and poverty would be treated to the same compassion the Right sheds on the 'unborn.'"[39] Sojourners has begun to partner with the NAE in seeking to broaden the pro-life agenda to include meeting all human needs.

Sojourners' prophetic evangelical vision is pro-life all the way down. Wallis affirms the prophetic work of evangelicals in the past who led the struggle on a number of issues, including the abolition of slavery, the end of child labor, and the support of women's rights. He sees the issue of extreme global poverty as the new front for an evangelical revival for justice. In the countries of both the global South and the North Atlantic, poverty eradication is the issue that is unifying the global church. As abolitionist preachers in the antebellum period called people to the altar to accept faith in Jesus Christ and sign up for the abolition movement, Jim Wallis is calling a new generation of people to come to the altar to accept faith in Jesus Christ and sign up for a justice movement to end extreme global poverty. Evangelicalism for Wallis is about the good news of Christ, and Jesus was anointed to bring good news to the poor (Isaiah 1, 11, 61; Luke 4). Wallis argues that "no matter what else the gospel does in our lives, if our gospel message is not 'good news to the poor,' it is simply not the gospel of Jesus Christ."[40]

In the spirit of Billy Graham, in 2008 Jim Wallis began a cross-country revival campaign. Starting in Ohio, Wallis plans to hold justice revivals in different cities throughout the United States. In his book *The Great Awakening,* he argues that we have entered "a post–Religious Right era" as progressive evangelicalism has become a national movement of justice, rooted in the social struggles of earlier religious awakenings. Wallis writes:

> It's time to remember the spiritual revivals that led to the abolition of slave trafficking in Britain and slavery in the United States, the centrality of the black church's leadership in the U.S. civil rights movement, the deeply Catholic roots of the Solidarity movement in Poland that led to the overthrow of communism. It's time to recall how liberation theology in Latin America helped pave the way for new democracies, how Desmond Tutu and the South African churches served to inspire victory over apartheid, how the Dalai Lama is keeping hope alive for millions of Tibetans, and, today, how the growing evangelical and Pentecostal churches of the global South (the developing or underdeveloped countries, primarily in the Southern Hemisphere) are mobilizing to challenge the injustice of the global economy. I believe that we are seeing the beginnings of a similar movement again, right here in America. I believe we are poised on the edge of what might become another spiritual revival or awakening that will change things—big things in the world. We may be seeing the beginning of a revival for justice.[41]

Wallis's proclamation of a message of Jesus and justice resonated with people of faith across the ecumenical spectrum, inspiring them to work together for the common good.

Many progressive Christian groups are better at doing social justice than they are at spiritual renewal, and conservative evangelicals have emphasized spiritual renewal while often neglecting a broader social ethic. Sojourners has the twin missions of holding those two biblical streams in constant connection. Wallis's message picks up how those who value social justice (e.g., mainliners) are looking for a more personal gospel, while evangelicals are looking for a more holistic gospel of justice. In addition to mainliners and evangelicals, Wallis's message also resonates with a group of spiritual seekers who are drawn to the notion of being a Christian to be an agent of spiritual transformation in the world, as well as people who are already social activists but do not have a spiritual grounding for their activism.

Justice revivals are an opportunity to focus on reviving hearts of a new generation in a way that can spark a movement to overcome the unnecessary economic and social injustice that plagues our country and world. Aaron Graham, coordinator of the justice revivals, says: "If we are going to continue building a movement to overcome poverty we will not only need to go upstream to get at the root causes of injustice to see who is throwing bodies into the river, but we also need to go upstream from politics itself and get back to the Gospel story that calls us to personal conversion. I believe our world is longing for the articulation of a gospel that integrates personal and social change, and I believe that Sojourners is uniquely positioned to facilitate that kind of revival in our country."[42]

Revival and reform go together more easily for those who are directly affected by injustice. Slaves during the abolition struggle and African Americans during the civil rights movement actively joined the struggle against injustice because they were the ones who were being oppressed. The contemporary experience of many white evangelicals is different: they are trying to repent for their racist sins through working with people of color and the poor to dismantle white racist institutions. White evangelicals are realizing that their faith is incomplete apart from participating in God's work of loosening the chains of injustice. Black suffering illuminated from the suffering of Jesus Christ becomes a Christ-centered entry point for white evangelicals to participate in the embodiment of a new political order of jubilee justice. Intercultural coalitions for justice are vital for the future of the church's mission of justice and reconciliation.

Sojourners has been successful in mobilizing an intercultural coalition for justice, but it is increasingly identified with the Democratic Party. After the 2004 presidential election, Democrats sought out Wallis to begin to understand the values of evangelical Americans. Many Democrats were completely flabbergasted that an issue like gay marriage could become such a big mobilizer for the Religious Right. Wallis began working with the Democratic Party to help them become more effective in discussing religious values in national political discourse. While popular campaigns, such as "God is not a Republican or a Democrat," argue for a theology that ignores partisan boundaries, Sojourners' framing sought to promote a growing movement of Democratic politicians who share many of the same value commitments as Sojourners.

In advance of the 2006 midterm elections, Wallis hosted the tenth annual Call to Renewal conference. On the last day, several hundred participants marched to the Capitol to call for Congress to hold up the issue of poverty as a legislative priority. During the 2006 midterm elections, Democrats took back both houses of Congress. On the airways of mainstream and Christian radio, new prophetic evangelical voices were heard from members of Sojourners, Faithful Democrats, and a growing number of young "Red-letter Christians." Along with Randall Balmer and Tony Campolo, Jim Wallis is one of the evangelical front men for this progressive evangelical political movement. After the midterm elections, when they were looking for a bridge, a voice able to reach a large segment of Americans, the Democratic Party turned to Wallis. He delivered the Democratic radio message on December 4, 2006, marking the first time a religious leader has delivered such an address.

After the midterm elections, Wallis's connections to the Democratic Party were strengthening, and he was committed to helping the Democrats take back the White House in 2008. On June 4, 2007, Sojourners hosted a "Presidential Forum on Faith, Values and Poverty," with a live broadcast on CNN of leading Democratic presidential contenders Hillary Clinton, John Edwards, and Barack Obama at Lisner Auditorium at George Washington University. But it did not host a similar event for Republican candidates. Through candidate forums, a justice revival in the critical swing state of Ohio, and informal support of the Matthew 25 Network, Sojourners actively provided its organizational infrastructure to deliver the progressive evangelical vote in the 2008 election. Sojourners' "Voting All of Your Values" campaign was able to successfully reverse engineer Focus on the Family's "I Vote Values," propelling Democratic success in the polls in the 2006 and 2008 elections. Wallis has a different message, but his tactics resemble those of the Religious Right. James Dobson and Jim Wallis are both evangelical pragmatists, they both think religious values play a determinative role in national politics. Although they disagree over what those values should be, their strategies and tactics for promoting those values are almost identical.

Increasingly concerned about its media exposure and influence on progressive politics, Sojourners has drifted from its earlier radical communitarian critique of American empire toward a much closer alignment with the Democratic Party. In order to maintain its prophetic platform, it is vital that Sojouners begins to articulate and embody what is ecclesial about prophetic evangelical politics. As a result of a broad spectrum of churches in Call to Renewal and Christian Churches Together in America, Sojourners has had the opportunity to work closely with leaders in the Roman Catholic and black churches, among others. Together this growing ecumenical, intercultural movement for justice will have to consider in more depth what it means to act politically as the church.

The church has to be distinct, a peculiar people, but it simultaneously has to bear prophetic witness in the public square. Because of the global interconnectedness of our society, the stakes are too high for the church not to stand up and work toward governmental policies that will end the suffering. Government programs should work in tandem with the community and with programs offered by faith-based communities so together they may work for the common good. The tension between ecclesial particularity and democratic universals is the uncomfortable place that Sojourners inhabits. The black Christian imagination of King and Perkins has helped Wallis navigate this rocky terrain, trying to hold Christ-shaped community and the call to reform governmental policies closely together.

From Detroit, Michigan, to Washington, DC, Wallis always remembers the depth of black suffering in our country. He continues to prophetically merge his work in racial reconciliation with campaigns to end domestic and extreme global poverty. For Sojourners, the commitment to end poverty arises out of their narrative vision of Jesus as a prophet, suffering with the poor but working for their salvation, even on this earth. Like John Perkins, Wallis sees himself working out of King's civil rights legacy. Wallis's awareness of black consciousness and his consistent addressing of racism is an important example of how white evangelicals can work with evangelicals of color in a Kingdom of God movement for justice.

The two evangelical social movements in the King line—the Christian Community Development Association and Sojourners—are trying to disentangle the assimilation of whiteness and evangelicalism. As prophetic evangelicals, Jim Wallis and John Perkins cease to equate evangelicalism with whiteness. At their best CCDA and Sojourners embody an intercultural, global prophetic evangelicalism, seeking to inhabit a space beyond the white hegemony and the circumscription of the American nation-state. By Jim Wallis arguing that evangelicalism is post-American and post-white, he is articulating a broader vision of what it means to be Christian. When evangelical Christianity lives into its truly global, intercultural identity, then it will be in a place where it can critique the whiteness and Americanism that plagues much of early twenty-first-century evangelicalism.

The relation between evangelicalism and whiteness is the root difference between the theological visions of Carl Henry and Martin Luther King Jr. Henry's uneasy conscience is attuned to racial injustice, but he is part of a midcentury white evangelical establishment embedded in a narrative of Caucasian racial unity and "Christian" American exceptionalism. In contrast, King's vision of beloved community envisions a radical intercultural, transnational Christianity that prophetically confronts systems of segregation, suffering, and social sin that reward white power and privilege, often under the guise of a conservative evangelical theological logic. In helping lead the Montgomery Improvement Association's bus boycott to a successful conclusion, King provided a new horizon for a prophetic evangelicalism that could be truly post-white and post-American. In the spirit of King, Wallis in his own way has remained a sojourner in the empire, while never hesitating to speak truth to power.

The prophetic evangelical political approaches of Perkins and Wallis complement each other. Whereas CCDA emphasizes the embodied practices of the local community—intentional living, conflict resolution dialogues, economic redistribution, community worship services, leadership training, prison ministries, and biblical study—Sojourners emphasizes public advocacy activities—congressional lobbying, candidate pledge campaigns, peaceful protests, political commentary, town hall meetings, candidates' forums, voter registration drives, and mobilizations to end poverty. Both embody communal practices and public advocacy activities that are important dimensions of the one mission of the church, a church that is called to proclaim and embody a new order—the inbreaking intercultural Kingdom of God.

9

EVANGELICAL POLITICS IN A SHADE OF BLUE GREEN

The maturation of evangelical public theology is cast in a shade of blue green. The long tragedy of black suffering is pitched in blue; against that backdrop, an emergent holism within evangelicalism is saturated in green. From colonial times to the present, black Christianity has continually induced a prophetic transformation of American evangelicalism from within. Now, in the third millennium, we are witnessing a historical unfolding through the reconstitution of a prophetic evangelicalism in the post–civil rights era. Evangelicalism is singing and listening to the blues; it is evolving and growing green.

Jesus Christ is at the center of this transformation of evangelical public theology. His message is the culmination of the prophets; his truth is right for yesterday, today, and tomorrow. His incarnation is a vision of God's love and justice as revealed in his Jewish flesh. Through his life, death, and resurrection, Jesus came to dwell with all humanity—Jew and Gentile, black and white, female and male—and to embrace the whole of creation. It is this all-encompassing message of mercy that prophetic evangelicals seek to proclaim and embody in all they say and do.

American evangelicals have labored and agonized for centuries in their attempt to manifest this message within their embattled national history. A colonial logic of manifest destiny severely hindered them from fully manifesting the egalitarian ideal of the Gospel. The enslavement of Africans in the New World is the contradiction on which America as a nation-state was founded, and this unjust racial order generated a moral and theological crisis that continues to this day. White evangelicalism is tragically, but deeply, implicated in a tenaciously racist regime. Those whose religious story conjoins with the story of the nation-state sadly reinforce institutional racism often without realizing it.

Out of the shameful past, however, comes an unexpected fruit and a promising future. As black slaves were being racialized and denied access to opportunity, capital, dignity, and true freedom, Christianity provided them with theological resources to acquire black selfhood, collective identity, social power, and redemption. Amidst their pain and suffering, black Christians turned their eyes upon Jesus. In Jesus they found empathy, in Jesus they found hope, in Jesus they found a glimpse of light in the darkness. It was through singing the blue notes of the Christian lexicon of faith that black folks were able to endure.

Black Christian hermeneutics focused on the blue places and spaces of Jesus's life, laying hold of scriptural stories of Jesus, claiming them amidst their own experiences of suffering and survival, grieving and victory. As Harriet Jacobs fled the advances of her white master, Dr. Norcrom, and took refuge in a small, lonely space, she identified with Christ's descent into hell on Holy Saturday. During the fires of the civil rights struggle, Martin Luther King Jr. preached that no matter how low you go and how dark it gets, you must still see the light of God's love and invoke the power of Christ's resurrection. After John Perkins was beaten in a jail cell in Brandon, Mississippi, he got up and started a national movement of community-building Christians. Jesus Christ was a stone of hope, a refuge in the storm, and an inspiring example of the nonviolent struggle for justice.

While evangelical Christianity imbued black Christianity with a social and spiritual heritage, black Christianity, at its best, imbued white evangelical Christianity with a more egalitarian and activist spirit, focused on Jesus the suffering prophet. The icon of Jesus as refracted through black Christianity functions as a mirror and a window. As a mirror it helps white evangelicals to see themselves against the piercing light of history, complicit in the theological defense of a white supremacist worldview upon which the American nation was built. From slavery to segregation, white evangelicals have often been blind to their role in perpetuating racism and often justified it through conservative evangelical theologies.

Jesus Christ viewed through black Christian eyes offers a reflective image through which the contradiction of racism is unveiled to Americans of all colors. As a window to eternity, Jesus the Jew seen from the vantage point of black Christianity opens up a new horizon for evangelical faith and politics: it offers the potential for a Christian counterpolitics lying fully outside of the modern racial imaginary of the American nation.

Christology from the black Christian point of view emphasizes the brokenness of Jesus's humanity and suffering but also the great hope that he offers. When humans suffer because they are being persecuted for their commitment to the Gospel, these Christians participate in the sufferings of Christ. This suffering, Christologically understood, is the entry point into a new order of life, another way of being in the world—a way of love, peace, and justice. King's Christology crystallizes on Jesus the Jew whose death on a cross showed humanity how to live—each one called to take up his or her own cross through joining a people's movement for justice. King's lived theology demonstrated that one can live a life of complete surrender to Jesus's teaching of the Kingdom of God in the spirit of shalom. Echoing Jesus's kingdom teaching, King's vision of a beloved community sparked a movement for peace and justice in the world in the 1950s and 1960s that is firing the imagination of a new generation of evangelicals across racial and religious divides.

For evangelicals to move ahead religiously and politically in the United States, whites must open themselves up to the prophetic confrontation and healing streams of the blues. From the Mississippi Delta to the Windy City, blues singers have soulfully shared the tragic tale of heartbreak, love lost, and the scourges of slavery and segregation. In spite of the new, infectious interest in a Christian politics of the common good, the lynching tree of Jim Crow America still stands in judgment of any Christian, black or white or any shade in between, who wants to be identified as an evangelical. Yet, the streams of American Christianity are flowing in new directions. Black evangelicals have been diverting the stream of white evangelicalism toward the deep river of prophetic black Christianity. Prophetic evangelicals are inspired by the dream of Martin Luther King Jr., through which all of God's children be they black, brown, or white can begin to heal wounds that are deep and painful, moving ahead together to begin to realize King's deepest aspirations.

Signs of the dream are bursting forth all over. King's dream, after decades of turbulence and uncertainty, is gradually moving toward reality today, four decades later. Christians of all ethnicities are disrupting the racialized black-white binary and together are forging a prophetic, inter-cultural evangelical life together. Out of this effort springs vibrant colors—deep and dark, blue and green, bold and beautiful—providing the pallet for a new mosaic of evangelical public life.

Such a cooperative effort comes with great strife, born as it is out of the two different theological streams of Martin Luther King Jr. and Carl F. H. Henry. It is King's tradition that has been the primary driver of an internal transformation within evangelicalism toward a more holistic Gospel. Certainly there are glimpses of this transformation in the Henry stream as well, but that tradition has had a much deeper resistance to racial and economic justice. If evangelicals are to direct these tributaries toward a singular river, a few dualities need to be addressed and unified. The first of these focuses on Christology; how each tradition views Christ has differed greatly based on social location. The second difference in focus relates to the importance of individuals versus institutions.

King emphasized Jesus Christ as a suffering prophet, whereas Henry emphasized Jesus as a divine Lord. Henry sought to courageously work out the logic of Lordship to all areas of human life; his socially engaged conservatism aspired to achieve true justice for all. Yet while Henry tri-umphantly proclaimed the Lordship of Christ over American culture, he was not able to reconcile this view with the severe social injustices of his day. Henry's uneasy conscience plagued him to his dying day. This deep moral anxiety is a pervasive problem for this form of evangelicalism be-cause its individualism and social conservatism do not allow it to dislodge itself from the narratives of the American nation and a collective identity steeped in white male dominance.

When the image of Christ as Lord over all is applied across races, each individual stands equal in obeisance before him. This dynamic is not harm-ful—indeed, on an individual level it is crucial—but it is insufficient in ad-dressing deep-seated racial inequalities in the United States. Since the Henry tradition often characterizes racial reconciliation as a matter of in-terpersonal relationships, efforts by Focus on the Family and the National Association of Evangelicals to make progress in this area have amounted to little more than including evangelicals of color in social and professional networks. The NAE has increased the number of evangelicals of color on its board, and Focus on the Family frames much of its racial reconciliation work as outreach to families and communities of color. These personal influence approaches to racial justice, however well intentioned and positive, are deeply limited in their efficacy in bringing about true and lasting racial justice for all.

Evangelical theology in the Henry line is waking up, many years later, to the moral and theological problem of white skin power and privilege; however, it is unsure how to chart a clear course toward racial justice and what tools need to be deployed to achieve it. Henry's conscience was awakened to the moral contradiction inherent in a separatist evangelicalism that turned its eyes and ears from the cries of the widows, orphans, strangers, and poor (Zechariah 7:9–10). The radical disconnect between the prophetic ideal and the separatist reality was the source of Henry's ongoing existential angst. Henry recognized the inability of evangelicals to understand religion as salvation from injustice in this earthly existence, but he was unable to provide a robust counterethic to the modern racial imaginary that dominated twentieth-century evangelicalism.

The hope for change lay outside the confines of establishment evangelicalism. It is prophetic black Christianity that would subtly and consistently redirect evangelicalism toward realizing its deepest gospel ideals. Like the silt and minerals of the Mississippi River that flowed and fertilized the farm land of the delta, King's theology drew deep on the wells of the black church, haunted and inspired by slave songs, blues, and spirituals that lifted up Jesus to speak to the pain of the downtrodden. The Christology of the King tradition grew naturally out of an oppressed people's need for empathy amidst the white evangelical power establishment. Synthesizing shalom and kingdom theologies through his vision of beloved community, King provided a theology that prophetically confronted the racial logic of modernity while simultaneously offering an alternative counterpolitics to that of the American nation. While the way of the American nation was a way of power and arrogant assertion, the way of Jesus Christ advocated by King was the way of justice, mercy, and humble service.

From slavery to segregation, black Christians have a heritage of being a suffering community in exile. Seen as a new Moses, King's Christ suffers for and with all of God's children. The suffering of black folks is illuminated by the suffering Jesus of Nazareth. From Sojourner Truth and Frederick Douglass to Martin Luther King Jr. and John Perkins, black Christian theology seeks to lodge the narrative of black folks into the narrative of Jesus. From a position of exile—a sojourn—black Christianity operates from a position of marginalization, giving it distance and traction to call the nation and the churches that undergird it to prophetic account.

In addition to focusing on different aspects of Christ, the two traditions have differences in their approaches to public policy: one emphasizes the transformation of individuals, the other the transformation of social structures. Carl Henry, Billy Graham, and many white evangelicals placed their primary theological and ministry focus on the redemption and mass conversion of individuals. Emerson and Smith's *Divided by Faith* posits that white evangelicalism puts an emphasis on the individual redemption, whereas African American evangelicals have high value for structural redemption as well.[1] In fact, they go so far as to say that white evangelicals lack the cultural tools to even recognize structures, and that the only way for them to gain these tools is to become fully immersed in ethnically marginalized communities.

The Henry tradition is revealed in Focus on the Family's narrative vision to evangelize the world through nurturing and defending the family. The family is a social structure, but Focus on the Family's ministry strategies often reinforce this individualistic, evangelistic paradigm. The evangelism of individuals is viewed in an apologetic mode, with a seeking to defend Christian values focused on the sanctity of life, the integrity of the family, and the freedom of evangelical expression. Focus on the Family has not been able to confront evangelicalism's legacy of racism and colonization. As a result, it has furthered the production of a white male Christian capitalist citizenry—all under the banner of "family values." Its commitments to providing resources for the cultivation of healthy and whole families is to be commended, but its inability to acknowledge the negative impacts of its socially conservative political movement, including failing to address racism and poverty, reveals that a portion of conservative evangelicals have big blind spots in their public theology. Fortunately, the warrior politics of the Religious Right is on decline and there are small signs—including Tony Perkins's collaboration with Harry Jackson Jr. and their new openness to discuss environmental justice—that Focus itself is experiencing a slow transformation.

The NAE's story in this context is a bit more complex. Its narrative vision—to unify evangelical churches to cooperate in common witness—along with the primary call to world evangelism in its mission statement, promising to "extend the kingdom of God," certainly intimates a sound focus on transforming individual lives. But given the NAE's recent work on racial reconciliation and international justice, its forms of public engagement are being transformed to include a new focus on shaping various social structures, including family, government, church, schools, and labor unions.

Although the NAE has grown in its understanding of institutional sin, it still struggles with the question of race, especially when it comes to the black evangelicals of the National Association of Black Evangelicals. Like all African Americans, black evangelicals are intimately connected to a social reality that denied them recognition. Since black evangelicals were not recognized in the initial formation of the NAE, they have continued to struggle in a small parallel institutional structure. Many white NAE presidents, including Argue, Mannoia, Haggard, and Anderson, intentionally reached out to African Americans, but racial reconciliation proved difficult. Black and white evangelicals in the NAE family have had to negotiate the conditions of their living in the United States in different ways. Yet the leadership of the NAE continues to fight for more intentional racial reconciliation through the recruiting and nurturing of a growing number of people of color to serve as NAE board members. The presence of Harry R. Jackson Jr. and Samuel Rodriguez indicates a slow yet rising movement toward a prophetic evangelical paradigm that draws on King's public theology as well as Carl Henry's.

In contrast to the individualist theology of many white evangelicals, Martin Luther King Jr., Jesse Jackson Sr., John Perkins, and other civil rights leaders were compelled to challenge unjust social structures. Sojourners and CCDA broadly work out of the King tradition of systemic transformation, so not surprisingly, racism is an important starting point for the strategies of both organizations. For Sojourners, though, race is merely an important social issue among issues, while for CCDA it is the controlling hermeneutic.

CCDA is immersed in the black freedom struggle that grew organically out of and continues to be fed by the civil rights movement in the United States. Its narrative vision is to be a multiracial coalition for racial and economic justice. Although the quiet revolution of CCDA is a vision for all God's children, the heart of the movement beats for African American freedom. John Perkins was able to translate lessons learned in the African American community in Mendenhall and Jackson, Mississippi, to the broader world. The CCDA movement continues to push out to engage issues of justice among all people, especially the poor and the ethnically marginalized.

Following Jesse Jackson's Rainbow/PUSH coalition, CCDA has provided a grassroots national network of evangelical Christians committed to social transformation from 1989 to today. As John Perkins had voted for Jesse Jackson in the 1980s, he would vote for President Barack Obama in 2008 elections. As a black evangelical, Perkins saw an Obama presidency as an exciting prospect for black America, and also important for white evangelicalism. In April 2008, Jim Wallis preached his evangelical social gospel to a capacity crowd in the strategic swing state of Ohio. A personal friend of President Obama, Wallis had been coaching him for several years about how to share his evangelical convictions with the American public: the massive mobilization of progressive evangelical voters culminated in an active evangelical reception of Barack Obama's theology of hope.

> As the months passed in Chicago, I found myself drawn not just to work with the church, but to be in the church. For one thing, I believed and still believe in the power of the African-American religious tradition to spur social change. Because of its past, the black church understands in an intimate way the biblical call to feed the hungry and clothe the naked and challenge powers and principalities. In its historical struggles for freedom and human rights, I was able to see faith as more than just a comfort to the weary or a hedge against death, but rather as an active, palpable agent in the world, as a source of hope.
>
> Perhaps it was out of this intimate knowledge of hardship—the grounding of faith in struggle—that the church offered me a second insight. You need to come to church in the first place precisely because you are first of this world, not apart from it. You need to embrace Christ precisely because you have sins to wash away—because you are human and need an ally in this difficult journey.

It was because of these newfound understandings that I was finally able to walk down the aisle of Trinity United Church of Christ on the South Side of Chicago one day and affirm my Christian faith. It came about as a choice and not an epiphany. I didn't fall out in church. The questions I had didn't magically disappear. But kneeling beneath that cross on the South Side, I felt that I heard God's spirit beckoning me. I submitted myself to God's will and dedicated myself to discovering God's truth.[2]

Obama reaffirms the Afro-Christian tradition's commitment "to spur social change," and he also connects to the narrative vision of Henry's tradition by acknowledging the need for personal forgiveness of sin. The King tradition provides an important foundation of social justice Christianity for Obama to build on as he taps into a deep root in the black church tradition, passionate personal piety, shared by evangelicals like Carl Henry, Billy Graham, and Rick Warren.

One white evangelical who experienced a deep cultural immersion in the black community that changed his life and the direction of his ministry is Jim Wallis. In inner-city Detroit, Wallis joined the black church, learning in detail about the suffering and pain of his African American friends yet experiencing joy and catharsis through worshiping in the black church with gospel music and passionate preaching. Wallis's cultural immersion experience began as a young boy in Detroit, Michigan, influenced by two streams of prophetic critique that called on the Exodus motif: Yoder's notion of the church as a counterculture to American nationalist culture and King's notion of beloved community as a contrasting vision to white supremacy separatism. The symbol of the sojourner—a wanderer whose identity lies both within and without the confines of the nation-state—reflected the exile character of the movement. In Sojourners' earliest years it was inspired less by issues of race than by the struggle for international peace precipitated by the war in Vietnam. In recent years, Sojourners' focus on antipoverty campaigns, first Call to Renewal and now the Mobilization to End Poverty, has drawn the movement back to an emphasis on racial reconciliation and justice. In the United States, the problem of poverty is coextensive with the problem of race.

Prophetic evangelical politics still needs to fully emerge from deep solidarity with the suffering of those who sing of a tragic past. From slavery through segregation, prophetic black Christians kept hope alive—not only for themselves but also for the white Christians, who sometimes wittingly and other times unwittingly perpetuated racist structures that continue to marginalize people of color. The prophetic activism of the black church opened a door to a new world for evangelical politics. Prophetic black Christianity has not only inspired evangelicals to become more politically engaged, but it has provided the theological resources to rethink theology and "the political." A radical evangelical political theology that is anti-racist, intercultural, and interdisciplinary is beginning to forcefully emerge in many pockets of the evangelical world.

In the wake of the civil rights movement, there have been growing attempts to achieve racial justice within evangelicalism. From InterVarsity's campus mission to reconcile all ethnic groups to Promise Keepers' goal of forging deep friendships between black and white men, all evangelical attempts to move toward racial justice are problematic yet hopeful. Reconciliation between black and white evangelicals has been a struggle, but some progress has been made. If evangelicals can bring the prophetic voice of King on board alongside the Henry tradition, transforming it and repudiating centuries of explicit and implicit racism, the blue green movement that is arising in the global south can begin to take root and grow in America.

As evangelicals listen to the voices of the blues, they hear primal spiritual echoes of the sad songs of slaves, and it sounds almost as if the earth itself is groaning. Evangelicals attuned to these reverberations are moved to pursue justice wherever suffering is found on earth, whether it be the poor or the diseased here or abroad, or the anguish of creation itself. Like the debates over slavery in the antebellum period, the environmental debate is more than one of science and economics—it is fundamentally a theological debate. Those of the premillennial dispensational camp of the *Left Behind* novels are opposed to environmental justice work because they think this earth will one day burn in the fiery flames of judgment, yet a burgeoning group of prophetic evangelicals, including a growing group of megachurch ministers like Rob Bell, Joel Hunter, and Tri Robinson, view creation care as a vital part of living out the Gospel. They are encouraging their congregations to recycle, compost, use sustainable energy sources, and drive hybrids.

Among young evangelicals, there is a growing hope in a green future. Richard Cizik has been a central architect of the NAE's creation care movement—the rise of a generation of evangelicals who are passionately committed to caring for creation, as well as ending poverty and AIDS— forging a strategic partnership between scientists and evangelicals who are working together to achieve environmental sustainability in the context of a world of environmental challenges. With a press release in January 2007, "An Urgent Call to Action: Evangelicals and Scientists Unite to Protect Creation," this new collaboration went public after a long, intense period of debate and struggle.[3] Although the alliance continued to field criticism from the Religious Right, it forged ahead and organized an environmental expedition. The Scientist-Evangelical Environmental Expedition, consisting of a team of five scientists and five evangelical leaders, journeyed together through Alaska to witness firsthand the dramatic effects of climate change on the local people and on the land, ocean, plants, and wildlife.

The expedition was an eye-opener for all involved, including Harry Jackson Jr., one of the highest profile black evangelical leaders of the Religious Right. As a result of the expedition, Jackson and Tony Perkins of the Family Research Council included a chapter on the environment to their new manifesto for the Religious Right.[4] The Religious Right has historically been interested almost exclusively in issues like abortion, gay marriage, and pornography, but the greening of Harry Jackson is a sign that the broader agenda of evangelicals is being increasingly internalized within the Religious Right. From the evangelical left to the Religious Right, America is witnessing an evangelical spring.

A new evangelical internationalism is also emerging, one that builds on the missionary work of people like Hudson Taylor in China and Jim Elliot in Central America. These and other evangelical missionaries, while seeking to convert individuals, confronted issues of cultural difference and political transformation in ways that the evangelical church in the United States was never fully able to comprehend. The work of prophetic evangelicals like Malinda Berry, Bart Campolo, Tony Campolo, Shane Claiborne, Ruth Padilla DeBorst, David Gushee, Lisa Sharon Harper, Gary Haugen,

Brian McClaren, Claude Nikondeha, Raymond Rivera, Sammy Rodriguez, Gabriel Salguero, Adam Taylor, Richard Twiss, and Jonathan Wilson-Hartgrove continues in this stream of prophetic evangelical internationalism. In the wake of the Ted Haggard scandal, the NAE has continued a coherent legislative strategy guided by its document *For the Health of the Nation*. The NAE actively works on environmental issues and is becoming more politically involved in international issues, such as the genocide in Darfur and AIDS epidemic in Africa. This worldwide approach is also found in the initiatives of the Micah Challenge, a global network of evangelicals committed to mobilizing Christians on issues of poverty related to the Millennium Development Goals. The NAE, Sojourners, and CCDA are joining with Bread for the World, the ONE Campaign, and the Micah Challenge to collectively seek to engage young Christians in the larger movement to end hunger and dramatically reduce global poverty.

Evangelical strategic partnerships now extend even to people of other faiths. At the NAE Global Leaders Forum in October 2007, the NAE issued its third Statement of Conscience on the Dalits, traditionally known as "untouchables," of India.[5] Dr. Joseph D'Souza, a prominent Indian evangelical and international president of the Dalit Freedom Network and president of the All India Christian Council, spoke passionately about the abuse and suffering endured by the lowest class and called for an end to India's caste system through holistic ministry. The board passed the resolution unanimously, signaling an important growth in NAE's global political activism: beyond helping Christians who suffer from persecution and protecting God's creation, the NAE seeks to enact justice for people of all faiths. The Dalit Statement of Conscience was the first of its kind from a non-Indian national ecumenical body.

Even the areas of evangelicalism most obviously ensconced within the Carl Henry tradition are undergoing a widening of moral scope. We witness a transition to holistic evangelism in the ministry of megachurch pastor Rick Warren. Warren's primary goal continues to be soul winning, but now he is increasingly interested in global social change. The transformation of Warren's politics is a symbol of a deeper transformation of evangelical politics taking place across the evangelical world. Historically, the issues of foremost importance to him were the pro-life and pro-marriage campaigns of the Religious Right, along with such lesser, related issues as opposition to stem cell research. In 2004, Warren released a short video message for his congregation asserting that a candidate's stance on these issues should be a decisive factor in determining one's vote. In the long run-up to the 2008 presidential election, Warren did not change or soften his stance on any of these traditional evangelical fronts, but he did add a host of progressive causes to them: global, prophetic causes such as poverty, education, and disease prevention. This extraordinary shift from Religious Right politics to a broader, greener agenda was summarized in his international PEACE Plan—a plan intended to revolutionize evangelical missionary work.

Warren attributes the shift to several factors: first, he made millions of dollars and attracted national attention by publishing *The Purpose Driven Life*, a runaway bestseller.[6] Warren says he realized in the face of unprecedented fame and fortune that his affluence and influence must be intended to speak for those who had no voice.

Second, and perhaps more important, his wife, Kay, became deeply burdened with the need for a church-led response to the global AIDS crisis.[7] Through the influence of Kay's dawning realization of the social implications of the Gospel, Rick found himself compelled to champion the church's role in bringing about social change, especially among the poor and the sick. It is along this front that he has attracted the most attention, not only for his and his wife's crusades for healing in Rwanda, but for hosting the annual Global Summit on AIDS and the Church. Warren has even applied this holistic approach to American politics; while still maintaining strong personal ties to President George W. Bush, Warren reached out to Senator Barack Obama and Senator Hillary Clinton during the 2008 election cycle. In the shadow of the lynching tree of Jim Crow America, an ethical question looms over Warren's purpose-driven paradigm: when will Rick Warren connect his passion for ending AIDS and poverty in Africa with an honest dismantling of institutional racism in the United States? In invoking Martin Luther King Jr. in his prayer at the presidential inauguration of Barack Obama on January 20, 2009, America's next Billy Graham is beginning to draw wisdom from the deep well of prophetic black Christianity in the Americas.

Although many commentators remain interested in the evangelical vote, the current transformation of evangelical politics goes far beyond elections. Prophetic black Christianity has transformed evangelicalism from within. This transformation has been taking place for a long time and it is not over, but we are beginning to the see the signs of an evangelical spring. No longer retreating into a sanctified conservative subculture, evangelicals of all colors are pulling together to proclaim and embody the Gospel through collaborative, subversive social witness.

As we have seen in our journey through the uneven terrain of evangelicalism, four leading personalities within the evangelical world have different passions: James Dobson is concerned with family integrity, while Richard Cizik is passionate about creation care; John Perkins is vigilant in his struggle for racial justice in local communities, and Jim Wallis is inspiring a new generation of evangelicals to join the struggle to end domestic poverty. Each evangelical leader has a primary issue they focus on, but they are united by their concern for a broader justice agenda. The four evangelical social movements studied in this book are a sample of the diversity of evangelical politics today, part of a broader evangelical social awakening that is rooted in the activist religion of nineteenth-century evangelicals. From physicians to megachurch ministers, evangelicals are moving on a variety of justice issues with the fervor of abolitionists.

At the beginning of the twenty-first century, evangelical politics stands at a crossroads. The warrior politics of the Religious Right has been an unbending, dominant stream of evangelical politics since the Jerry Falwell founded the Moral Majority in 1979, with an agenda focused on two primary issues—the sanctity of human life and the institution of marriage—while also maintaining strong commitments to militarism and free-market capitalism. Right-wing evangelicals have successfully mobilized the pro-family movement using strong-arm tactics, and they will continue to do so. But this form of evangelical politics is in rapid decline. We have witnessed a massive transition from the warrior politics of the Religious Right to the prophetic politics of prophetic evangelicals.

As we enter a new millennium, the legacy of Martin Luther King Jr., the lionized hero of the civil rights movement, is massive, shaping not only the prophetic black Christian tradition but through it transforming the whole of American evangelicalism. The King legacy within evangelicalism lives on in the CCDA movement of John Perkins and the Sojourners movement of Jim Wallis, reminding us that this country was built on slavery and continues to struggle to overcome racism and embody the beloved community. If white evangelicals cannot hear the call of the blues and let it reverberate in the pages of their theology and practices of their politics, then they will have unwittingly reconstituted whiteness yet again, and sadly, in the name of Christ. The new prophetic evangelical ethic will never be completely just if it does not begin with America's original sin—racism. Prophetic evangelical politics will not move toward a full Gospel of love and justice if it does not reach for *all* of the Gospel, both the suffering Savior and the loving Lord.

White evangelical theology of the Henry ilk has emphasized the deity of Christ. The primary evangelical task was seen to be the verbal proclamation of salvation through the divine Son of God. Yet Henry saw that unless this message had "world relevance," Christianity in the Americas would not be able to be truly Christ-like. Martin Luther King Jr. and the civil rights movement demonstrated that Christianity was not only relevant to black suffering and selfhood, but through Christ's suffering and selfhood provided the conditions through which a black Christ-consciousness could arise. The fires of antebellum revivalism that ignited the antebellum abolition movement blazed again in Christians who joined King in his struggle to achieve the beloved community by working together to end racism, poverty, and war. As a result of his prophetic activism, King lost his life, but his dream continues to inspire a new generation of evangelical activists.

It was in the suffering humanity of Jesus Christ that King saw the key to social ethics. Through the Incarnation, Jesus entered fully into the human experience as a Jew, a member of the tribe that God has covenantally chosen to bear salvation to the whole world. Through Jesus's suffering and wounded Jewish flesh, the whole world would be invited to be redeemed and empowered to participate with him in a struggle to achieve love and justice. John Perkins and Jim Wallis heard in King's cry an echo of the cry in Gethsemane of Jesus the Jew. They have worked tirelessly to help a new generation of evangelicals—black, white, and every shade in between—follow a Jesus who is fully human and fully divine, confront sin in both its personal and social dimensions, and through grace live out salvation through a collective struggle to embody God's shalom. Decades after his death, King's life and theological vision bear a powerful imprint on a growing prophetic evangelical movement.

The evangelical church, cast in a shade of blue, listens to and lives the black experience as a growing intercultural collective: from slave songs to spirituals, blues to jazz, black music in America tells a story of suffering that must be heard. White evangelical theology will never confront its whiteness and work toward a true antiracist, proreconciliation future until it inhabits the suffering embodied in black music, arts, and culture. As King and Perkins enfolded the narratives of their black freedom struggles into the narratives of Jesus Christ in the Gospels, they created the conditions of a deep theological and cultural transformation of the very fabric of American evangelical religion and politics. With the Christological architecture of the prophetic black evangelical imagination as an anchor, evangelicals of all colors are beginning to think structurally about race issues, with white evangelicals working with evangelical people of color in the pursuit of justice today. An evangelical politics in the shade of blue green is an intercultural prophetic movement of the poor in action on behalf of the good creation.

Evangelical politics is maturing into a deeper shade of blue green. Prophetic evangelicalism is moving from white homogenization toward a multicultural rainbow, from egocentrism to empathetic compassion for the Other, from militarism toward peace-making, from consumptive consumerism toward environmental sustainability, from affluence to solidarity with the poor, from self-security to prophetic witness. With roots in the prophetic black church, prophetic evangelical politics is growing tall like a mighty oak tree whose branches are reaching out for renewal, as green leaves quickly emerge and flowers begin to bloom.

Evangelicalism is searching for itself, a self that was buried in an ancient, painful past. Evangelicalism is looking to Jesus, looking to his Jewish flesh, broken and blue, bowing before the neighbor and the good, green creation, learning to discern the divine presence in all things and to see glimpses of the earthing of the Kingdom of God.

Evangelicalism is moving, and moving quickly, to embody justice around the world.

NOTES

Chapter 1. The Lion Is Roaring

1. David Brooks, "The Two Earthquakes," *New York Times,* January 4, 2008, http://www.nytimes.com/2008/01/04/opinion/04brooks.html?_r=1&hp&oref =slogin (accessed January 7, 2008).

2. For my initial discussions of "prophetic evangelicalism," see my "Prophetic Evangelicals: Toward a Politics of Hope," in *The Sleeping Giant Has Awoken: The New Politics of Religion in the United States,* ed. Jeffrey W. Robbins and Neal Magee (New York: Continuum, 2008), 25–40; Robin Rogers and Peter Goodwin Heltzel, "The New Evangelical Politics," *Society* 45:5 (2008): 412–14. This paragraph draws on these two essays.

3. Carl F. H. Henry, *Evangelicals in Search of Identity* (Waco, TX: Word Books, 1976), 96.

4. Esther Kaplan, *With God on Their Side: How Christian Fundamentalists Trampled Science, Policy, and Democracy in George W. Bush's White House* (New York: New Press, 2004), 7. Dana Milbank, "Religious Right Finds Its Center in Oval Office: Bush Emerges as Movement's Leader after Robertson Leaves Christian Coalition," *Washington Post,* December 24, 2001.

5. Fourth National Survey of Religion and Politics, Post-Election Sample (November–December 2004, University of Akron), as cited by John C. Green, "How the Faithful Voted: Religious Communities and the Presidential Vote in 2004," Pew Forum on Religion and Public Life, University of Akron. Presented at "A Matter of Faith? Religion in the 2004 Election," December 2005, University of Notre Dame.

6. For a thoughtful account of how Jesus's teachings are at odds with the warrior politics that was forged through a synthesis of the Religious Right and the Republican Party as embodied in the presidential administrations of Ronald Reagan, George H. W. Bush, and George W. Bush, see Obery M. Hendricks Jr., *The Politics of Jesus: Rediscovering the True Revolutionary Nature of Jesus' Teachings and How They Have Been Corrupted* (New York: Doubleday, 2006).

7. Naomi Schaefer Riley, "The Press and Patrick Henry College," *Chronicle of Higher Education,* July 14, 2006, p. B12.

8. Kevin Phillips, *American Theocracy: The Peril and Politics of Radical Religion, Oil, and Borrowed Money in the 21st Century* (New York: Viking, 2006), 64. On the recent rise of evangelicals in American public life, see Monique El-Faizy, *God and Country: How Evangelicals Have Become America's New Mainstream* (New York: Bloomsbury, 2006); David P. Gushee, *The Future of Faith in American Politics: The Public Witness of the Evangelical Center* (Waco, TX: Baylor University Press, 2008); Amy Sullivan, *The Party Faithful: How and Why Democrats Are Closing the God Gap* (New York: Scribner, 2008).

9. D. Michael Lindsay, "Is the National Prayer Breakfast Surrounded by a 'Christian Mafia'? Religious Publicity and Secrecy within the Corridors of Power," *Journal of the American Academy of Religion* 74:2 (June 2006): 390–419.

10. D. Michael Lindsay, "Elite Power: Social Networks within American Evangelicalism," *Sociology of Religion* 67 (2006): 207–27. Cf. D. Michael Lindsay, *Faith in the Halls of Power: How Evangelicals Joined the American Elite* (Oxford: Oxford University Press, 2007).

11. Lindsay, "Elite Power"; Lindsay, *Faith in the Halls of Power.*

12. Donald W. Dayton, "Some Doubts about the Usefulness of the Category 'Evangelical,'" in *Varieties of American Evangelicalism,* ed. Donald W. Dayton and Robert K. Johnston (Knoxville: University of Tennessee, 1991), 245–51.

13. David Bebbington, *Evangelicalism in Modern Britain: A History from the 1730s to the 1980s* (London: Unwin Hyman, 1989), 2–19.

14. Mark A. Noll, *Scandal of the Evangelical Mind* (Grand Rapids: Eerdmans, 1994), 8.

15. Nathan O. Hatch, *Democratization of American Christianity* (New Haven: Yale University Press, 1991). I am using the term "democratic" to indicate the fact that U.S. churches have been less hierarchical and have had fewer rules governing the relationships between people and God.

16. See John G. Stackhouse Jr., "Evangelical Theology Should Be Evangelical," in *Evangelical Futures: A Conversation on Theological Method,* ed. John G. Stackhouse Jr. (Grand Rapids: Baker, 2000), 42; idem, *Canadian Evangelicalism in the Twentieth Century: An Introduction to Its Character* (Toronto: University of Toronto Press, 1993), 6–12.

17. Timothy Larsen, "Defining and Locating Evangelicalism," in *The Cambridge Companion to Evangelical Theology,* ed. Timothy Larsen and Daniel Treier (Cambridge: Cambridge University Press, 2007), 1–14. For a focused account of the origins of the black national consciousness of Afro-Christian interpretations of the biblical story of Exodus, see Eddie S. Glaude Jr., *Exodus! Religion, Race, and Nation in Early Nineteenth-Century Black America* (Chicago: University of Chicago Press, 2000).

18. Thomas Kidd points out the absence of the person of the Holy Spirit in Bebbington's definition, especially as it relates to revivals. Thomas S. Kidd, *The Great Awakening: The Roots of Evangelical Christianity in Colonial America* (New Haven: Yale University Press, 2007), xiv. By adding the person of the Holy Spirit to Bebbing-

ton's definition, most of global Pentecostalism would be evangelical with the exception of the Oneness Pentecostals, who reject the Trinity. See Amos Yong, *The Spirit Poured Out on All Flesh: Pentecostalism and the Possibility of Global Theology* (Grand Rapids: Baker Academic, 2005) for an important discussion of the complexities and promise that Oneness Pentecostalism brings to broader evangelicalism.

19. For the best overview of evangelical politics in the antebellum period, see Richard J. Carwardine, *Evangelicals and Politics in Antebellum America* (New Haven: Yale University Press, 1993).

20. Mark A. Noll, "Forum: Public Theology in Contemporary America," *Religion and American Culture* 10:1 (Winter 2000): 8–12; 11.

21. J. Kameron Carter, "Race and the Experience of Death: Theologically Reappraising American Evangelicalism," in *The Cambridge Companion to Evangelical Theology*, ed. Timothy Larsen and Daniel Treier (Cambridge: Cambridge University Press, 2007), 177–98.

22. Ibid., 179.

23. Harriet Jacobs, *Incidents in the Life of a Slave Girl*, ed. Jean Fagan Yellin (Cambridge: Harvard University Press, 1987).

24. Carter, "Race and the Experience of Death," 191.

25. Ibid., 194.

26. See J. Kameron Carter, *Race: A Theological Account* (Oxford: Oxford University Press, 2008); Reginald Horsman, *Race and Manifest Destiny: The Origins of American Racial Anglo-Saxonism* (Cambridge: Harvard University Press, 1981).

Chapter 2. Revival, Race, and Reform

1. John B. Boles, *The Great Revival: Beginnings of the Bible Belt* (Lexington: University Press of Kentucky, 1996); Paul Keith Conkin, *Cane Ridge: America's Pentecost* (Madison: University of Wisconsin Press, 1990); Christine Leigh Heyrman, *Southern Cross: The Beginnings of the Bible Belt* (New York: Alfred A. Knopf, 1997).

2. David W. Wills, "The Central Themes of American Religious History: Pluralism, Puritanism, and the Encounter of Black and White," *Religion and Intellectual Life*, no. 1 (Fall 1987): 30–41.

3. Ibid., 35.

4. For the best brief overview of black fundamentalism and evangelicalism, see Albert G. Miller, "The Rise of African-American Evangelicalism in American Culture," in *Perspectives on American Religion and Culture*, ed. Peter W. Williams (Oxford: Blackwell, 1999), 259–69; W. H. Bentley, "Bible Believers in the Black Community," in *The Evangelicals: What They Believe, Who They Are, Where They Are Changing*, ed. D. F. Wells and J. D. Woodbridge (Nashville: Abingdon Press, 1975), 108–21; Milton G. Sernett, "Black Religion and the Question of Evangelical Identity," in *The Variety of American Evangelicalism*, ed. Donald W. Dayton and Robert K. Johnston (Knoxville: University of Tennessee Press, 1991), 135–47; William E. Pannell, "The Religious Heritage of Blacks," in *The Evangelicals: What They Believe, Who They Are, Where They Are Changing*, ed. David F. Wells and John D. Woodbridge (Nashville: Abingdon Press,

1975), 95–107; Ronald C. Potter, "The New Black Evangelicals," in *Black Theology: A Documentary History, 1966–1979,* ed. Gayraud S. Wilmore and James H. Cone (Maryknoll, NY: Orbis Books, 1979), 302–9; Albert J. Raboteau, "The Black Experience in American Evangelicalism: The Meaning of Slavery," in *The Evangelical Tradition in America,* ed. Leonard I. Sweet (Macon: Mercer University Press), 181–89. James Melvin Washington, "The Origins of Black Evangelicalism and the Ethical Functions of Evangelical Cosmology," *Union Seminary Quarterly Review* 32:2 (1977): 104–16; cf. William E. Pannell, *My Friend the Enemy* (Waco, TX: Word Books, 1968).

5. Randall Balmer, *Mine Eyes Have Seen the Glory: A Journey into the Evangelical Subculture in America,* 3rd ed. (Oxford: Oxford University, 2000), 176–92; David Bebbington, *The Dominance of Evangelicalism: The Age of Spurgeon and Moody* (Downers Grove, IL: InterVarsity Press, 2005), 227–33; Donald W. Dayton, "Piety and Radicalism: Antebellum Social Evangelicalism in the U.S.," *Radical Religion* 3:1 (1976): 34–40; Curtis J. Evans, *The Burden of Black Religion* (Oxford: Oxford University Press, 2008); David Hempton, "James Baldwin—Preacher and Prophet: Evangelicalism and Race," *Evangelical Disenchantment: 9 Portraits of Faith and Doubt* (New Haven: Yale University Press, 2008), 163–86. Hempton, *Methodism,* 131–50; Douglas Jacobsen, "Theology and Race," *Thinking in the Spirit: Theologies of the Early Pentecostal Movement* (Bloomington: Indiana University Press, 2003), 260–85; Thomas S. Kidd, *The Great Awakening: The Roots of Evangelical Christianity in Colonial America* (New Haven: Yale University Press, 2007), 213–33. Charles Marsh, *God's Long Summer: Stories of Faith and Civil Rights* (Princeton: Princeton University Press, 1997); idem, *The Beloved Community: How Faith Shapes Social Justice, from the Civil Rights Movement to Today* (New York: Basic Books, 2005); idem, *Wayward Christian Soldiers: Freeing the Gospel from Political Captivity* (Oxford: Oxford University Press, 2007). Mark A. Noll, *The Civil War as Theological Crisis* (Chapel Hill: University of North Carolina Press, 2006); idem, *God and Race in American Politics: A Short History* (Princeton: Princeton University Press, 2008); Douglass A. Sweeney, *The American Evangelical Story: A History of the Movement* (Grand Rapids: Baker Academic, 2005), 107–32. Anthea D. Butler, *Women in the Church of God in Christ: Making a Sanctified World* (Chapel Hill: University of North Carolina, 2007); Cheryl Jeanne Sanders, *Saints in Exile: The Holiness-Pentacostal Experience in African American Religion and Culture* (New York: Oxford University Press, 1996).

6. A few recent examples of this literature include James B. Bennett, *Religion and the Rise of Jim Crow in New Orleans* (Princeton: Princeton University Press, 2005); Edward J. Blum, *Reforging the White Republic: Race, Religion, and American Nationalism, 1865–1898* (Baton Rouge: Louisiana State University Press, 2005); Paul Harvey, *Freedom's Coming: Religious Culture and the Shaping of the South from the Civil War through the Civil Rights Movement* (Chapel Hill: University of North Carolina Press, 2005); and Michele Mitchell, *Righteous Propagation: African Americans and the Politics of Racial Destiny After Reconstruction* (Chapel Hill: University of North Carolina Press, 2004).

7. For this point I am indebted to Patrick Provost-Smith. See Patrick Provost-Smith, "Historians and the Past Tense: 'Evangelium' and 'Imperium' as Genealogies of

the Concept of Sovereignty," in *Evangelicals and Empire,* ed. Bruce Ellis Benson and Peter Goodwin Heltzel (Grand Rapids: Brazos Press, 2008), 107–19.

8. David W. Wills, "The Central Themes of American Religious History: Pluralism, Puritanism, and the Encounter of Black and White," *Religion and Intellectual Life,* no. 1 (Fall 1987): 30–41.

9. Kidd, *Great Awakening,* 213–33. While Kidd refers to this group of socially engaged Protestants as "radical evangelicals," I prefer the term "prophetic evangelicals."

10. See Michael J. Crawford, *Seasons of Grace: Colonial New England's Revival Tradition in Its British Context* (New York: Oxford University Press, 1991); Leigh Eric Schmidt, *Holy Fairs: Scottish Communions and American Revivals in the Early Modern Period* (Princeton: Princeton University Press, 1989).

11. See George Marsden, *Jonathan Edwards: A Life* (New Haven: Yale University Press, 2003).

12. See Mark A. Noll, *The Rise of Evangelicalism: The Age of Edwards, Whitefield, and the Wesleys* (Downers Grove, IL: InterVarsity Press, 2003), 174. Cf. Harry S. Stout, *The Divine Dramatist: George Whitefield and the Rise of Modern Evangelicalism* (Grand Rapids: Eerdmans, 1991).

13. Milton C. Sernett, "Black Religion and the Question of Evangelical Identity," in *The Variety of American Evangelicalism,* ed. Donald W. Dayton and Robert K. Johnston (Knoxville: University of Tennessee Press, 1991), 135–47; 138. For a thoughtful discussion of the ways in which African American religion was shaped by its African past, its context within slavery, and the forms of white evangelical religion, see Albert J. Raboteau's *Slave Religion: The Invisible Institution in the Antebellum South,* 2nd edition (New York: Oxford University Press, 2004).

14. Kidd, *Great Awakening,* 214.

15. Ibid., 217, 218. Cf. Sylvia R. Frey and Betty Wood, *Come Shouting to Zion: African American Protestantism in the American South and British Caribbean to 1830* (Chapel Hill: University of North Carolina Press, 1998).

16. Richard Allen, *The Life Experience and Gospel Labors of the Rt. Rev. Richard Allen* (Nashville: Abingdon Press, 1983), 20–21. I am grateful to Dale T. Irvin for bringing this passage to my attention.

17. For theologically erudite accounts of the rise of transatlantic Methodism, see David Hempton, *The Religion of the People: Methodism and Popular Religion, 1750–1900* (London: Routledge, 1996); idem, *Methodism: Empire of the Spirit* (New Haven: Yale University Press, 2005).

18. See Timothy L. Smith, *Revivalism and Social Reform in Mid-Nineteenth-Century America* (New York: Abingdon Press, 1957); Donald W. Dayton, *Discovering an Evangelical Heritage* (New York: Harper and Row, 1976).

19. Richard J. Carwardine, *Evangelicals and Politics in Antebellum America* (New Haven: Yale University Press, 1993), 44.

20. Mechal Sobel, *The World They Made Together: Black and White Values in Eighteenth-Century Virginia* (Princeton: Princeton University Press, 1987), 180. Dry christening ceremonies dedicated infants to God without the use of water. These cere-

monies were conducted by some Baptist churches in eighteenth-century Virginia and continue in many churches today.

21. Ann Taves, *Fits, Trances, and Visions: Experiencing Religion and Explaining Experience from Wesley to James* (Princeton: Princeton University Press, 1999), 79–117.

22. Hempton, *Methodism*, 134.

23. Ibid., 135.

24. Nathan Hatch, *The Democratization of American Christianity* (New Haven: Yale University Press, 1989), 106.

25. For example, Virginia planter Robert Carter III freed 450 slaves out of evangelical convictions beginning in 1791. Kidd, *Great Awakening*, 250.

26. Thornton Stringfellow, "A Brief Examination of Scripture Testimony in the Institution of Slavery" (1841), in *The Ideology of Slavery: Proslavery Thought in the Antebellum South, 1830–1860,* ed. Drew Gilpin Faust (Baton Rouge: Louisiana State University Press, 1981), 154; For a thoughtful analysis of southern proslavery thought, see Elizabeth Fox-Genovese and Eugene D. Genovese, *The Mind of the Master Class: History and Faith in the Southern Slaveholders' Worldview* (New York: Cambridge University Press, 2005).

27. Eugene D. Genovese, *The Political Economy of Slavery: Studies in the Economy of the Slave South* (Middletown, CT: Wesleyan University Press, 1989), 34.

28. Orlando Patterson, *Slavery and Social Death: A Comparative Study* (Cambridge: Harvard University Press, 1982), 76.

29. John Hope Franklin, *The Militant South* (Boston: Beacon Press, 1964), 34–35, as quoted by Patterson, *Slavery and Social Death,* 95. Cf. Bertram Wyatt-Brown, *Southern Honor: Ethics and Behavior in the Old South* (New York: Oxford University Press, 1982); idem, *Yankee Saints and Southern Sinners* (Baton Rouge: Louisiana State University Press, 1985); cf. Donald G. Mathews, *Religion in the Old South* (Chicago: University of Chicago Press, 1977). For a thoughtful genealogy of honor and shame culture in ancient Christianity, see Virginia Burrus, *Saving Shame: Martyrs, Saints, and Other Abject Subjects* (Philadelphia: University of Pennsylvania Press, 2007).

30. Genovese, *Political Economy of Slavery,* 270.

31. Robert J. C. Young, *Colonial Desire: Hybridity in Theory, Culture and Race* (New York: Routledge, 1995), 97.

32. Recent monographs that discuss race and sex in the Americas include Hilary Beckles, *Centering Woman: Gender Discourses in Caribbean Slave Society* (Princeton: M. Wiener, 1999); Sharon Block, *Rape and Sexual Power in Early America* (Chapel Hill: University of North Carolina Press, 2006), 163–209; Victoria Bynum, *Unruly Women: The Politics of Social and Sexual Control in the Old South* (Chapel Hill: University of North Carolina Press, 1992); Cassandra Jackson, *Barriers Between Us: Interracial Sex in Nineteenth-Century America* (Bloomington: Indiana University Press, 2004); Anne McClintock, *Imperial Leather: Race, Gender, and Sexuality in the Colonial Contest* (New York: Routledge); Joane Nagel, *Race, Ethnicity, and Sexuality: Intimate Intersections, Forbidden Frontiers* (Oxford: Oxford University Press, 2003); Mason Boyd Stokes, *The Color of Sex: Whiteness, Heterosexuality, and the Fictions of White Supremacy* (Durham: Duke University Press, 2001); idem, "Someone's in the Garden

with Eve: Race, Religion, and the American Fall," *American Quarterly* 50:4 (December 1998): 718 – 44; Deborah White, *Ar'n't I a Woman? Female Slaves in the Plantation South* (New York: W. W. Norton, 1999).

33. Edward J. Blum, *Reforging the White Republic: Race, Religion, and American Nationalism, 1865–1898* (Baton Rouge: Louisiana State University Press, 2005); idem, *W. E. B. Du Bois: American Prophet* (Philadelphia: University of Pennsylvania Press, 2007), 13, 52, 63 – 67, 71–75.

34. Samuel George Morton, *Crania Americana; or, A Comparative View of the Skulls of Various Aboriginal Nations of North and South America; to Which Is Affixed an Essay on the Variety of the Human Species* . . . (Philadelphia: J. Pennington, 1839); idem, *Crania Aegyptiaca; or, Observations on Egyptian Ethnology, Derived from Anatomy, History and Monuments* (Philadelphia: J. Pennington, 1844).

35. Patterson, *Slavery and Social Death,* 75.

36. Robert L. Dabney, *A Defense of Virginia (and through Her, of the South) in Recent and Pending Contests against the Sectional Party* (New York: Negro University Press, 1969), 353.

37. Linda Brent, *Incidents in the Life of a Slave Girl;* Eugene D. Genovese, *Roll, Jordon, Roll* (New York: Vintage Books, 1972), 413 – 31; Frantz Fanon, *Black Skin, White Masks* [1952], trans. Charles Lam Markmann (London: Pluto, 1986), 41–62; bell hooks, "Sexism and the Black Female Experience," in *Ain't I a Woman: Black Women and Feminism* (Boston: South End Press, 1981), 15 – 49; Melton A. McLaurin, *Celia, a Slave* (Athens: University of Georgia Press, 1991).

38. Sander L. Gilman, *Difference and Pathology* (Ithaca: Cornell University Press, 1985), 109 – 27.

39. Young, *Colonial Desire,* 152.

40. Harriet Jacobs, *Incidents in the Life of a Slave Girl,* ed. Jean Fagan Yellin (Cambridge: Harvard University Press, 1987).

41. See Kevin Belmonte, *Hero for Humanity: A Biography of William Wilberforce* (Colorado Springs: NavPress, 2002).

42. See Adam Hochschild, *Bury the Chains: Prophets and Rebels in the Fight to Free an Empire's Slaves* (New York: Houghton Mifflin/Mariner, 2005).

43. See Kidd, *Great Awakening,* 217 – 19.

44. Charles E. Hambrick-Stowe, *Charles G. Finney and the Spirit of American Evangelicalism* (Grand Rapids: Eerdmans, 1996); Keith J. Hardman, *Charles G. Finney, 1792–1875: Revivalist and Reformer* (Syracuse: Syracuse University Press, 1987); David L. Weddle, *The Law as Gospel: Revival and Reform in the Theology of Charles G. Finney* (Metuchen, NJ: Scarecrow Press, 1985).

45. Richard Carwardine, "The New Measures in the Cities," *Journal of American History* 59 (1972): 327 – 40.

46. Charles G. Finney, *Lectures on Revivals of Religion,* ed. William G. McLoughlin (Cambridge: Harvard University Press, 1960).

47. See James D. Bratt, "The Reorientation of American Protestantism, 1835 – 1845," *Church History* 67:1 (March 1998): 52 – 82; idem, "Religious Anti-Revivalism in Antebellum America," *Journal of the Early Republic* 24 (Spring 2004): 66 – 106; David

Hampton, "Theodore Dwight Weld—The American Century," *Evangelical Disenchantment,* 70–91.

48. Sojourner Truth, *Narrative of Sojourner Truth* (Mineola, NY: Dover Publications, 1997), 4.

49. Ibid.

50. Ibid., 16.

51. Sarah Hopkins Bradford, *Harriet, the Moses of Her People* (New York: George R. Lockwood and Son, 1897), 90–91, as quoted by Jean M. Humez, *Harriet Tubman: The Life and the Life Stories* (Madison: University of Wisconsin Press, 2003), 259. Italics are in the original. I am grateful to Osagyefo Uhuru Sekou for this reference.

52. Bradford, *Harriet, the Moses of Her People,* 134–35. For an insightful discussion of the exodus motif in the African American theological imagination, see Eddie S. Glaude, *Exodus! Religion, Race, and Nation in Early Black America* (Chicago: University of Chicago Press, 2000).

53. Harriet Beecher Stowe, "Sojourner Truth: The Libyan Sibyl," *Atlantic Monthly* 11 (April 1863): 473–81, as quoted by Corey D. B. Walker, "Empire and the Ethics of Opacity: The End of Theology and the Beginning(s) of Theological Thinking," in *Evangelicals and Empire,* ed. Bruce Ellis Benson and Peter Goodwin Heltzel (Grand Rapids: Brazos, 2008), 235. Corey D. B. Walker writes of this episode, "the question, 'Frederick, is God dead?' is not one which so much requires an absolute answer—as so many evangelicals would like to offer—inasmuch as it requires a deep and probing interrogation of the myriad methods, categories, norms, and substantive commitments that in/form the material and ideological constructions of Empire *and* evangelicalism. . . . At stake in the openness of Truth's question is nothing less than the present and future possibility of a critical response to Empire as well as a fundamental rethinking of the relation of theology and politics."

54. Noll, *Civil War as Theological Crisis,* 50.

55. Ibid., 32–33.

56. Ibid., 75–94.

57. Harry S. Stout, *Upon the Altar of the Nation: A Moral History of the Civil War* (New York: Penguin Books, 2006), 295–424.

58. *Christian Observer,* February 2, 1865, as cited by Stout, *Upon the Altar of the Nation,* 409.

59. Stout, *Upon the Altar of the Nation,* 409.

60. Noll, *Civil War as Theological Crisis,* 52.

61. Ibid., 161.

62. Stout, *Upon the Altar of the Nation,* 458.

63. Edward J. Blum, "'O God of a Godless Land': Northern African American Challenges to White Christian Nationhood, 1865–1906," in *Vale of Tears: New Essays in Religion and Reconstruction,* ed. Edward J. Blum and W. Scott Poole (Macon, GA: Mercer University Press, 2005), 93–111.

64. See W. Scott Poole, *Never Surrender: Confederate Memory and Conservatism in the South Carolina Upcountry* (Athens: University of Georgia Press, 2003); Charles

Reagan Wilson, *Baptized in Blood: The Religion of the Lost Cause, 1868–1920* (Athens: University of Georgia Press, 1980).

65. Stout, *Upon the Altar of the Nation*, 292; cf. Harry S. Stout and Christopher Grasso, "Civil War, Religion, and Communications: The Case of Richmond," in *Religion and the American Civil War*, ed. Randall M. Miller, Harry S. Stout, and Charles Reagan Wilson (Oxford: Oxford University Press, 1998), 313–59.

66. Ted Ownby, *Subduing Satan: Religion, Recreation, and Manhood in the Rural South, 1865–1920* (Chapel Hill: University of North Carolina Press, 1990), 15.

67. Heyrman, *Southern Cross*, 128ff.

68. Jean E. Friedman, *The Enclosed Garden: Women and Community in the Evangelical South, 1830–1900* (Chapel Hill: University of North Carolina Press, 1985).

69. Kimberly R. Kellison, "Parameters of Promiscuity: Sexuality, Violence, and Religion in Upcountry South Carolina," in *Vale of Tears: New Essays on Religion and Reconstruction*, ed. Edward J. Blum and W. Scott Poole (Macon, GA: Mercer University Press, 2005), 35.

70. Edward J. Blum, "Black Messiahs and Murderous Whites: Violence and Faith in Literary Expression," in *W. E. B. Du Bois: American Prophet* (Philadelphia: University of Pennsylvania Press, 2007), 134–80. My discussion of the cultural and theological significance of lynching that follows is indebted to several conversations with Edward J. Blum, J. Kameron Carter, James Cone, Jennifer Heckart, and K. Christine Pae, and especially to James Cone's argument in "The Cross and the Lynching Tree," *Harvard Divinity Bulletin*, Vol. 35, No. 1 (Winter 2007): 47–55.

71. Patterson, *Slavery and Social Death*, 39.

72. Richard Slotkin, *Regeneration through Violence: The Mythology of the American Frontier, 1600–1860* (Middletown, CT: Wesleyan University Press, 1973), 5.

73. Patterson, *Slavery and Social Death*, 83.

74. Ibid.; Orlando Patterson, *Rituals of Blood: Consequences of Slavery in Two American Centuries* (New York: Basic Civitas Books, 1998).

75. Genovese, *Roll, Jordon, Roll*, 4.

76. Patterson, *Slavery and Social Death*, 39, 46, 98.

77. Donald G. Mathews, "The Southern Right of Human Sacrifice," *Journal of Southern Religion* (August 22, 2000), http://jsr.fsu.edu/mathews.htm (accessed September 15, 2007).

78. See Bynum, *Unruly Women;* Martha Hodes, "The Sexualization of Reconstruction Politics: White Women and Black Men in the South after the Civil War," in *American Sexual Politics: Sex, Gender, and Race since the Civil War*, ed. John C. Fout and Maura Shaw Tantillo (Chicago: University of Chicago Press, 1993), 59–74; idem, *White Women, Black Men: Illicit Sex in the Nineteenth-Century South* (New Haven: Yale University Press, 1997).

79. Peter Ehrenhaus and Susan Owen, "Race Lynching and Christian Evangelicalism: Performances of Faith," *Text and Performance Quarterly* 24:3–4 (July and October 2004): 276–301.

80. W. Scott Poole, "Confederate Apocalypse: Theology and Violence in the White

Reconstruction South," in *Vale of Tears: New Essays on Religion and Reconstruction*, ed. Edward J. Blum and W. Scott Poole (Macon, GA: Mercer University Press, 2005), 40.

81. Blum, *W. E. B. Du Bois*, 138.

82. W. E. B. Du Bois, *Black Reconstruction in America* (1932; reprint, New York: Atheneum, 1992), 634, as quoted by Blum, "'O God of a Godless Land,'" 93–107.

83. W. E. B. Du Bois, "The Crucifixion of God," W. E. B. Du Bois, Papers, microfilm, reel 88, frames 1211–13 (typed, 6 pages), University of Massachusetts—Amherst. Reference provided by Edward J. Blum.

84. Ida B. Wells, *A Red Record: Tabulated Statistics and Alleged Causes of Lynchings in the United States, 1892–1893–1894* (1895), in *Selected Works of Ida B. Wells-Barnett*, ed. Trudier Harris (New York: Oxford University Press, 1991), 149.

85. Blum, *Reforging the White Republic*, 140–41.

86. As quoted by Blum, "'O God of a Godless Land,'" 101.

87. For important studies on the origins and nature of the black Christianity in the United States see Wallace D. Best, *Passionately Human, No Less Divine: Religion and Culture in Black Chicago, 1915–1952* (Princeton: Princeton University Press, 2005). John Hope Franklin, *From Slavery to Freedom: A History of Negro Americans*, 5th ed. (New York: Alfred A. Knopf, 1980); Sylvia R. Frey and Betty Wood, *Come Shouting to Zion;* Evelyn Brooks Higginbotham, *Righteous Discontent: The Women's Movement in the Black Baptist Church* (Cambridge: Harvard University Press, 1993); C. Eric Lincoln and Lawrence H. Mamiya, *The Black Church in the African American Experience* (Durham: Duke University Press, 1990); Michele Mitchell, *Righteous Propagation;* Raboteau, *Slave Religion;* Daniel W. Stowell, *Rebuilding Zion: The Religious Reconstruction of the South, 1863–1877* (New York: Oxford University Press, 1998); and James Melvin Washington, *Frustrated Fellowship: The Black Baptist Quest for Social Power* (Macon, GA: Mercer University Press, 1986).

Chapter 3. Martin Luther King Jr.'s Theology of the Cross

1. John Alexander, "Is Dr. Martin Luther King, Jr., a Communist?" and "Is Dr. Martin Luther King, Jr., a Fundamentalist?" *Freedom Now*, 2, no. 3, June 1, 1966.

2. Charles Marsh presents King and the civil rights movement as being a formative influence on evangelicals, including Ed King and John Perkins. Charles Marsh, *The Beloved Community: How Faith Shapes Social Justice, from the Civil Rights Movement to Today* (New York: Basic Books, 2005).

3. Frederick Douglass, *Narrative of the Life of Frederick Douglass: An American Slave Written by Himself*, ed. Benjamin Quarles (Cambridge: Belknap Press of Harvard University Press, 1960), 37, 38.

4. David W. Wills, "The Central Themes of American Religious History: Pluralism, Puritanism, and the Encounter of Black and White," *Religion and Intellectual Life*, no. 1 (Fall 1987): 30–41.

5. Brian Steensland, Jerry Park, Mark Regnerus, Lynn Robinson, W. Bradford Wilcox, and Robert Woodberry, "The Measure of American Religion: Toward Improving the State of the Art," *Social Forces* 79:1 (2000): 291–318.

6. James H. Cone, "Martin Luther King, Jr., Black Theology—Black Church,"

Theology Today 40:4 (January 1984): 409–20; idem, "The Theology of Martin Luther King, Jr.," Union Seminary Quarterly Review 40:4 (January 1986): 21–39. Cf. Lewis V. Baldwin, *There is a Balm in Gilead* (Minneapolis: Fortress Press, 1991), 159–228.

7. Ibid., 30.

8. James H. Cone, *Martin and Malcolm: A Dream or a Nightmare* (Maryknoll, NY: Orbis Books, 1991). Cf. Lewis V. Baldwin, *Between Cross & Crescent: Christian and Muslim Perspectives on Malcolm and Martin* (Gainesville: University Press of Florida, 2002), 349–50.

9. Gary Dorrien, *The Making of American Liberal Theology: Imagining Progressive Religion, 1805–1900*, vol. 1 (Louisville: Westminster, 2001); idem, *The Making of American Liberal Theology: Idealism, Realism and Modernity, 1900–1950*, vol. 2 (Louisville: Westminster, 2003); idem, *The Making of American Liberal Theology: Crisis, Irony, and Postmodernity, 1950–2005*, vol. 3 (Louisville: Westminster John Knox Press, 2006). Dorrien's discussion of King is found in *Making of American Liberal Theology*, 3:143–61.

10. Dorrien, *Making of American Liberal Theology*, 2:10.

11. Ibid., 2:426–30.

12. On the black social gospel, see Clayborne Carson, "Martin Luther King, Jr., and the African-American Social Gospel," in *African-American Christianity*, ed. Paul E. Johnson (Berkeley: University of California Press, 1994), 159–77.

13. Martin Luther King Jr., *A Testament of Hope: The Essential Writings and Speeches of Martin Luther King, Jr.*, ed. James Melvin Washington (San Francisco: Harper Collins, 1986), 37 (hereafter *Testament of Hope*).

14. Ibid.

15. For a concise introduction to personalism that includes a discussion of King, see Rufus Burrow Jr., *Personalism: A Critical Introduction* (St. Louis: Chalice Press, 1999).

16. Rufus Burrow Jr.'s work shows that King was not only shaped by Boston personalism, but he advanced this school of thought, particularly in the ethical personalism that he embodied through leading the civil rights movement. See Rufus Burrow Jr., "Martin Luther King, Jr., Personalism, and Moral Law," *Asbury Theological Journal* 52:2 (Fall 1997): 32–39; idem, "Personal-Communitarianism and the Beloved Community," *Encounter* 61:1 (Winter 2000): 23–43.

17. In 1955, King defended his dissertation, "A Comparison of the Conceptions of God in the Thinking of Paul Tillich and Henry Nelson Wieman." His dissertation can be found in *The Papers of Martin Luther King, Jr.*, ed. Clayborne Carson (Berkeley: University of California Press, 1992), vol. 2, 339–547. In his dissertation King critiques Tillich and Wieman and offers a constructive personalist conception of God in the spirit of Edgar S. Brightman and L. Harold DeWolf.

18. See L. Harold DeWolf, *The Religious Revolt against Reason* (New York: Harper and Brothers, 1949).

19. Dorrien, *Making of American Liberal Theology*, 3:133–34

20. Rufus Burrow, "Personalism, the Objective Moral Order, and Moral Law," in Lewis V. Baldwin with Rufus Burrow Jr., Barbara A. Holmes, and Susan Holmes Winfeild, *The Legacy of King: The Boundaries of Law, Politics, and Religion* (Notre Dame: University of Notre Dame Press, 2002), 217.

21. Mark A. Noll, "Forum: Public Theology in Contemporary America," *Religion and American Culture* 10:1 (Winter 2000): 8.

22. Dorrien, *Making of American Liberal Theology*, 3:144.

23. I agree with Richard Lischer that even amidst his studies in liberal theology, King never fully embraced a liberal theological identity and began to fall out with white liberals during the final years of his life. Lischer writes, "In seminary and graduate school King internalized the vocabulary and values of theological liberalism; he did not become a liberal but embraced a new language with which to rationalize his more original religious instincts." Richard Lischer, *The Preacher King* (Oxford: Oxford University Press, 1995), 53.

24. Martin Luther King Jr., *Stride Toward Freedom: The Montgomery Story* (New York: Harper, 1958), 134.

25. Noel Leo Erskine, *King among the Theologians* (Cleveland: Pilgrim Press, 1994), 154.

26. On the importance of biblical narratives on the formation of Afro-Christian theological identity, see the essays in Cane Hope Felder, ed. *Stony the Road We Trod: African American Biblical Interpretation* (Minneapolis: Fortress Press, 1991); Vincent L. Wimbush, ed. *African Americans and the Bible: Sacred Texts and Social Textures* (New York: Continuum, 2000).

27. Vincent Harding, "The Anointed Ones: Hamer, King, and the Bible in the Southern Freedom Movement," in *African Americans and the Bible: Sacred Texts and Social Textures*, ed. Vincent L. Wimbush (New York: Continuum, 2000), 537–45; 540.

28. Lischer, *Preacher King*, 11.

29. David L. Chappell, *A Stone of Hope: Prophetic Religion and the Death of Jim Crow* (Chapel Hill: University of North Carolina Press, 2004), 96–98, 140–44.

30. Taylor Branch, *Parting the Waters: America in the King Years, 1954–63* (New York: Simon and Schuster, 1988), 24.

31. Ibid., 594–95.

32. Ibid.

33. Ibid., 227.

34. Lischer, *Preacher King*, 243–44.

35. Mark A. Noll, *God and Race in American Politics: A Short History* (Princeton: Princeton University Press, 2008), 108.

36. Chappell, *Stone of Hope*, 97.

37. Martin Luther King Jr., "Letter from Birmingham City Jail," (1963) in *Testament of Hope*, 298.

38. Martin Luther King Jr., "Transformed Nonconformist," in *Strength to Love* (Philadelphia: Fortress Press, 1981), 21–29.

39. King, *Testament of Hope*, 50, 294–95, 356–57.

40. Martin Luther King Jr., "Pilgrimage to Nonviolence" (1960), *Testament of Hope*, 35.

41. Martin Luther King Jr., "Contemporary Continental Theology" (Boston University paper, January 15, 1952), in Martin Luther King Jr., *The Papers of Martin Luther King, Jr.*, ed. Clayborne Carson (Berkeley: University of California Press, 1992), vol. 2, 137.

42. King, *Testament of Hope,* 45.

43. Martin Luther King Jr., "Love, Law, and Civil Disobedience" (1961), *Testament of Hope,* 49.

44. Ibid., 51.

45. Ibid.

46. Lewis V. Baldwin, *Toward the Beloved Community: Martin Luther King, Jr. and South Africa* (Cleveland: Pilgrim Press, 1995); Charles Marsh, *The Beloved Community: How Faith Shapes Social Justice, from the Civil Rights Movement to Today* (New York: Basic Books, 2005); cf. Rufus Burrow Jr., "Graham, King, and the Beloved Community," in *The Legacy of Billy Graham: Critical Reflections on America's Greatest Evangelist,* ed. Michael G. Long (Louisville: Westminster John Knox, 2008), 161–78.

47. King, "Love, Law, and Civil Disobedience" (1961), *Testament of Hope,* 42.

48. King, *Testament of Hope,* 20.

49. Martin Luther King Jr., "An Experiment in Love" (1958), *Testament of Hope,* 21.

50. Martin Luther King Jr., "The American Dream" (1961), *Testament of Hope,* 215.

51. Ibid.

52. Ibid., 209.

53. My understanding of the relation between love and justice in King's Christology is indebted to many conversations with Malinda Berry. See her forthcoming doctoral dissertation at Union Theological Seminary, "The Axis of the Cross Is Where We Find Our Humanity: Reinhold Niebuhr, Martin King, and Christian Social Responsibility."

54. Martin Luther King Jr., "A Tough Mind and Tender Heart," *Strength of Love* (Philadelphia: Fortress Press, 1981), 18.

55. King, "An Experiment in Love" (1958), *Testament of Hope,* 16.

56. King, *Testament of Hope,* 11.

57. King, "A Tough Mind and Tender Heart," *Strength of Love,* 13–20.

58. King, "Love, Law, and Civil Disobedience" (1961), *Testament of Hope,* 16–20.

59. King, "Experiment in Love" (1958), *Testament of Hope,* 46.

60. Ibid., 20.

61. Ibid., 19.

62. King, "Love, Law, and Civil Disobedience" (1961), *Testament of Hope,* 47.

63. King, "Experiment in Love" (1958), *Testament of Hope,* 19.

64. Martin Luther King Jr., "Pilgrimage to Nonviolence" (1960), *Testament of Hope,* 38.

65. Martin Luther King Jr., "Suffering and Faith" (1960), *Testament of Hope,* 41.

66. Martin Luther King Jr., "Stride toward Freedom" (1958), *Testament of Hope,* 487.

67. King, "Suffering and Faith" (1960), *Testament of Hope,* 487.

68. Womanist theologians are women of African descent who share many of the concerns of feminist theologians but are committed to the Afrocentric character of theologizing within black theology.

69. Dolores Williams, *Sisters in the Wilderness: The Challenge of Womanist God-Talk* (Maryknoll, NY: Orbis Books, 1993), 167. Williams writes, "[Joanne Carlson] Brown and [Rebecca] Parker claim, as I do, that most of the history of atonement theory in Christian theology supports violence, victimization and undeserved suffering. . . .

Their critique of Martin Luther King, Jr.'s idea of the value of the suffering of the oppressed in oppressed-oppressor confrontations accords with my assumption that African-American Christian women can, through their religion and its leaders, be led passively to accept their own oppression and suffering—if the women are taught that suffering is redemptive" (ibid., 199–200). See Emilie M. Townes, *In a Blaze of Glory: Womanist Spirituality as Social Witness* (Nashville: Abingdon Press, 1995), 121: "A womanist spirituality is drawn to question continually the inordinate amount of suffering that is the lot of the oppressed. Spirituality is challenged to a new awareness of God's presence within humanity as a liberating event. Situations of oppression do not reveal the mystery of God's love. The revelation of God's love manifests itself in work to end oppression." See Karen Baker-Fletcher, "The Strength of My Life," in *Embracing the Spirit: Womanist Perspectives on Hope, Salvation and Transformation*, ed. Emilie M. Townes (Maryknoll, NY: Orbis Books, 1997): "What both authors [Dolores Williams and Jacquelyn Grant] demonstrate is that however well-intentioned ministers who glorify suffering and servanthood may be, the effects of such ministry is detrimental. It effectively supports suffering, oppression, and exploitation. It is disempowering" (p. 134). Cf. Emilie M. Townes, ed., *A Troubling in My Soul: Womanist Perspectives on Evil and Suffering* (Maryknoll, NY: Orbis Books, 1993).

70. David J. Garrow, *Bearing the Cross: Martin Luther King, Jr., and the Southern Christian Leadership Conference* (New York: Vintage Books, 1988). As Vincent Harding has persuasively argued, Martin Luther King Jr.'s theological vision and activism became increasingly radical after his march on Washington in 1963, especially illustrated in his public denouncements of the Vietnam War and his organization of the Poor People's Campaign. Theologically, King turned increasingly to his personal faith in Jesus Christ to sustain him during the suffering and violence of his final years. He understood the suffering he experienced during the civil rights movement as his cross to bear, as he actively participated in the suffering life, death on a cross, and resurrection life of Jesus of Nazareth. With a common source in antebellum revivalism, the black Christian and evangelical streams of King's theology converged in his Christ-centered personal piety and radical social ethic. See Vincent Harding, *Martin Luther King, Jr.: The Inconvenient Hero* (Maryknoll, NY: Orbis Press, 1970).

71. Martin Luther King Jr., "Letter from Birmingham Jail," in *Testament of Hope*, 295.

Chapter 4. Carl F. H. Henry's Uneasy Conscience

1. Carl F. H. Henry, *The Uneasy Conscience of Modern Fundamentalism*, 3rd ed. (Grand Rapids: Eerdmans, 1982).

2. Henry, *Uneasy Conscience*, 17.

3. Mark G. Toulouse, "*Christianity Today* and American Public Life: A Case Study," *Journal of Church and State* 35 (Spring 1993): 255–57, 272–74. Michael O. Emerson and Christian Smith found fewer than two articles per year on race issues in *Christianity Today,* on average, during the period 1957–65. Michael O. Emerson and Christian Smith, *Divided by Faith: Evangelical Religion and the Problem of Race in America* (Oxford: Oxford University Press, 2000), 46.

4. Barry Hankins, *Uneasy in Babylon: Southern Baptist Conservatives and American Culture* (Tuscaloosa: University of Alabama Press, 2002), 22.

5. Carl F. H. Henry, *God, Revelation and Authority*, 6 vols. (Waco, TX: Word Books, 1976–83).

6. Barry Hankins writes, "It would not be going too far to say that Henry has been a mentor for nearly the entire SBC conservative movement. Indeed, he helped officiate at the installation of Richard Land at the Christian Life Commission, Albert Mohler as president of Southern Seminary, Timothy George as dean of the Beeson Divinity School, and Mark Coopenger as president of Midwestern Baptist Seminary in Kansas City." Barry Hankins, *Uneasy in Babylon: Southern Baptist Conservatives and American Culture* (Tuscaloosa: University of Alabama Press, 2002), 22. Cf. Russell D. Moore, "God, Revelation, and Community: Ecclesiology and Baptist Identity in the Thought of Carl Henry," *Southern Baptist Journal of Theology* 8:4 (Winter 2004): 26–43.

7. Carl F. H. Henry, "A Troubled Conscience Fifty Years Later," unpub. MS, 1997, Carl F. H. Henry Archives, Trinity Evangelical Divinity School, Deerfield, Illinois, p. 8. Henry writes, "Any current theology worthy to be called Christian vindicates the propriety and indispensability of the deity, virgin birth, substitutionary death, bodily resurrection, and second coming of Christ." *Evangelical Responsibility in Contemporary Theology* (Grand Rapids: Eerdmans, 1957), 66.

8. Henry, *God, Revelation and Authority*, 2:21.

9. For helpful secondary analyses of Henry's social ethic, see Augustus Cerillo Jr. and Murray W. Dempster, "Carl F. H. Henry's Early Apologetic for an Evangelical Social Ethic, 1942–1956," *Journal of the Evangelical Theological Society* 34:3 (September 1991): 365–79; David L. Weeks, "Carl F. H. Henry's Moral Arguments for Evangelical Political Activism," *Journal of Church and State* (Winter 1998): 83–106; idem, "The Uneasy Politics of Modern Evangelicalism," *Christian Scholar's Review* 30:4 (Summer 2001): 403–18; David F. Wells, "Evangelical Theology," in *The Modern Theologians*, 3rd ed., ed. David F. Ford with Rachel Muers (Oxford: Blackwell, 2005), 608–10.

10. Carl F. H. Henry, *Has Democracy Had Its Day?* (Nashville: ERLC, Christian Life Commission of the Southern Baptist Convention, 1996), vii.

11. Henry, *Uneasy Conscience*, 30, 45.

12. Ibid., 36.

13. Ibid., 17.

14. Ibid., 18–19.

15. Carl Henry, letter to Harold John Ockenga, January 22, 1948, Harold John Ockenga Archive, Gordon-Conwell Theological Seminary, South Hamilton, Massachussetts. I would like to thank Garth Rosell for giving me access to the Ockenga archives. My understanding of Ockenga's contribution to twentieth-century evangelical public theology has been deepened through many conversations with him.

16. See George Marsden, *Reforming Fundamentalism: Fuller Seminary and the New Evangelicalism* (Grand Rapids: Eerdmans, 1987).

17. Marsden, *Reforming Fundamentalism*, 70.

18. Henry was influenced by Abraham Kuyper's theology of Christ's Lordship over all creation: "No single piece of our mental world is to be hermetically sealed off from

the rest, and there is not a square inch on the whole plane of human existence over which Christ, who is Sovereign over all, does not cry: 'Mine.'" Abraham Kuyper, "Sphere Sovereignty," in *Abraham Kuyper: A Centennial Reader,* ed. James D. Bratt (Grand Rapids: Eerdmans, 1998), 488. Cf. Vincent Bacote, *The Spirit in Public Theology: Appropriating the Legacy of Abraham Kuyper* (Grand Rapids: Baker Academic, 2005).

19. H. Richard Niebuhr, *Christ and Culture* (New York: Harper, 1951).

20. Henry, *Uneasy Conscience,* 27, 76.

21. Carl F. H. Henry, *A Plea for Evangelical Demonstration* (Grand Rapids: Baker, 1971), 31.

22. Carl Henry, letter to Harold John Ockenga, April 23, 1947. Harold John Ockenga Archive, Gordon-Conwell Theological Seminary.

23. Henry, like King, completed his Ph.D. at Boston University. Both were drawn to Boston personalism but for different reasons. While King appropriated personalist notions in his theology of neighbor love, Henry sought to critique the personalistic impulse in Strong's theology on epistemological and theological grounds. Although Henry brought a Reformed Baptist reading to personalism and King a black church progressive appropriation of it, they both remained at heart prophetic Baptists whose Baptist public theologies had been shaped by extensive interaction with the personalist tradition.

24. Some Baptists were originally part of the Congregationalist break with the Puritans, who had themselves separated from Anglicanism in England, and others are rooted in the Anabaptist experience in Europe, when many of these religious dissenters were persecuted by the state. In the United States, the Baptists largely came from the Congregationalist split with the Puritans. Baptists have always emphasized that the individual is free to choose his or her own religious affiliation. On the impact of individualism on evangelical ethics see Dennis P. Hollinger, *Individualism and Social Ethics: An Evangelical Syncretism* (Lanham, MD: University Press of America, 1983).

25. Marsden, *Reforming Fundamentalism,* 91.

26. Robert N. Bellah, "Is There a Common American Culture?" *Journal of the American Academy of Religion* 66 (1998): 613–26.

27. Carl F. H. Henry, "Friendly Persuasion," *Eternity* 34:7 (July–August 1983): 48. On Schaeffer's theology, see Barry Hankins, *Francis Schaeffer and the Shaping of Evangelical America* (Grand Rapids: Eerdmans, 2008).

28. Henry's desire for the United States to be shaped by the moral law of the Bible should be clearly distinguished from the ideas of Rousas John Rushdoony, the father of Christian reconstructionism, who believed that the civil law of the Old Testament should be binding on contemporary governments. Henry is not calling for a literal application of Old Testament civil law but follows the mainstream Reformed tradition of Abraham Kuyper, which sees the moral vision of the "whole counsel" of scripture as being an important guide to governmental affairs.

29. Henry, *Plea for Evangelical Demonstration,* 48.

30. Ibid., 107.

31. I am drawing here on Dennis P. Hollinger's interpretation of Henry's regenerational ethic. Hollinger writes, "The regenerational approach does not totally reject so-

cial change and public policy concerns, but it finds its roots in personal redemption."
Hollinger, *Individualism and Social Ethics*, 109.

32. Henry, *Plea for Evangelical Demonstration*, 109.

33. Ibid., 107. Dennis P. Hollinger notes that *Christianity Today* addressed communism more than any other political issue between 1956 and 1976. Hollinger, *Individualism and Social Ethics*, 187–90.

34. Henry, *Uneasy Conscience*, 65.

35. Editorial, "Why Christianity Today?" *Christianity Today* 1:1 (October 15, 1956): 20.

36. Henry, *Uneasy Conscience*, 53.

37. Ibid., 38.

38. Ibid., 54.

39. Marsden, *Reforming Fundamentalism*, 93.

40. Henry, *Uneasy Conscience*, 78.

41. Henry, "Troubled Conscience Fifty Years Later," 42. Henry, *Uneasy Conscience*, 53.

42. Henry, *Uneasy Conscience*, 54.

43. Henry, *Plea for Evangelical Demonstration*, 108.

44. Henry, *Uneasy Conscience*, 47.

45. Ibid., 31. Cf. Carl F. H. Henry, "Evangelicals in the Social Struggle," *Christianity Today* 10:1 (October 8, 1965): 11.

46. Henry, *Uneasy Conscience*, 76.

47. United Press International, "Billy Graham Hits State Liquor System, Scores Segregation in the Church," *Jackson (Mississippi) Daily News*, July 9, 1952.

48. David L. Chappell, *A Stone of Hope: Prophetic Religion and the Death of Jim Crow* (Chapel Hill: University of North Carolina Press, 2004), 96–97, 140–44; For thoughtful analyses of Graham on race, see Michael G. Long, *Billy Graham and the Beloved Community: America's Evangelist and the Dream of Martin Luther King, Jr.* (Houndmills, Eng.: Palgrave MacMillan, 2006). Gary Dorrien, "Niebuhr and Graham: Modernity, Complexity, White Supremacism, Justice, Ambiguity," in *The Legacy of Billy Graham: Critical Reflections on America's Greatest Evangelist*, ed. Michael G. Long (Louisville: Westminster John Knox, 2008), 141–60; Rufus Burrow Jr., "Graham, King, and the Beloved Community," in *The Legacy of Billy Graham*, ed. Michael G. Long, 161–78. For helpful overviews of evangelical participation in the civil rights movement, see Curtis J. Evans, "Evangelicals and the Civil Rights Movement," (master's thesis, Gordon-Conwell Theological Seminary, 1999); Michael D. Hammond, "Conscience in Crisis: Neo-Evangelicals and Race in the 1950s" (master's thesis, Wheaton College, 2002).

49. Long, *Billy Graham and the Beloved Community*, 226.

50. Carl F. H. Henry, editorial, "Race Tensions and Social Change," *Christianity Today* 3:8 (January 19, 1959): 21.

51. For a thoughtful political history of whiteness that includes an account of the cultural constitution of white Americans as a unified Caucasian race during the period 1924 to 1965, see Matthew Frye Jacobson, *Whiteness of a Different Color: European Immigrants and the Alchemy of Race* (Cambridge: Harvard University Press, 1998), 1–136.

52. Mark A. Noll, *Scandal of the Evangelical Mind* (Grand Rapids: Eerdmans, 1994), 156; Edward L. Moore, *Billy Graham and Martin Luther King, Jr.: An Inquiry into White and Black Revivalistic Traditions* (Ph.D. diss., Vanderbilt University, 1979), 468, 471–72.

53. William Pannell, "The Religious Heritage of Blacks," *The Evangelicals: What They Believe, Who They Are, Where They Are Changing* (Nashville: Abingdon Press, 1975), 102–6; 96–107.

54. Henry, *Plea for Evangelical Demonstration*, 13.

Chapter 5. Focus on the Family

1. From this point forward I will refer to Focus on the Family as Focus.

2. Gary Bauer, phone interview, April 14, 2006.

3. Carl F. H. Henry, *The Uneasy Conscience of Modern Fundamentalism*, 3rd ed. (Grand Rapids: Eerdmans, 1982), 10.

4. Carl F. H. Henry, "Coming Home to Say Good-bye," *Wheaton Alumni* 57 (June–July 1990): 12–14.

5. In the foreword to his latest book, Richard Land writes in the acknowledgments, "I must add a special word of gratitude to the late, great theologian Dr. Carl F. H. Henry, who long ago began to challenge me persistently to take up the task of grappling with the major issues involved with Christians and their engagement with their society—a challenge to which this book is a partial reply." *The Divided States of America? What Liberals and Conservatives Are Missing in the God-and-Country Shouting Match!* (Nashville: Thomas Nelson, 2007), viii.

6. Barry Hankins, *Uneasy in Babylon: Southern Baptist Conservatives and American Culture* (Tuscaloosa: University of Alabama Press, 2002), 22.

7. Henry, *Uneasy Conscience*, 54. Francis Schaeffer also argued that the Lordship of Christ "covers *all* of life and *all* of life equally." Francis A. Schaeffer, *A Christian Manifesto* (Westchester, IL: Crossway Books, 1981), 19.

8. Carl F. H. Henry, *Twilight of a Great Civilization: The Drift toward Neo-Paganism* (Westchester, IL: Crossway, 1988). Cf. James A. Patterson, "Cultural Pessimism in Modern Evangelical Thought: Francis Schaeffer, Carl Henry, and Charles Colson," *Journal of the Evangelical Theological Society* 49:4 (December 2006): 807–20.

9. In 1908 at Pilot Point, Texas, the Church of the Nazarene merged with two other churches that had grown out of the Holiness Movement: the Association of Pentecostal Churches in America and the Holiness Church of Christ.

10. Darren Dochuk, "From Bible Belt to Sunbelt: Plain Folk Religion, Grassroots Politics, and the Southernization of Southern California, 1939–1969" (Ph.D. diss., Notre Dame University, 2005).

11. Susie C. Stanley, "Social Holiness Ministries," *Holy Boldness: Women Preachers' Autobiographies and the Sanctified Self* (Knoxville: University of Tennessee Press, 2002), 172–94; 173. Stanley describes a progressive and feminist stream of social holiness within the Wesleyan/Holiness tradition. Cf. Norris Magnuson, *Salvation in the Slums*, ATLA Series, no. 10 (Metuchen, NJ: Scarecrow Press, 1977); Timothy L. Smith,

Revivalism and Social Reform in Mid-Nineteenth-Century America (New York: Ab-ingdon Press, 1957); Douglass M. Strong, *Perfectionist Politics: Abolitionism and the Religious Tensions of American Democracy* (Syracuse: Syracuse University Press, 1999).

12. Bresee's proclamation on social holiness can be attributed to John Wesley, who wrote, "The gospel of Christ knows of no religion, but social; no holiness but social holiness. 'Faith working by love' is the length and breadth and depth and height of Christian perfection." John Wesley, "Preface" to *Hymns and Sacred Poems* (1739) as quoted in *From the Margins: A Celebration of the Theological Work of Donald W. Dayton*, ed. Christian T. Collins Winn (Eugene, OR: Pickwick Publications, 2007), vii. Cf. Carl Bangs, *Phineas F. Bresee: His Life in Methodism, the Holiness Movement, and the Church of the Nazarene* (Kansas City, Mo.: Beacon Hill Press, 1995).

13. Dale Buss, *Family Man: The Biography of Dr. James Dobson* (Wheaton, IL: Tyn-dale House, 2005), 24.

14. As quoted by Donald W. Dayton, *Theological Roots on Pentecostalism* (Metu-chen, NJ: Scarecrow Press, 1987), 21.

15. James Dobson, *The New Dare to Discipline* (Wheaton, IL: Tyndale House, 1992), 247.

16. James Dobson and panelists, "The Essential Role of Men's Ministry," Focus on the Family (panel), CD, 2004: B00154D/32025.

17. James Dobson and panelists, "The Essential Role of Men's Ministry," Focus on the Family (panel), CD, 2004: B00154D/32025.

18. Ibid.

19. Francis Schaeffer founded L'Abri, an alternative Christian community in the Swiss Alps. During the 1960s and 1970s, L'Abri became the pilgrimage site for a gener-ation of restless evangelical youth. A creative intellectual and Presbyterian theologian, Schaeffer provided these young minds with a critique of the excesses of Western culture and a vision of Christianity as a dynamic and creative learning community. Schaeffer's reputation as a charismatic teacher rivaled that of Carl Henry and C. S. Lewis, inspiring the theological imaginations of evangelicals in the late twentieth century. For the definitive work on the life and thought of Francis Schaeffer see Barry Hankins, *Francis Schaeffer and the Shaping of Evangelical America* (Grand Rapids: Eerdmans, 2008).

20. Randall Balmer, *God in the White House: A History* (New York: Harper One, 2008), 115.

21. H. B. London, interview with the author, Focus on the Family, Colorado Springs, CO, August 2006.

22. Thomas Hess, interview with the author, Focus on the Family, Colorado Springs, CO, August 2006. Unlike Henry's *Uneasy Conscience,* which was a manifesto for evangelical activism in 1947, Francis Schaeffer's *Christian Manifesto* was a mani-festo for the Religious Right in 1981. Schaeffer's *Christian Manifesto* was the third vol-ume in a trilogy starting with *How Should We Then Live?* documenting how the mod-ern worldview shifted toward humanism, and *Whatever Happened to the Human Race?* which explained how humanism was redefining human life in law and medical science. Francis Schaeffer and Dr. C. Everett Koop, later surgeon general of the United States,

dedicated their 1979 book and film *Whatever Happened to the Human Race?* to "those who were robbed of life, the unborn, the weak, the sick, and the old." In contrast to humanism as the religion of the secularized state, which led to "the dark ages of madness, selfishness, lust and greed for which the last decades of the twentieth centuries are remembered," Schaeffer presented a fresh call for a public evangelical theology. He saw evangelical social witness as vital and necessary antidote to the poison of secular humanism that was eroding the Judeo-Christian foundation of American society.

23. For Randall Balmer's argument that the lawsuit against Bob Jones University's racially discriminatory policies is the true origin of the Religious Right, see Randall Balmer, "The Abortion Myth," in *Thy Kingdom Come* (New York: Basic Books, 2006), 1–34; Balmer, *God in the White House*, 94–101; 157. Cf. Michael Cromartie, ed., *No Longer Exiles: The Religion New Right in American Politics* (Washington, DC: Ethics and Public Policy Center, 1993), 26ff. For an introduction to the southern fundamentalist character of Bob Jones, see Mark Taylor Dalhouse, *An Island in a Lake of Fire: Bob Jones University, Fundamentalism, and the Separatist Movement* (Athens: University of Georgia Press, 1996).

24. Michael O. Emerson and Christian Smith, *Divided by Faith: Evangelical Religion and the Problem of Race in America* (New York: Oxford University Press, 2000), 7.

25. Ibid., 9.

26. Buss, *Family Man*, 88.

27. Mark A. Noll, "Civil Rights, the Republican—White Evangelical Alliance, and the Endurance of Evil in the Land of the Free," Stafford Little Lectures at Princeton University, October 17–19, 2007, 21–22. Cf. idem, *God and Race in American Politics: A Short History* (Princeton: Princeton University Press, 2008), 161.

28. As quoted in Buss, *Family Man*, 165–67.

29. President George W. Bush's inaugural address, January 20, 2001, http://www .whitehouse.gov/news/inaugural-address.html (accessed December 14, 2007).

30. See Sébastien Fath's eschatological analysis of Bush's "compassionate conservatism." Sébastien Fath, "Empire's Future Religion: The Hidden Competition between Postmillennial American Expansionism and Premillennial Evangelical Christianity," in Benson and Heltzel, *Evangelicals and Empire*, 120–29.

31. As quoted in Buss, *Family Man*, 7.

32. Dan Gilgoff, *The Jesus Machine: How James Dobson, Focus on the Family, and Evangelical America Are Winning the Culture War* (New York: St. Martin's Press, 2007), 38–140.

33. "Debate-Tested Sound Bites on Defending Marriage" by Glenn T. Stanton. Family.org, available at http://www.family.org/cforum/fosi/marriage/ssuap/a0032017 .cfm (original post date: May 14, 2004).

34. Pew Research Center for the People and the Press, "Religion and the Presidential Vote: Bush's Gains Broad-Based," available at http://people press.org/commentary/ display.php3?AnalysisID=103 (accessed December 6, 2004). Although there is some suggestion that evangelicals voted in larger numbers in 2004 than in 2000, they did not

increase in proportion to the rest of the population, making up an estimated 23 percent of voters in both elections.

35. James Dobson as quoted by Peter H. Stone and Bara Vaida, "Christian Soldiers: The Religious Right Now Includes Many Influential and Politically Astute Groups That Work Together on Issues," *National Journal,* December 4, 2004, p. 3601.

36. United Press International, "Billy Graham Hits State Liquor System, Scores Segregation in the Church," *Jackson (Mississippi) Daily News,* July 9, 1952.

37. See Susan Faludi, *Stiffed: The Betrayal of the American Man* (New York: William Morrow, 1999); Dana D. Nelson, *National Manhood: Capitalist Citizenship and the Imagined Fraternity of White Men* (Durham: Duke University Press, 1998).

38. James Davison Hunter, *Evangelicalism: The Coming Generation* (Chicago: University of Chicago Press, 1987), 90.

39. Maxine Van de Wetering, "The Popular Concept of 'Home' in Nineteenth-Century America," *Journal of American Studies* 18 (April 1984): 5–28.

40. Barbara Welter, "The Cult of True Womenhood, 1820–1860," *American Quarterly* 18 (Summer 1966): 151–74.

41. Ted Ownby, *Subduing Satan: Religion, Recreation, and Manhood in the Rural South, 1865–1920* (Chapel Hill: University of North Carolina Press, 1990), 5.

42. James Dobson, *Dr. Dobson Answers Your Questions* (Wheaton, IL: Tyndale House, 1980), 407.

43. Ibid., 416.

44. James Dobson, *Dare to Discipline* (Wheaton, IL: Tyndale House, 1980). Dobson was developing arguments about the "traditional family" that were shared by Jerry Falwell, *Listen America* (New York: Harper and Row, 1980); cf. Tim LaHaye, *The Battle for the Family* (Old Tappan, NJ: Revell, 1982).

45. Dobson, *Dr. Dobson Answers Your Questions,* 159.

46. Ibid., 409.

47. Ibid., 407.

48. Ibid., 408.

49. Ibid., 405–6.

50. Ibid., 406.

51. Recent empirical research may lend itself to explaining in part why James Dobson's pop psychology resonates with some women. Wilcox, a sociologist who concentrates on the family, argues that it is men's emotional work in producing happiness—and not equality—that makes wives content in their marriages. W. Bradford Wilcox and Steven Nick, "What's Love Got to Do with It? Equality, Equity, Commitment and Women's Marital Quality," *Social Forces* 84:3 (March 2006): 1321–45.

52. James Dobson, *Straight Talk to Men and Their Wives* (Waco, TX: Word Books, 1982), 21.

53. Eithne Johnson, "Dr. Dobson's Advice to Christian Women: The Story of Strategic Motherhood," *Social Text* 16:4 (Winter 1998): 55–82; Colleen McDannell, "Beyond Dr. Dobson: Women, Girls, and Focus on the Family," in *Women and Twen-*

tieth-Century Protestantism, ed. Margaret Lamberts Bendroth and Virginia Lieson Brereton (Urbana: University of Illinois Press, 2001), 113–31.

54. Wilcox and Nick, "What's Love Got to Do with It?"

55. Christian Smith, *Christian America? What Evangelicals Really Want* (Berkeley: University of California Press, 1998).

56. Paul Asay, "Dobson's Impact Widely Felt," *Colorado Springs Gazette,* January 18, 2005.

57. Hunter, *Evangelicalism,* 76–77.

58. Joel Carpenter, "From Fundamentalism to the New Evangelical Coalition," in *Evangelicalism and Modern America,* ed. George Marsden (Grand Rapids: Eerdmans, 1983), 10.

59. Tom Minnery, e-mail to author, February 15, 2007.

60. Hunter, *Evangelicalism,* 114.

61. Harry R. Jackson Jr. and Tony Perkins, *Personal Faith and Public Policy* (Lake Mary, FL: Strang Communications, 2008).

62. See George Barna and Harry R. Jackson Jr., *High Impact African-American Churches: Leadership Concepts from Some of Today's Most Effective Churches* (Ventura, CA: Regal Books, 2004); Harry R. Jackson Jr., *The Black Contract with America on Moral Values: Protecting America's Moral Compass* (Lake Mary, FL: Charisma House, 2005); idem, *The Truth in Black and White* (Lake Mary, FL: FrontLine/Strang, 2008). Jackson writes, "Fifty years ago, the national evangelical movement missed a great opportunity to help direct the civil rights movement. If the white church in the South had preached against racism and called for local churches to lead the movement for justice on biblical grounds, they could have helped navigate the nation through many strife-filled years. The church of the 1950s opted, instead, to maintain the status quo. They could have led the nation through a very delicate transition, but now the task falls to us." Jackson, *The Truth in Black and White,* 213.

63. Jackson and Perkins, *Personal Faith and Public Policy,* 203–19. Jackson and Perkins write, "We must exercise dominion and lead the way in the caring for the earth. We cannot simply repeat the mantra 'I do not believe in global warming,' even if we don't. We have a responsibility to encourage our political leaders and scientists to give real options for bettering our stewardship of this planet God has given to use to tend and rule over." Ibid., 207.

64. Jackson and Perkins, *Personal Faith and Public Policy,* 136.

65. Jackson, *Truth in Black and White,* 20, 21.

66. Jackson and Perkins, *Personal Faith and Public Policy,* 133.

67. Ibid., 138.

68. Jim Wallis writes, "What form racial restitution or reparations should take is a matter of intense debate. I don't have the ideal formula or answer. But for the healing of the nation, and the genuine task of counteracting an injustice, some form of restitution could still be very significant. Few believe that solutions such as cash payments to individuals or families are the best option now, but there is growing interest in explor-

ing what might be the equivalent of 'forty acres and a mule.'" Jim Wallis, *The Great Awakening* (San Francisco: Harper One, 2008), 165.

69. Jackson and Perkins, *Personal Faith and Public Policy,* 142.

70. Ibid., 144, 145.

71. The ideas in this paragraph I developed in conversation with Robin Rogers. See Robin Rogers and Peter Godwin Heltzel, "The New Evangelical Politics," *Society* 45:5 (2008): 412–14.

Chapter 6. National Association of Evangelicals

1. Member denominations of the National Association of Evangelicals include the Assemblies of God, Association of Vineyard Churches—USA, Baptist General Conference, Brethren in Christ Church, Christian Reformed Church in North America, Church of God, Church of the Nazarene, Conservative Baptist Association of America, Conservative Lutheran Association, Evangelical Assembly of Presbyterian Churches, Free Methodist Church of North America, Hispanic World Harvest Churches, International Church of the Foursquare Gospel, International Pentecostal Church of Christ, Open Bible Churches, Presbyterian Church in America, Reformed Episcopal Church, Southern Pacific Latin American Churches, the Brethren Church, the Christian and Missionary Alliance, the Salvation Army, U.S. Conference of Mennonite Brethren Churches, and the Worldwide Church of God.

2. Arthur H. Matthews, *Standing Up, Standing Together: The Emergence of the National Association of Evangelicals* (Carol Stream, IL: National Association of Evangelicals, 1992), 52.

3. Bruce L. Shelley, *Evangelicalism in America* (Grand Rapids: Eerdmans, 1967), 70.

4. Ibid., 104.

5. As quoted by Joel A. Carpenter, *Revive Us Again: The Reawakening of American Fundamentalism* (Oxford: Oxford University, 1997), 149.

6. Ibid., 207.

7. Statement on Prejudice and Racism, National Association of Evangelicals and National Black Evangelical Association, January 26–27, 1990; Ronald J. Sider and Diane Knippers, eds., *Toward an Evangelical Public Policy: Political Strategies for the Health of the Nation* (Grand Rapids: Baker Books, 2005). For a thoughtful account of the "centrist" evangelical coalition that has been centered in the Governmental Affaris Office of the NAE, see David P. Gushee, *The Future of Faith in American Politics: The Public Witness of the Evangelical Center* (Waco, TX: Baylor University Press, 2008). Gushee himself has prophetically led evangelicals and Baptists to engage issues of torture and climate change, among other social justice issues.

8. The five central doctrines of the fundamentalist movement that the NAE emerged from were the inerrant Bible, the virgin birth, Jesus Christ's substitutionary atonement, bodily resurrection, and the second coming.

9. Sider and Knippers, eds., *Toward an Evangelical Public Policy,* 365.

10. On the influence of Catholic social teaching on the NAE, see Kristin E. Heyer,

"Insights from Catholic Social Ethics and Political Participation," in *Toward an Evangelical Public Policy,* ed. Sider and Knippers, 101–16.

11. Carpenter, *Revive Us Again.*

12. William H. Bentley writes, "Though unknown outside the parochialism of our endemic Black evangelicalism, NBEA early manifested the potential of becoming a pace-setter. Before 'Black Power' became the rallying cry it later did, some Black evangelicals among us were thinking seriously in terms of group consciousness." William H. Bentley, "Factors in the Origin and Focus of the National Black Evangelical Association," in *Black Theology: A Documentary History, 1966–1979,* ed. Gayraud S. Wilmore and James H. Cone (Maryknoll, NY: Orbis Books, 1979), 310–21; idem, *National Black Evangelical Association: Evolution of a Concept of Ministry,* rev. ed. (Chicago: The Author, 1979); idem, *The Meaning of History for Black Americans* (Chicago: National Black Evangelical Association and the National Black Christian Students Conference, 1979); idem, *National Black Evangelical Association: Bellwether of a Movement, 1963–1988* (Chicago: National Black Evangelical Association, 1988).

13. For some of the historical background on this tradition of prophetic evangelical politics, see Randall Balmer and Lauren F. Winner, "Protestantism and Social Justice," in their *Protestantism in America* (New York: Columbia University Press, 2002), 179–93; cf. Christian Smith, *American Evangelicalism: Embattled and Thriving* (Chicago: University of Chicago, 1998), 196–98.

14. Ronald J. Sider, *The Scandal of the Evangelical Conscience* (Grand Rapids: Baker Books, 2005).

15. Don Argue, phone interview, December 12, 2006.

16. Statement on Prejudice and Racism, National Association of Evangelicals and National Black Evangelical Association, January 26–27; cover letter from Don Argue, NAE and Russ Knight, NBEA, http://www.nae.net/images/Racial%20Reconciliation.pdf (accessed October 29, 2008); Jim Jones, "Still Playing Catch-Up: NBEA, NAE Move Slowly to Heal Racial Rifts," *Christianity Today,* May 19, 1997, p. 56.

17. John W. Kennedy, "NAE Issues 'Evangelical Manifesto,'" *Christianity Today,* April 8, 1996, p. 101.

18. Rick Miesel, "National Association of Evangelicals (NAE) or 'National Association of Neo-Evangelicals?'" available at http://www.rapidnet.com/~jbeard/bdm/Psychology/nae/nae.htm (accessed October 2006).

19. Ibid.

20. Worldwide Church of God, "Transformed Church Finds Acceptance and Fellowship in Evangelical Community: NAE Accepts Worldwide Church of God," May 7, 1997, http://www.wcg.org/lit/AboutUs/media/nae.htm (accessed October 6, 2006).

21. Ibid.

22. Jim Jones, "Breaking up Isn't Hard to Do," *Christianity Today International,* April 2, 2001, available at http://www.christianitytoday.com/ct/2001/005/13.26.html (accessed October 3, 2006).

23. Ted Haggard, interview with author, Colorado Springs, CO, August 15, 2006.

24. Don Argue, phone interview, December 12, 2006.

25. Ted Haggard, interview with the author, Colorado Springs, CO, August 15, 2006.

26. Tim Stafford, "Good Morning, Evangelicals," *Christianity Today,* November 2005.

27. Paul Asay and Deedee Correll, "SHOCK. DISBELIEF. DENIAL," November 2, 2006, http://www.gazette.com/display.php?id=1326038&secid=14 (accessed November 2, 2006).

28. Luis Lugo, Allen Hertzke, Richard Cizik, and Joel H. Ronethal, "Evangelical Reflections on the U.S. Role in the World," Carnegie Council, www.cceia.org/resources/transcripts/5230.html (accessed September 12, 2008).

29. Sammy Rodriguez Jr., interview with author, Washington, DC, October 2007.

30. Ibid.

31. Jesse Miranda, telephone interview, December 18, 2006. My understanding of Hispanic evangelicalism in the paragraphs below are indebted to Juan F. Martínez, "Stepchildren of the Empire: The Formation of a Latino *Evangélico* Identity," *Evangelicals and Empire,* ed. Bruce Ellis Benson and Peter Goodwin Heltzel (Grand Rapids: Brazos Press, 2008), 141–51.

32. Samuel Rodriguez, telephone interview, December 18, 2006.

33. Ibid.

34. Allen D. Hertzke, *Freeing God's Children: The Unlikely Alliance for Global Human Rights* (Lanham, MD: Rowman and Littlefield, 2004), 59.

35. "Sudan: Coalition Works for War's End," *Atlanta Journal-Constitution,* August 30, 2004, p. A8.

36. For the best portrait of Rich Cizik's new form of evangelical politics, see Jeff L. Sheler, "Capital Crusaders: Washington DC," *Believers: A Journey into Evangelical America* (New York: Viking, 2006), 227–70.

37. Link to The Great Warming, http://www.thegreatwarming.com/revrichard cizik.html.

38. Quoted in Richard Cizik's open letter to James Dobson, previously available on the National Association of Evangelical's Web site, www.nae.net (accessed May 23, 2006).

39. Richard Cizik, "For Those Who Will Believe in Me," John 18:20–23, keynote address at the spring board meeting of the NAE Wooddale Church, Eden Prairie, MN, March 8, 2007. Transcribed by the author.

Chapter 7. The Christian Community Development Association

1. From the CCDA Web site, www.ccda.org (accessed October 15, 2006).

2. Charles Marsh, *The Beloved Community: How Faith Shapes Social Justice, from the Civil Rights Movement to Today* (New York: Basic Books, 2005), 153–88; for a thoughtful discussion of John Perkins's black evangelical contribution to the growing evangelical movement for justice, see Lisa Sharon Harper, *Evangelical Does Not Equal Republican . . . or Demoract* (New York: New Press, 2008), 48–61. My interpretation of John Perkins is indebted to conversations with Marsh and Harper.

3. John Perkins, *Let Justice Roll Down* (Ventura, CA: Regal Books, 1976), 72.

4. Ibid., 51.

5. Ibid., 86.

6. Ibid., 92, 93.

7. Ibid., 99, 107. Emphasis in original.

8. Ibid., 99.

9. John Perkins, interview with the author, September 14, 2008.

10. John Perkins, "Foreword," in Lowell Noble, *From Oppression to Jubilee Justice* (Jackson, MS: Urban Verses, 2007), i–ii; Perkins's "Christ on the Cross" quote is cited by Charles Marsh, *Beloved Community,* 171. Perkins thinks that the Lordship of Christ should be embodied in the life of the Christian community, including race relations and economic justice. For Perkins, black suffering is illuminated through the redemptive suffering of Jesus Christ. It is only when people across racial lines are honest about past hurts and their current pain that true healing and reconciliation can take place. Perkins, *Let Justice Roll,* 101.

11. Chris Rice, "A Tribute to J.P." June 6, 2008. A tribute that was presented to John Perkins during the first John M. Perkins Visionary Award ceremony at Envision: The Gospel, Politics and the Future Conference, Princeton University, June 10, 2008, http://www.divinity.duke.edu/reconciliation/pages/journeys/20080610perkins .html (accessed September 28, 2008).

12. Perkins, *Let Justice Roll,* 101.

13. Marsh, *Beloved Community,* 168. Perkins writes of his positive experiences with white evangelicals while he was in Pasadena, California, in the late 1940s and 1950s: "Then there was the Christian Businessmen's Committee, where men like John McGill also nutured and disciplined me. At that time I was the only black attending, yet I felt accepted and loved within this Christian community in a way I had never felt before. I had experienced racism and bigotry as a boy. I had watched as whites murdered my brother. I had watched all types of brutalization back in Mississippi, but here was a group of white Christians encouraging me in my newfound faith. I can remember David Peacock who loved me so dearly, Ed Anthony, and others who were very conservative Christians, but who put their arms around me and loved me. And I loved them back." John M. Perkins, *Beyond Charity: The Call to Christian Community Development* (Grand Rapids: Baker Books, 1993), 13, 14.

14. Perkins, *Let Justice Roll,* 107–16.

15. "Demands of the Black Community," December 23, 1969, in John Perkins, *A Quiet Revolution: Meeting Human Needs Today: A Biblical Challenge to Christians,* rev. ed. (Pasadena, CA: Urban Family Publications, 1985), 225–26.

16. Ronald C. Potter, "The New Black Evangelicals," in *Black Theology: A Documentary History, 1966–1979,* ed. Gayraud S. Wilmore and James H. Cone (Maryknoll, NY: Orbis, 1979), 304; William Bentley, "Black Christian Nationalism: An Evangelical Perspective," *Black Books Bulletin* 4:1 (Spring 1976): 26–31.

17. Ron Sider, "Introduction: A Historic Moment for Biblical Social Concern," in *The Chicago Declaration,* ed. Ronald J. Sider (Carol Stream, IL: Creation House, 1974), 21–22.

18. Pamela Cochran, *Evangelical Feminism: A History* (New York: New York University Press, 2005).

19. For helpful accounts of John Perkins, Voice of Calvary, and the Christian Community Development Association, see John M. Perkins, *Restoring At-Risk Communities: Doing It Together and Doing It Right* (official handbook of the Christian Community Development Association) (Grand Rapids: Baker Books, 1995); Randall Balmer, *Mine Eyes Have Seen the Glory: A Journey into the Evangelical Subculture in America* (New York: Oxford University Press, 2000), 176–92; Stephen E. Berk, *A Time to Heal: John Perkins, Community Development, and Racial Reconciliation* (Grand Rapids: Baker Books, 1997).

20. Michael Emerson and Christian Smith, *Divided by Faith* (New York: Oxford University Press, 2000), 53.

21. Perkins, *A Quiet Revolution*, 220.

22. Eddie S. Glaude, *In a Shade of Blue: Pragmatism and the Politics of Black America* (Chicago: University of Chicago Press, 2007), 132. I have heard Glaude's call for community in a deeper shade of blue and have responded through trying to work out the implications of this call for American evangelical political life. I affirm Glaude's poetic and profound discussion of black suffering through the color blue, a symbol of the social and existential anguish that people of African descent have suffered in the Americas since 1619. Glaude and I both see suffering as a commonality of the human community that must be named and then overcome through collective political action. Although we affirm a similar problem (suffering) and social end (the alleviation of suffering), we disagree in terms of our theo-social imaginary and political strategy.

Glaude's pragmatic narrative opens up a secular space for the realization of democracy, distancing himself from the Gospel narrative that opens up the life, death, and resurrection of Jesus Christ. Thus, Glaude's pragmatic vision needs to take a "theological turn" toward the suffering flesh of Jesus Christ. Black suffering in the Americas is illuminated not through pragmatic theory but through the wounded and redemptive flesh of a disinherited Jew, Jesus of Nazareth. The *Christian* identity of black Christians is the theological site of an ongoing decolonization of the white evangelical racist imagination. While evangelical Christian theology is one of the sources of the problem of the modern logic of racism, black evangelical theology is the source of a new horizon through which the evangelical theological imagination can be decolonized in order to actualize a transformed evangelicalism that is prophetic, intercultural, and radically democratic. John Perkins's Christology provides a black evangelical counterpolitics to a white evangelical theology of triumph, offering a communitarian political strategy that seeks to unveil the new social order of the Kingdom of God through concrete acts of love and justice in the community. Perkins provides us with a black evangelical theology in a deeper shade of blue.

23. Ibid., 18.

24. Rice, "Tribute to J.P." June 6, 2008. Relocating to the abandoned places of empire is one of the twelve marks of a new monasticism advocated by Shane Claiborne and

Jonathan Wilson-Hartgrove. See *School(s) for Conversion: 12 Marks of New Monasticism,* ed. Rutba House (Eugene, OR: Wipf and Stock, 2005).

Chapter 8. Sojourners

1. For a concise history of *Sojourners* magazine, see Mark G. Toulouse, "Sojourners," in *Popular Religious Magazines of the United States,* ed. Mark Fackler and Charles H. Lippy (Westport, CT: Greenwood, 1995), 444–51.

2. Jim Wallis, *God's Politics: Why the Right Gets It Wrong and the Left Doesn't Get It* (New York: HarperSan Francisco, 2005).

3. Wallis, *God's Politics,* xiv.

4. Jim Wallis, *The Great Awakening: Reviving Faith and Politics in a Post-Religious Right America* (New York: HarperCollins, 2008), 68. On King's kitchen table experience, see Wallis, *Great Awakening,* 21. Other thinkers with whom Wallis was in conversation about King's vision of beloved community, discussed in the paragraph below, include William Stringfellow, *My People Is the Enemy* (New York: Holt, Rinehart and Winston, 1966); William Pannell, *My Friend, the Enemy* (Waco, TX: Word Books, 1968). I initially began to interpret Jim Wallis and the Sojourners movement through the lens of black Christianity as a result of a research project with my colleague Eleanor Moody Shepherd. This chapter draws on the following essay: Eleanor Moody Shepherd and Peter Goodwin Heltzel, "Empire, Race, and the Evangelical Multitude: Jesse Jackson, Jim Wallis, and Evangelical Coalitions for Justice," in *Evangelicals and Empire: Christian Alternatives to the Political Status Quo,* ed. Bruce Ellis Benson and Peter Goodwin Heltzel (Grand Rapids: Brazos Press, 2008), 152–68.

5. Jim Wallis, *Agenda for Biblical People* (New York: Harper and Row, 1976), 13.

6. See David Gutterman's treatment of Call to Renewal's antipoverty initiative as part of the King tradition, *Prophetic Politics* (Ithaca: Cornell University Press, 2005), 129–60.

7. Jim Wallis, "Introduction," to "Getting Ready for the Hero: Reflections on Martin Luther King, Jr.—and Us," in *The Rise of Christian Conscience: The Emergence of a Dramatic Renewal Movement in Today's Church,* ed. Jim Wallis (San Francisco: Harper and Row, 1987), 127–44.

8. Gutterman, *Prophetic Politics,* 148.

9. Wes Granberg Michaelson, phone interview with the author, December 8, 2006. John Howard Yoder, *The Politics of Jesus* (Grand Rapids: Eerdmans, 1972). See Wallis's discussion and expansion of Yoder's *Politics of Jesus* in Wallis, *Great Awakening,* 57–78.

10. John Howard Yoder, *The Priestly Kingdom: Social Ethics as Gospel* (South Bend, Ind.: University of Notre Dame Press, 1984), 158; idem, *The Christian Witness to the State* (Scottdale, PA: Herald Press, 2002) For other theologians that were influenced by Yoder that are discussed in the paragraph below, see Jacques Ellul, *The Kingdom and the Presence* (New York: Helmers and Howard, 1989); William Stringfellow, *An Ethic for Christians and Other Aliens in a Strange Land* (Waco, TX: Word Books, 1973); Bill Wylie Kellermann, ed., *A Keeper of the Word: Selected Writings of William Stringfellow* (Grand Rapids: Eerdmans, 1994). Another book that was extremely influential in the

Sojourners circle in the 1970s was Arthur G. Gish, *The New Left and Christian Radicalism* (Grand Rapids: Eerdmans, 1970).

11. Wesley Granberg-Michaelson, phone interview with the author, December 8, 2006.

12. Wallis, *Great Awakening*, 61, 62.

13. Jim Wallis, *Revive Us Again: A Sojourners Story* (Nashville: Abingdon Press, 1983), 92–93.

14. Jim Wallis, *The Call to Conversion: Why Faith Is Always Personal but Never Private*, rev. ed. (New York: HarperCollins, 2005), 9. Wallis writes, "We will need societal transformation for real social change, and that never comes about without personal transformation as well. Faith can provide the fire, the passion, the strength, the perseverance, and the hope necessary for social movements to win, and to change politics." Wallis, *Great Awakening*, 21.

15. Wallis, *Call to Conversion*, 30.

16. Wallis, *God's Politics*, 15–17.

17. Ibid., xv.

18. Wallis, *Great Awakening*, 57–78. Influenced by Yoder and James Cone, Wallis connects Jesus's Jewish flesh as unveiling his vulnerability and suffering with the call to care for a suffering humanity that is made in the image of Jesus Christ. In contrast to the Jewish zealots who sought a violent overthrow of the Roman regime, Yoder describes Jesus's ministry was "one of suffering" and his disciples would have to be ready to "bear with that cross." Yoder, *Politics of Jesus*, 42. James Cone writes, "The historical Jesus emphasizes the social context of Christology and thereby establishes the importance of Jesus' racial identity. *Jesus was a Jew!* The particularity of Jesus' person as disclosed in his Jewishness is indispensable for Christological analysis. On the one hand, Jesus' Jewishness pinpoints the importance of his humanity for faith, and on the other, connects God's salvation drama in Jesus with the Exodus-Sinai event." James Cone, *God of the Oppressed* (New York: Seabury Press, 1975), 119.

19. The Chicago Declaration of Evangelical Social Concern, http://www.esa online.org/Images/mmDocument/Declarations%20&%20Letters/Chicago%20 Declaration%20of%20Evangelical%20Social%20Concern.doc (accessed October 25, 2007).

20. Mark Toulouse, *God in Public: Four Ways American Christianity and Public Life Relate* (Louisville: Westminster John Knox, 2006), 229, 238

21. For Wallis's most recent discussion of racism see Wallis, *Great Awakening*, 157–88.

22. Ibid., 161, 166.

23. Adam Taylor, "Just Son," in *The Emergent Manifesto of Justice*, ed. Brian McClaren, Ashley Bunting Seeber, and Elisa Padilla (Grand Rapids: Baker Books, 2009).

24. Adam Taylor, interview with the author, February 15, 2008.

25. Michael Emerson and Christian Smith, *Divided by Faith: Evangelical Religion and the Problem of Race in America* (Oxford: Oxford University Press, 2000), 91.

26. See Wallis's chapter, "Truth Telling about Race: America's Original Sin," in

God's Politics, 307–20. Also he wrote many articles on racism in *Sojourners* during the 1990s, and Sojourners has produced many educational guides for churches to implement antiracist ministries.

27. See Ernst R. Sandeen, *The Roots of Fundamentalism* (Chicago: University of Chicago Press, 1970); George Marsden, *Fundamentalism and American Culture* (New York: Oxford University Press, 1980). On anti-intellectualism within evangelicalism, see Mark A. Noll, *The Scandal of the Evangelical Mind* (Grand Rapids: Eerdmans, 1994).

28. See Douglas W. Frank, *Less than Conquerors: How Evangelicals Entered the Twentieth Century* (Grand Rapids: Eerdmans, 1986).

29. Wallis, *God's Politics,* 35.

30. Ibid., 61–64.

31. Ibid., 154. Jim Wallis, "Dangerous Religion: George W. Bush's Theology of Empire," in *Evangelicals and Empire: Christian Alternatives to the Political Status Quo,* ed. Bruce Ellis Benson and Peter Goodwin Heltzel (Grand Rapids: Brazos Press, 2008), 25–32.

32. Wallis, *God's Politics,* 64.

33. Ibid., 3.

34. Martin Durham, "Evangelical Protestantism and Foreign Policy in the United States after September 11," *Patterns of Prejudice* 38:2 (2004): 145–58; 153.

35. Wallis, *God's Politics.*

36. Alan Cooperman, "Evangelicals Broaden Their Moral Agenda," *Washington Post,* October 19, 2006, p. A19.

37. Michael Kazin, "A Difficult Marriage: American Protestants and American Politics," *Dissent* (Winter 2006): 52.

38. Wallis, *God's Politics,* 4.

39. Wallis, *Great Awakening,* 227; Kazin, "Difficult Marriage," 53.

40. Wallis, *Great Awakening,* 133

41. Ibid., 6.

42. Aaron Graham, interview with author, December 10, 2007. Jim Wallis's justice revivals are self-consciously modeled after Charles Finney's revival services that enlisted new converts to join the struggle to abolish slavery. Wallis writes, "Finney, who has been called the father of American evangelism, directly linked revival and reform and popularized the altar call . . . to sign up his converts for the antislavery campaign! They would commit their lives to Christ and then enlist for God's purposes in the world." Wallis, *Great Awakening,* 19. Like Finney, Wallis offers a call to personal conversion to Christ *and* to join a social movement to end racism, poverty, and war. Wallis's first justice revival was held at the Vineyard Church of Columbus in Ohio 2008, in the swing state where the "evangelical vote" helped re-elect George W. Bush in 2004 and elect Barack Obama in 2008. Sojourners deployed the collective intelligence of its organization and its community-organizing capacity to help mobilize evangelicals in Ohio to embrace a fully pro-life agenda that included poverty, health care, education, the environment, and immigration reform, an agenda more in line with the platform of the

Democratic Party. Wallis was able to effectively deploy a two-prong strategy to help the Democratic Party in advance of the 2008 election. He helped the Democrats become more adept at discussing religious values, and he helped organize and mobilize a large group of evangelicals committed to social justice issues. Wallis learned these moves (in part) from James Dobson and the pro-family movement, but he deployed them on behalf of an alternative form of prophetic evangelical politics. For an account of this broader transformation of the Democratic party, including an analysis of the prominent evangelical contribution to a new form of Democratic politics, see Amy Sullivan, *The Party Faithful: How and Why Democrats Are Closing the God Gap* (New York: Scribner, 2008).

Chapter 9. Evangelical Politics in a Shade of Blue Green

1. Michael O. Emerson and Christian Smith, *Divided by Faith: Evangelical Religion and the Problem of Race in America* (New York: Oxford University Press, 2000).

2. Barack Obama, "One Nation . . . under God?" excerpt from speech printed in *Sojourners,* November 2006; John Perkins, interview with the author, September 14, 2008.

3. "An Urgent Call to Action: Evangelicals and Scientists Unite to Protect Creation," National Press Club, Washington, DC, January 17, 2007, "Appendix 6," in David P. Gushee, *The Future of Faith in American Politics: The Public Witness of the Evangelical Center* (Waco, TX: Baylor University Press, 2008), 283–85.

4. Harry R. Jackson Jr. and Tony Perkins, "Core Value #7: The Environment and Global Warming," *Personal Faith and Public Policy* (Lake Mary, FL: Strang Communications, 2008), 203–19.

5. The NAE statement on religious freedom, mentioned in chapter 6, dealt with religious freedom and led to the International Religious Freedom Act in 1998; the second statement on religious freedom was a clarification and expansion of the first.

6. Richard Warren, *The Purpose Driven Life: What on Earth Am I Here For?* (Grand Rapids: Zondervan, 2002).

7. Kay Warren, *Dangerous Surrender* (Grand Rapids: Zondervan, 2007).

INDEX

abolition movement, 9, 16–18, 26–32, 54, 60–61, 98, 106, 116, 142, 153, 160, 179, 187, 197–98, 217
abortion, 4, 91, 92, 93, 100, 102–6, 107, 108, 113, 116, 125, 137–38, 197, 213. *See also* pro-life movement
activism, 7, 8, 49, 56, 59, 63, 120, 154, 155, 167, 178–79, 199, 212, 214, 217, 232n70, 237n22
African Methodist Episcopal Church, 43
agape, 64–65. *See also* God, love of.
Alaskan Expedition, Scientist-Evangelical, 119–20, 213
Allen, Richard, 18
American Council of Christian Churches (ACCC), 135
Anderson, Leith, 145, 149, 156, 209
antiracism, 14, 83, 143, 150, 180, 190, 191, 212, 218, 248n26
Argue, Don, 128, 139–44, 209; and Bill Clinton, 142
Arlington Group, 109, 124, 156
Asbury, Francis, 18, 20
Atlanta, Georgia, 49, 55, 123

Baldwin, Lewis, 63
Ball, Jim, 120, 153–54
Balmer, Randall, 103, 200, 238n23
Baptist church, 49, 54, 57, 62. *See also* Southern Baptist Convention (SBC)

Barth, Karl (Barthian), 180, 181, 184, 185
Bauer, Gary, 5, 94, 107, 157
Bebbington, David, 7–9
Bell, L. Nelson, 83–84
Bell, Rob, 212
Bellah, Robert, 76
beloved community. *See* Martin Luther King, Jr.
Bible: authority of, 7, 8, 9, 45, 48, 58, 72, 130, 190; inerrancy of, 72, 73, 96, 241n8; interpretation of, 21, 32–33, 34, 58, 62, 196; slavery and, 20, 21, 32–34
Billy Graham, 5, 14, 43, 102, 122, 151, 171; Carl F.H. Henry and, 71–72; Martin Luther King, Jr. and, 48, 59–61; and racial justice, 82–83, 235n48
black Christianity: prophetic forms of, 4, 11–12, 13–26, 40–41, 43, 46, 48–50, 58, 62, 74, 85, 161, 165, 168, 174–75, 185, 211–12, 218; Exodus story appropriated by, 31, 58, 62, 165, 167, 207–208; of Martin Luther King, Jr., 53, 54, 58; roots in slavery, 29–32. *See also* black church; evangelicalism, black
black church, xxi–xxii, 15, 45–46, 121, 141, 162, 168, 181, 187, 190–94, 211–12; Martin Luther King, Jr., and, 48–50, 55, 58, 62. *See also* black theology; evangelicalism, black; black Christianity